DELIUS KLASING

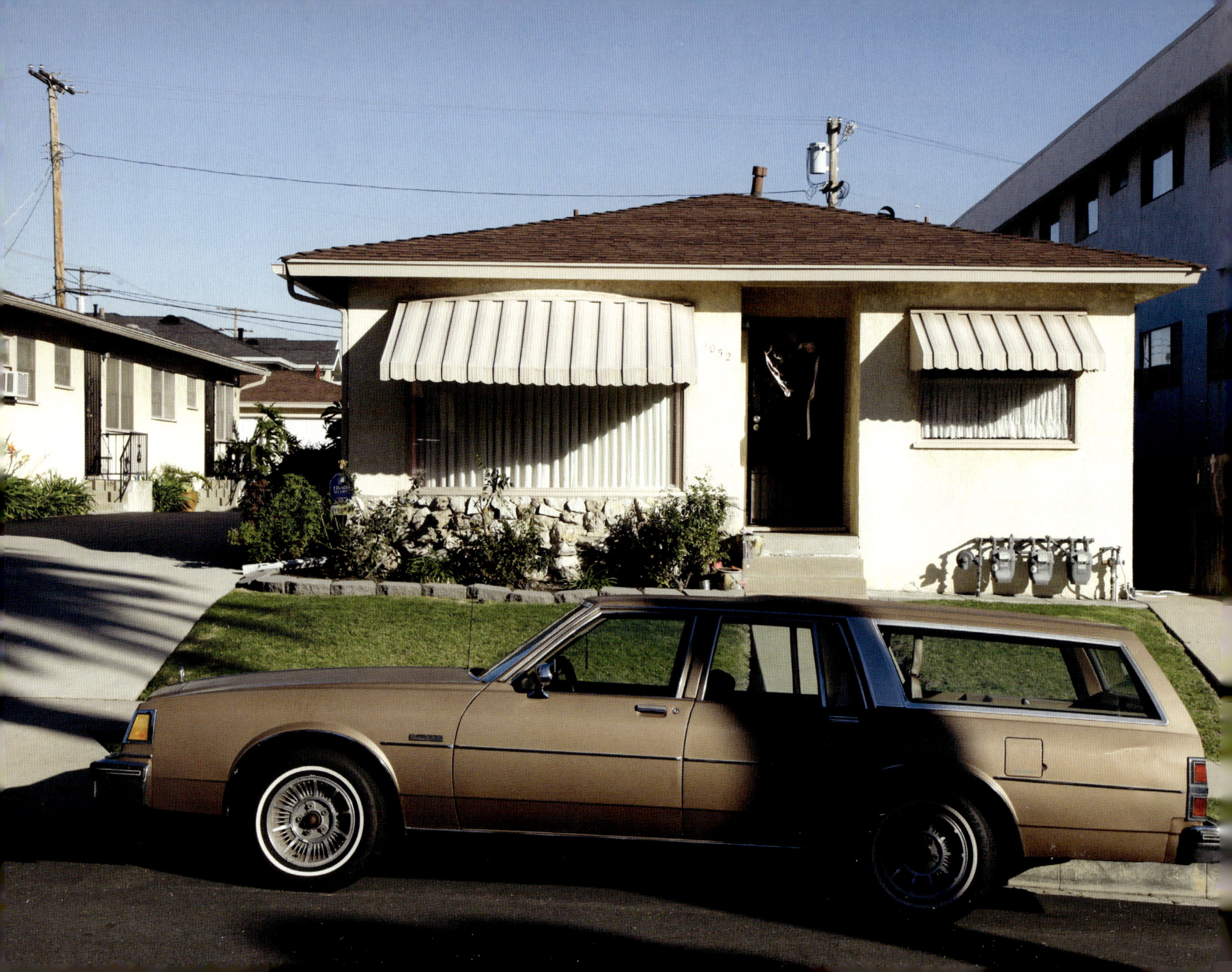

HOME ALONE

AUTO-ALLEIN ZU HAUS

TIM MAXEINER

DELIUS KLASING VERLAG

Von Henryk M. Broder

MOBILE IMMOBILIEN

Was braucht der Amerikaner zum Glücklichsein? Ein Haus, ein Auto, eine Familie, um die er sich sorgen kann, dazu ein Portemonnaie voller Debit- und Kreditkarten. Und natürlich auch einen Job, manchmal sogar zwei oder drei, damit er das Haus und das Auto abbezahlen und die Familie ernähren kann.

Im Prinzip, könnte man meinen, sind sie Menschen wie du und ich. Aber der erste Eindruck täuscht, zwischen Europa und Amerika liegt mehr als nur der Atlantik – ein Kulturgraben. Europa ist ein Haus, das von Generation zu Generation vererbt wurde. Im Keller ruhen die Gebeine von Karl dem Großen, Martin Luther, Napoleon und Kaiser Wilhelm, in der Belle Etage hängen die Bilder der holländischen Meister neben denen der deutschen Expressionisten, und auf dem Speicher liegt alles, womit man nicht täglich zu tun haben möchte: der Erste und der Zweite Weltkrieg, der Völkermord an den Hereros, der Holocaust und demnächst auch der »Vertrag von Lissabon«, aus dem beinah die Verfassung von Europa geworden wäre.

In Amerika dagegen gilt alles, was älter als 30 Jahre ist, als »antique« oder »vintage«: Möbel, Geschirr, Autos, Kleider, Bücher. Die Amerikaner trennen keinen Müll, aber sie recyceln alles in den sogenannten Thrift Shops der Heilsarmee oder bei den Yard- oder Garage-Sales, wo die Familien bis auf Oma und Opa alles zum Verkauf anbieten, das sie loswerden möchten.

Ist man in einer ganz normalen Familie zu Besuch, stellt man sich nicht selten die Frage: Sind die Leute gerade eingezogen und haben noch nicht alles einsortiert? Oder ziehen sie gerade aus und haben nicht genug Kisten, um die Habe zu verstauen? Den gleichen Eindruck bekommt man in vielen Städten, die so unfertig wirken wie eine Lego-Landschaft, an der die Kinder die Lust verloren haben. In Chattanooga z. B. hat eine Bürgerinitiative den alten Bahnhof vor dem Verfall gerettet und in eine Hotel- und Konferenzanlage umgewandelt. Die alten Waggons dienen jetzt als Appartments für Touristen, die es etwas uriger als im »Holiday Inn« haben möchten. Aber die Gegend rund um den Bahnhof ist so leblos wie die Innenstadt von Dessau nach Mitternacht.

Der Besucher aus Europa, der Alkmaar, Bern und Krakau gesehen hat, fragt sich, wieso Grundstücke in bester Innenstadtlage nicht bebaut, sondern als Parkplätze genutzt werden. Warum historische Gebäude nicht restauriert, sondern dem Verfall preisgegeben werden. Weshalb die Eisenbahn, einst das Kapillarsystem der USA, nur noch Gegenstand nostalgischer Zuneigung ist.

Bis ihm irgendwann klar wird: Amerika, das ist »Work in Progress«, eine Versuchsanstalt für angewandte Mobilität, eine Uhr, die mal vor- und mal nachgeht, aber niemals stillsteht.

Amerikaner warten nicht, bis Arbeit zu ihnen kommt, sie ziehen dahin, wo es Arbeit gibt. Howard, 63, fährt an fünf Tagen in der Woche im Morgengrauen 30 Meilen in die eine und am frühen Nachmittag 30 Meilen in die andere Richtung. Er arbeitet als Bäcker, in einem Beruf, den er nie gelernt hat. Nach 35 Jahren als Berufssoldat könnte er auch von seiner Pension leben, aber zu Hause sitzen und Rasen mähen, ist nicht seine Sache. Also verfährt er jeden Monat 1200 Meilen mit seinem Pickup. Er kann die Fahrtkosten nicht von der Steuer absetzen, eine »Pendlerpauschale«, wie es sie in Deutschland gibt, ist in den USA unbekannt.

Nicht nur die Menschen sind mobil, die Immobilien sind es auch. Sie gehen von Hand zu Hand. Bis vor kurzem war es einfacher, ein Haus zu kaufen, als eines zu mieten. In dieser Beziehung sind die Amerikaner vollkommen unsentimental. Ein Dach über dem Kopf soll vor Wind und Wetter schützen. Es verpflichtet nicht dazu, sein Leben an einem Ort zu verbringen.

Dennoch gibt es eine symbiotische Verbindung zwischen dem Haus und seinen Bewohnern, dem Auto und seinem Benutzer, dem Haus und dem Auto. Sie ergänzen einander und bilden eine organische Einheit. Wenn man mit dem Haus zur Arbeit fahren und im Auto wohnen könnte, würden die Amerikaner es auch tun. Und einige tun es tatsächlich. Sie hängen ihren Wohnwagen an den Pick-up und rollen dahin, wo es Arbeit gibt.

By Henryk M. Broder

MOBILE PROPERTIES

What does an American need to be happy? A house, a car, a family to care for, and a wallet filled with debit and credit cards. An American needs a job – sometimes two or three – in order to pay for the house, the car and the needs of the family.

One could say that Americans are just like you and I. However, first impressions can be misleading. Something more than just the Atlantic Ocean separates Europe and the U.S. of A.: a cultural rift. Europe is a house that was passed on from one generation to the next. The bones of Charlemagne, Martin Luther, Napoleon and Kaiser Wilhelm rest in the basement. Paintings by Dutch masters and German Expressionists hang in the piano nobile. The attic contains everything with which one does not want to be confronted on a daily basis: World Wars I and II, the massacre on the Herero tribe and the Holocaust. Soon, this will include the Treaty of Lisbon, which (almost) became the European Constitution.

In America, if something is older than 30 years, it is considered to be »antique« or »vintage«: furniture, dishes, cars, dresses and books. Americans don't separate their garbage, but they recycle all sorts of things in Salvation Army thrift shops or at garage sales. There, with the exception of Grandma and Grandpa, Americans sell everything they want to get rid of.

When one visits a normal American family, it is not clear whether they have just moved in or are on their way out. Have they just not finished unpacking their boxes or are they missing boxes to finish their packing? Many cities make a similar impression. These can seem as unfinished as a LEGO landscape abandoned by its young creators. In Chattanooga, for example, a citizens' action group fought to save an old railway station, turning it into a hotel and convention center. The old railway carriages serve as apartments for tourists in search of something more rustic than a Holiday Inn. The surrounding area, however, is as lifeless as the city center of eastern Germany´s Dessau at midnight.

The European visitor, who has been to Alkmaar, Bern and Cracau, is left wondering. Why are central plots of land in cities left undeveloped or used as parking lots? Why are historical buildings left to rot rather than being restored? Why are the railways – once the capillaries of the USA – now only objects of nostalgic affection?

Then, it becomes clear. America is work in progress. It is an experimental station for applied mobility. It is a clock, sometimes fast and sometimes slow, but never standing still.

Americans don't wait until work comes to them. They move to where there is work. Howard, 63, drives 30 miles each morning at the crack of dawn. In the early afternoon, he drives 30 miles in the opposite direction. He does this 5 days a week. Howard works as a baker. However, this has not been his main occupation in life. After having served as a professional soldier for 35 years, he could live from his retirement funds. But to sit at home and mow the lawn is just not his thing. So, each month, he drives 1,200 miles in his pickup truck. His travel costs are not tax-exempt and a »commuter allowance«, such as those in Germany, is unheard of in the USA.

It is not only the people, who are mobile. Properties are mobile, too. They are passed on from hand to hand. Until recently, it was easier to buy a house than to rent one. Americans are not sentimental in this respect. The roof over one's head should protect against wind and weather.

Nobody is obligated to spend his or her whole life in one place.

Nevertheless, there is a symbiotic relationship between the house and its inhabitants, the car and its passengers, and the house and the car. These complement one another and form a unit. If it were possible to drive to work in one's house and to live in one's car, an American would do it. Some even do. They hitch their campers to their pickup trucks and roll along ... until they've found a job.

Von Tim Maxeiner

DÉJÀ VU AUF DER SIEBTEN STRASSE

Die Leistung, der Preis oder die Technik eines Autos haben mich noch nie sonderlich interessiert. Mich beschäftigt stattdessen eine andere Frage: Was kann man damit erleben? Und oft würde ich auch gern wissen: Was hat dieses Auto schon erlebt? Seitdem ich in die USA gegangen bin, besitze ich nun das dritte Fahrzeug. Das Erste war ein betagter Volvo 240, dessen Kilometerzähler bei 300 000 Meilen stehengeblieben war. Da er ursprünglich im kanadischen Victoria herumfuhr, gab ich dem Schwedenpanzer den gleichen Namen. »Victoria« und ich fuhren zusammen bis nach Mexiko und zurück. Dann musste ich Victoria mit gebrochener Antriebswelle und gebrochenem Herzen am Straßenrand zurücklassen. Ich kam mir vor wie jemand, der seinen treuen Hund auf einem Autobahn-Rastplatz aussetzt. Noch heute plagt mich ein schlechtes Gewissen. Victoria, I miss you.

Es folgte ein Chevrolet Caprice Station Wagon, der mir eine Weile als erster Wohnsitz diente. Er war Baujahr 1988 und hatte fast genau mein Alter. Sanft schaukelnd teilte er die Fahrbahn wie ein Dampfer die Wellen. Beim Parken kam ich mir vor wie der Kapitän eines Kreuzfahrtschiffes, das vor Anker geht. Inzwischen bin ich sesshaft geworden und fahre einen alten Ford-Van, der zuvor für »Coca-Cola« unterwegs war. Jetzt transportiert er meine Surfbretter. Zum Ausgleich der Sesshaftigkeit lebe ich in San Pedro, dem Hafenviertel von Los Angeles. Kriterium: Möglichst nah am Meer und möglichst preiswert zum Leben. Ergebnis: Zimmer mit Meerblick, 15 Quadratmeter, keine Heizung, keine Klimaanlage, keine Küche. Durch einen Maschendrahtzaun mit wehrhaften Stacheln obendrauf streift mein Blick über ein ausgedehntes Flachdach, dann vorbei an einer entfernten »Stars and Stripes«-Fahne, trifft nach einigen Kilometern schließlich auf die Spitzen riesiger Ladekräne und entdeckt dahinter einen blauen Schimmer: der Pazifik!

San Pedro, oder »San Pidro«, wie es die Einheimischen aussprechen, wurde 1909 von Los Angeles eingemeindet, hat sich aber seinen eigenständigen Stolz bewahrt. Für einen wirklichen »San Pedrian« ist Los Angeles weit weg. Das lokale Sprichwort »Pidro kids never leave« beschreibt die Zuneigung zur Heimat. »Pidro« steht für Vielfalt: ethnische, kulturelle und architektonische. Viele Bewohner stammen aus Italien, Kroatien oder Mittelamerika. Die Häuser sind bunt und im Baustil wild zusammengewürfelt. Kleine Holzhäuser behaupten sich neben modernen Appartement-Anlagen. San Pedro zieht sich den östlichen Hang der Palos Verdes-Halbinsel hinauf; viele Straßen führen durch in den Berg geschnittene Canyons. Die übliche amerikanische Straßeneinteilung »Block after Block« kann hier nicht durchgehalten werden. Auf der Pacific Avenue, einer der Hauptschlagadern der Stadt, cruist der San Pedrian gern mit seinem »classic car« – egal, ob am Tag oder in der Nacht.

Ich habe mir angewöhnt, eine neue Umgebung erstmal zu Fuß zu erkunden. So auch San Pedro. Ich schaue mir gern die Häuser an und stelle mir vor, wie es sich darin lebt. Und wer darin lebt: Hafenarbeiter, Künstler, Automechaniker oder die Kassiererin vom Kiosk um die Ecke. So bekommt man ein gutes Gefühl für eine Gegend und versteht, wie die Bewohner ticken. Alle Aufnahmen in diesem Buch entstanden in einem Umkreis von wenigen Kilometern.

Ich liebe Autos, die vom Leben gezeichnet sind. Sie haben keine Beulen, sondern tragen würdevolle Narben. Auch vom Wind abgeschliffener Lack und von der Hitze spröde Dichtungen machen sie mir sympathisch. Schon bald fiel mir auf, dass in San Pedro Haus und Auto oft harmonieren, sich irgendwie ähnlich sind. So, wie man das von Herr und Hund sagt.

Ich fing an, diese Paarungen zu fotografieren. Erst unbewusst, später gezielt. Ich kann gar nicht mehr anders, als meine Umgebung nach solchen Motiven abzuscannen. Am liebsten früh morgens oder am frühen Abend, dann ist das Licht am schönsten. So entstanden zahlreiche amerikanische Stillleben. Früher arrangierten Maler gern Blumen oder Speisen zu Bildkompositionen. Ich mache das mit Autos und Häusern. Nur, dass sie niemand extra für mich hingestellt hat. Ich dokumentiere die Situation, wie sie ist. Die Leute haben einfach nur geparkt. Manchmal suche ich stundenlang nach einem Motiv, manchmal fliegen sie mir auf einem kurzen Spaziergang um den Block nur so zu. Ich habe die Autos immer genau von der Seite aufgenommen. Nur Autos, die im Profil gut aussehen, sind für mich wirklich schön. Daher die Wahl dieser Perspektive für dieses Buch.

Manche dieser Autos begegnen mir inzwischen wie alte Bekannte. Fast täglich habe ich irgendein Déjà-vu. Hat der alte Käfer letzte Woche nicht zwei Straßen weiter geparkt? Umgezogen? Neue Freundin? Kenne ich den großen schwarzen Cadillac im Gegenverkehr nicht von der 7th Street? Hat das putzige Holzhaus einen neuen Anstrich bekommen? Neuer Mieter? Oder verkauft? Doch Autos und Häuser behalten ihre Geheimnisse für sich. Welche es sind, bleibt der Fantasie des Betrachters überlassen.

By Tim Maxeiner

DÉJÀ VU ON 7TH STREET

I have never been especially interested in the performance, price or technology of a car. Much more interesting to me has always been the question: »what can one experience with a car?« Or »what has this car experienced throughout its lifetime?« I have owned three cars since my arrival in the United States. The first was an elderly Volvo 240, whose odometer stopped counting at 300,000 miles. I named the Swedish tank after its first home: Victoria, Canada. »Victoria« and I drove all the way to Mexico and back. Eventually, I had no choice but to abandon Victoria on the roadside with a broken drive shaft and a broken heart. I felt like someone who had just set his loyal dog out at a highway rest stop. Even now, I suffer from a guilty conscience. Victoria, I miss you.

Next was a Chevrolet Caprice station wagon, which also served as my home for a while. Its model year was 1988, making it almost exactly as old as I was at the time. Swaying gently, it parted the road like a steamer parts waves. When I parked, I felt like the captain of a cruise ship, dropping the anchor. By now, I have settled down. I drive an old Ford van, which used to be on the road for Coca-Cola. Now, it transports my surfboards. The trade-off for being settled is that I live in San Pedro, the port district of Los Angeles. Wanted: near the ocean and affordable, if possible. Result: 15 square meters, ocean view, no heating, no air conditioning and no kitchen. My gaze wanders through a chain link fence, which is fortified with barbed wire. It wanders across an expansive, flat roof, past a distant »Stars and Stripes« flag, towards the tip of a huge loading crane and settles, finally, on a sliver of blue. The Pacific Ocean!

San Pedro, or »San Pidro«, which is how the locals pronounce it, was annexed by the city of Los Angeles in 1909. Still, it has retained its independent pride. For a real »San Pedrian«, Los Angeles is far away. The local saying, »Pedro kids never leave«, describes this loyalty. »Pedro« means diversity: ethnic, cultural and architectural. Many residents originate from Italy, Croatia or Central America. The houses are colorful and thrown together wildly. Small, wooden houses assert themselves next to modern apartment complexes. San Pedro stretches along the eastern slope of the Palos Verdes Peninsula. Many of its streets cut through canyons, which have cut through the hills. The usual, American grid plan, »block by block«, does not apply here. One of the main arteries of the city is Pacific Avenue. San Pedrians like to cruise up and down in their classic cars, regardless of whether it is day or night.

I have taken to exploring new surroundings by foot, at first. It was the same when I arrived San Pedro. I enjoy looking at the houses and trying to imagine what it might be like to live there. I try to imagine who might live there: port workers, artists, mechanics or the cashier from the kiosk on the corner. This helps me get a sense of the neighborhood and understand how the people who live there think. The photos in this book were all taken within the same area of only a few square miles.

I love cars with visible signs of wear and tear. These carry dignified scars rather than small dents. I like them even if their coats of paint have been sanded down by the wind and their window seals are brittle from the heat. It soon occurred to me that, in San Pedro, there is a certain harmony between the houses and the cars that are parked in front of them. In a sense, they often fit together, just like a dog and his owner fit together.

I began photographing pairs. First, it was unintentional. Then, I began searching for them. By now, I can't help but to scan my surroundings for subjects like these. The light is most beautiful early in the morning and early in the evening. These are the best times to photograph. Out came American still lifes. Painters used to arrange flowers and fruits, thereby creating compositions for their works. I do this with cars and houses. Only that they aren't placed there just for me. I capture situations as they are. These cars were simply parked. Sometimes, I spend hours looking for subjects to photograph. Sometimes, they come at me from all directions during a short walk around the block. I photographed all of my subjects directly from the side. For me, only cars with nice profiles can be truly beautiful. That is why I chose this perspective for the book.

Some of these cars seem like old friends now. I experience »déjà vu« almost every day. Wasn't the old VW Bug parked two streets over last week? Did it move? New girlfriend? Don't I know that black Cadillac, which is coming towards me, from 7th Street? Did this cute house get a new paint job? New tenants? Was it sold? Cars and houses, however, keep their secrets to themselves. Imagining what they might be is up to the fantasy of the beholder.

BLACK AND WHITE. THE POWERFUL LOVE BLACK CARS AND WHITE HOUSES. COMMON PEOPLE TAKE THE LIBERTY OF CHOOSING

SCHWARZ UND WEISS.

DIFFERENT SHADES.

DIE MÄCHTIGEN LIEBEN

SCHWARZE AUTOS UND WEISSE HÄUSER. DAS VOLK ERLAUBT SICH AUCH ZWISCHENTÖNE.

»And I told about equality and it's true. Either you're wrong or you're right. But, if you're thinkin' about my baby, it don't matter if you're black or white.«
Michael Jackson

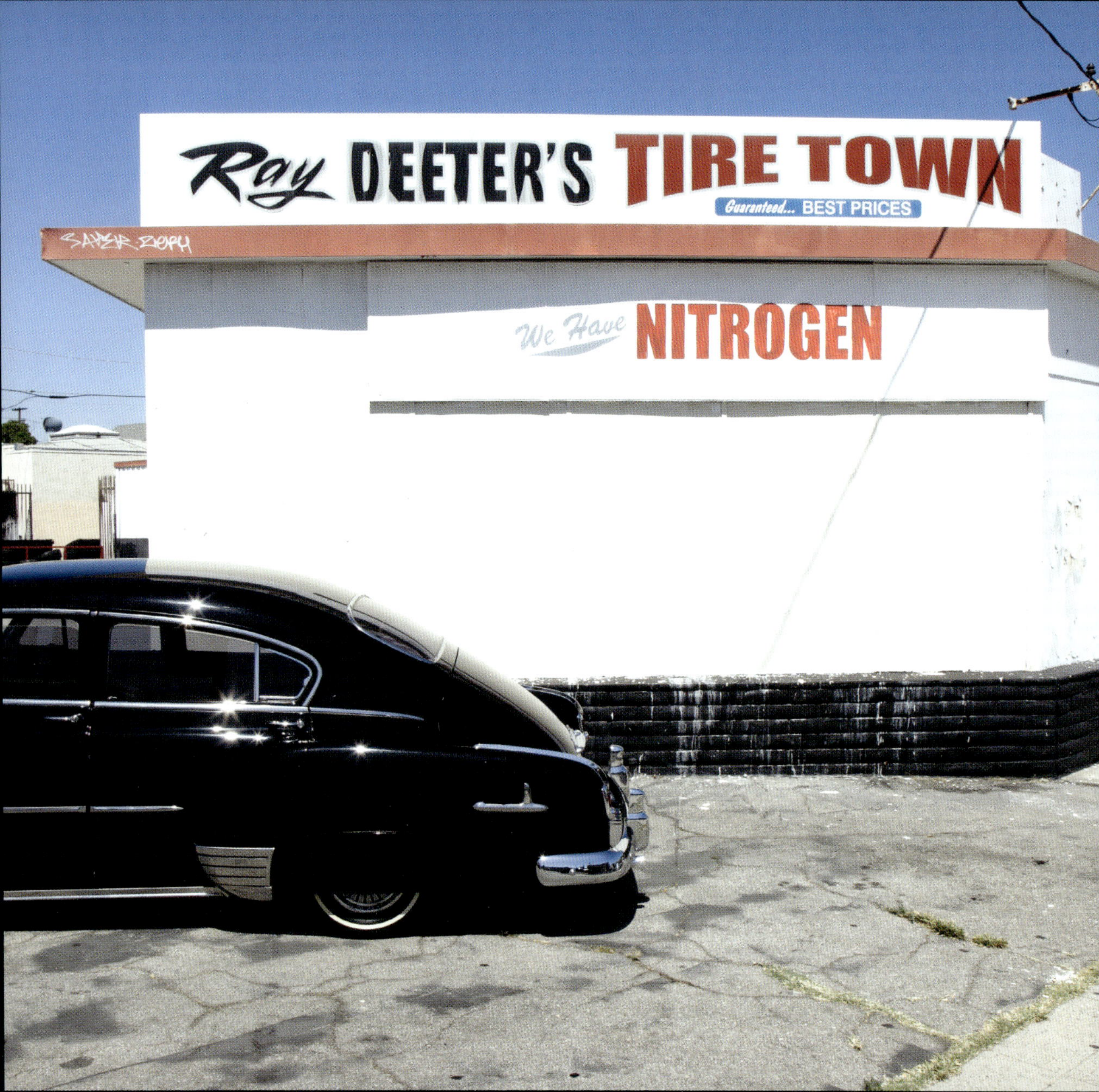

Tiefergelegter Buick aus den 1940er-Jahren vor stickstoffhaltiger Kulisse.
Lowered Buick from the 1940s in front of nitrogen-rich backdrop

Christliches Schattenspiel auf der Pacific Avenue.
Christian shadow play on Pacific Avenue.

002

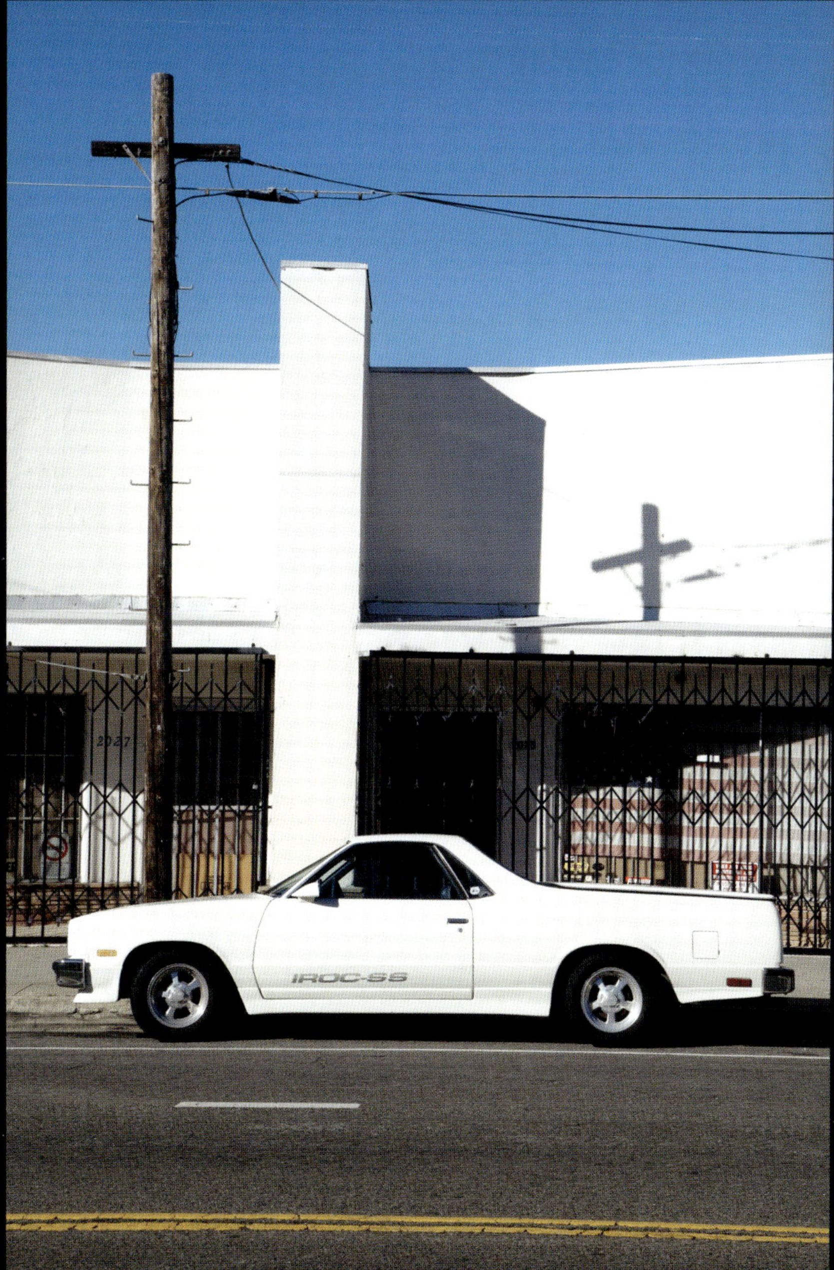

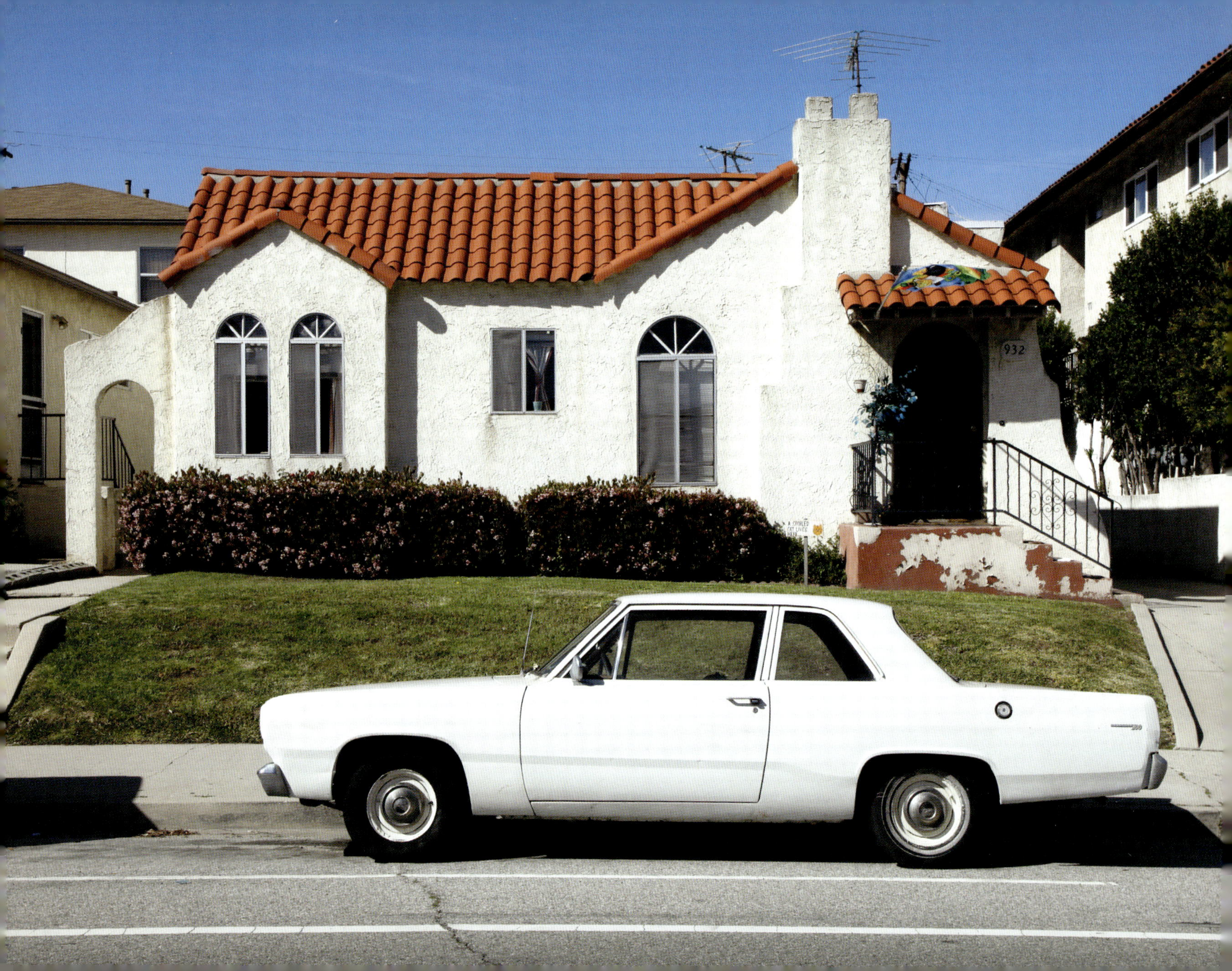
932

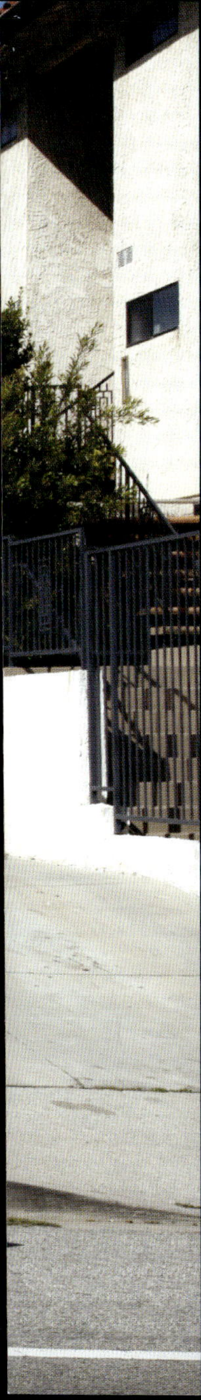

003

Meine durchgehende Sitzbank, mein Rasen, meine Hacienda. *My bench, my lawn, my Hacienda*

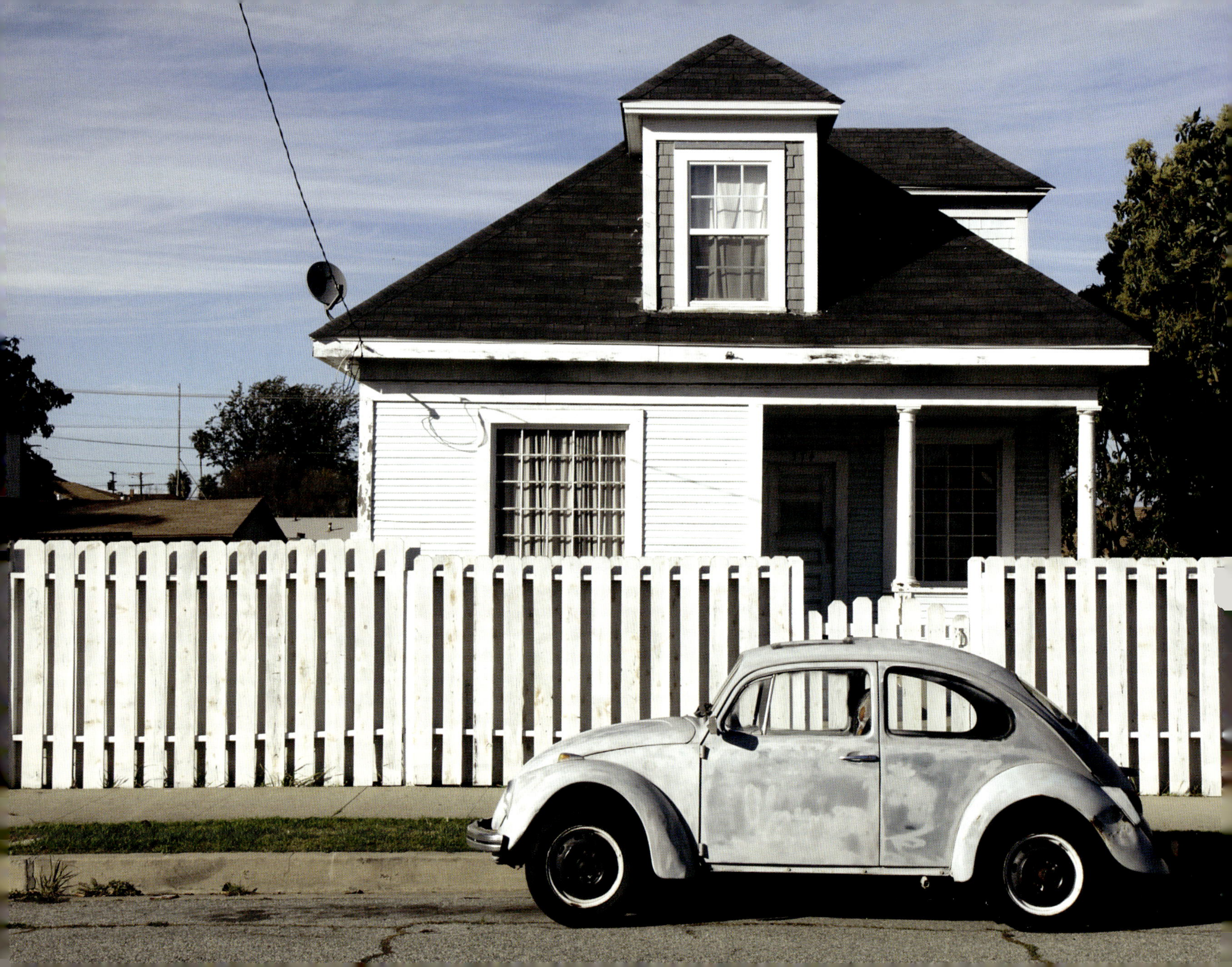

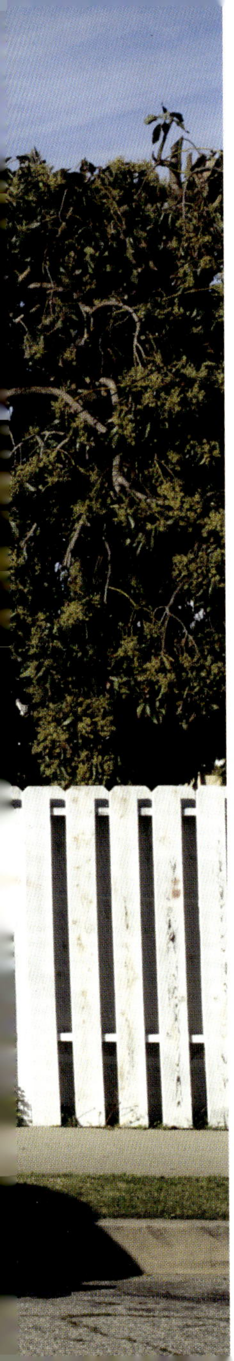

004

Abblätternder Lack ist einfach cool. Als Stilmittel eint er Haus und Auto.
Peeling paint is just cool. In style, the house and the car match.

005

Tiefergelegt und blickdicht. Genau wie der hohe Gartenzaun.
Lowered and opaque, just like the tall fence.

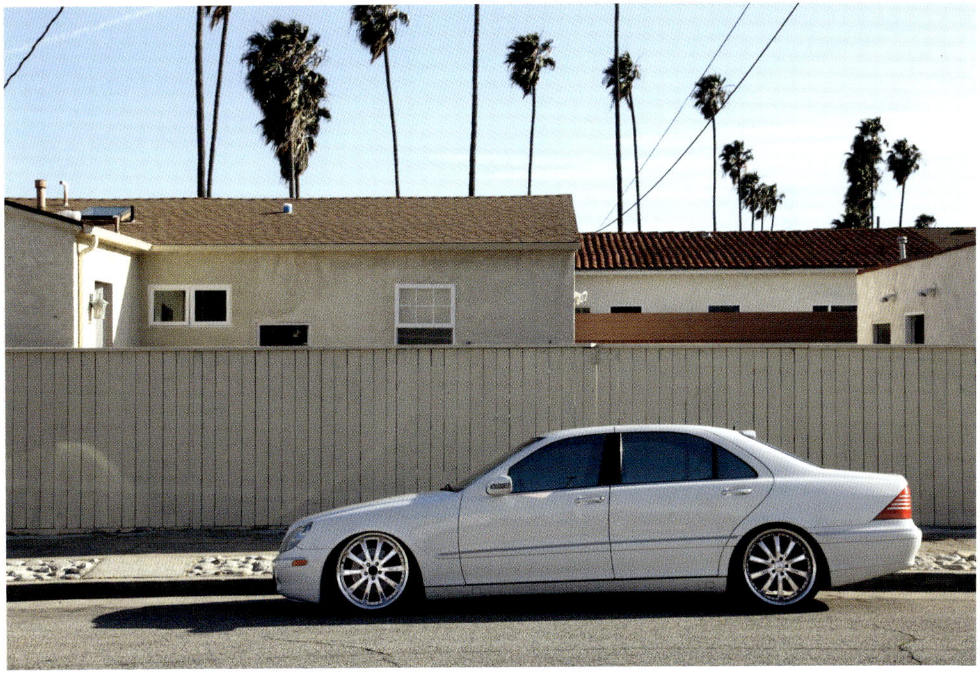

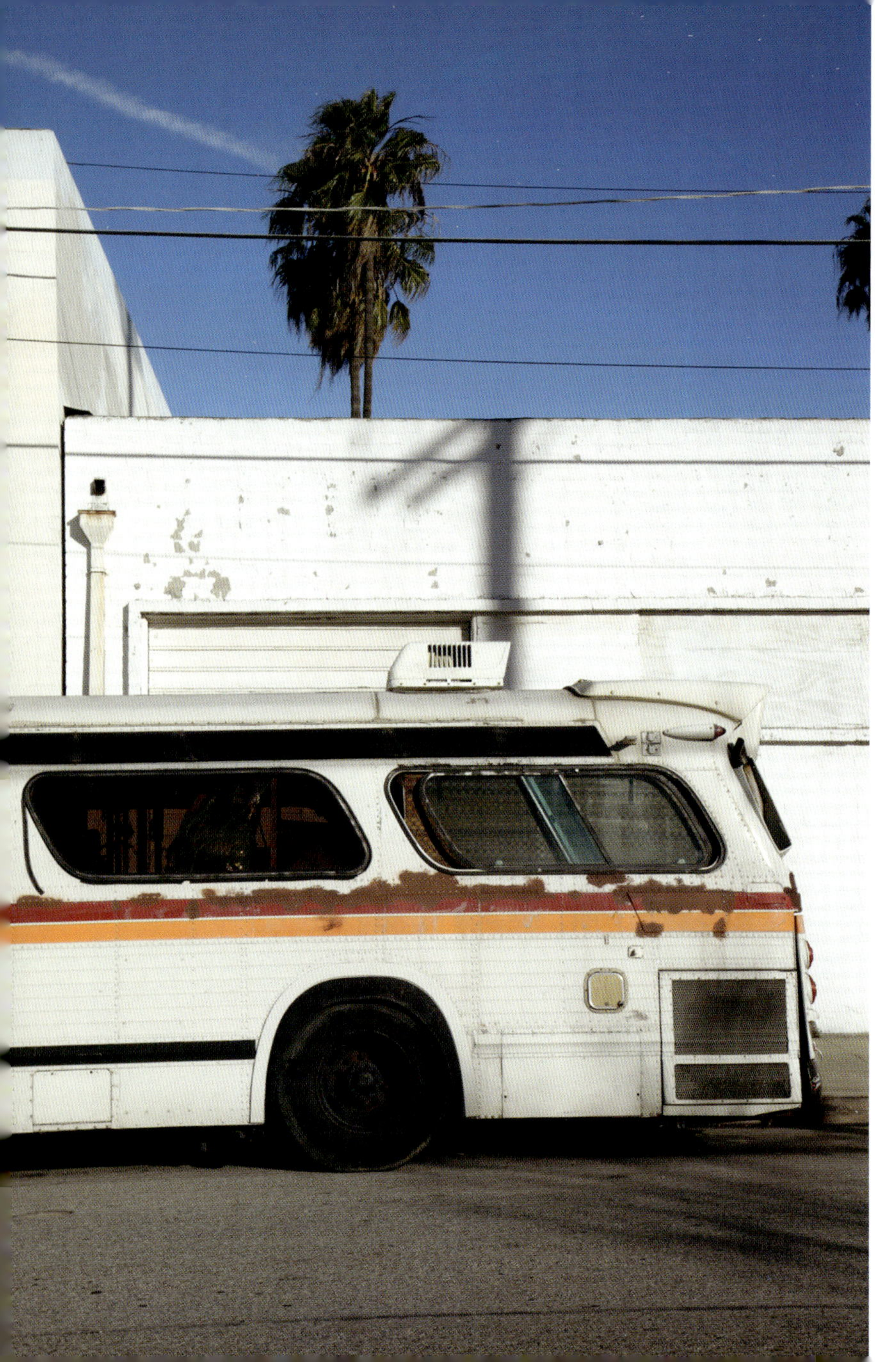

006

Zu Hause im Bus. Vier Räder und vier Wände bedeuten hier das gleiche.
At home in the bus: four wheels and four walls are one and the same.

007

Der Parkplatz fürs Haus war leichter zu finden.
It was easier to find a parking space for the house.

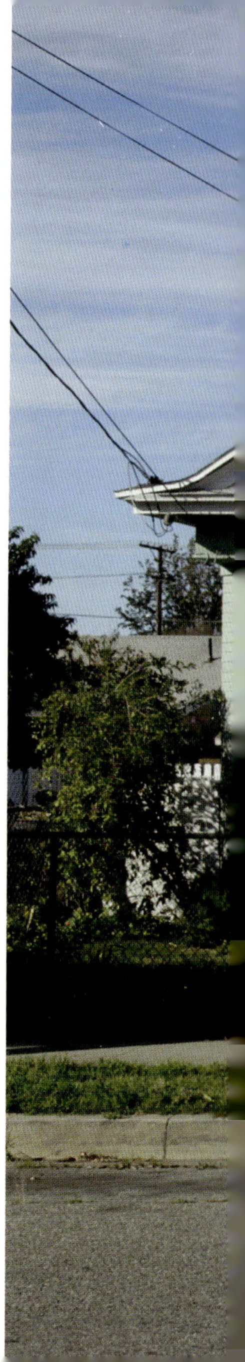

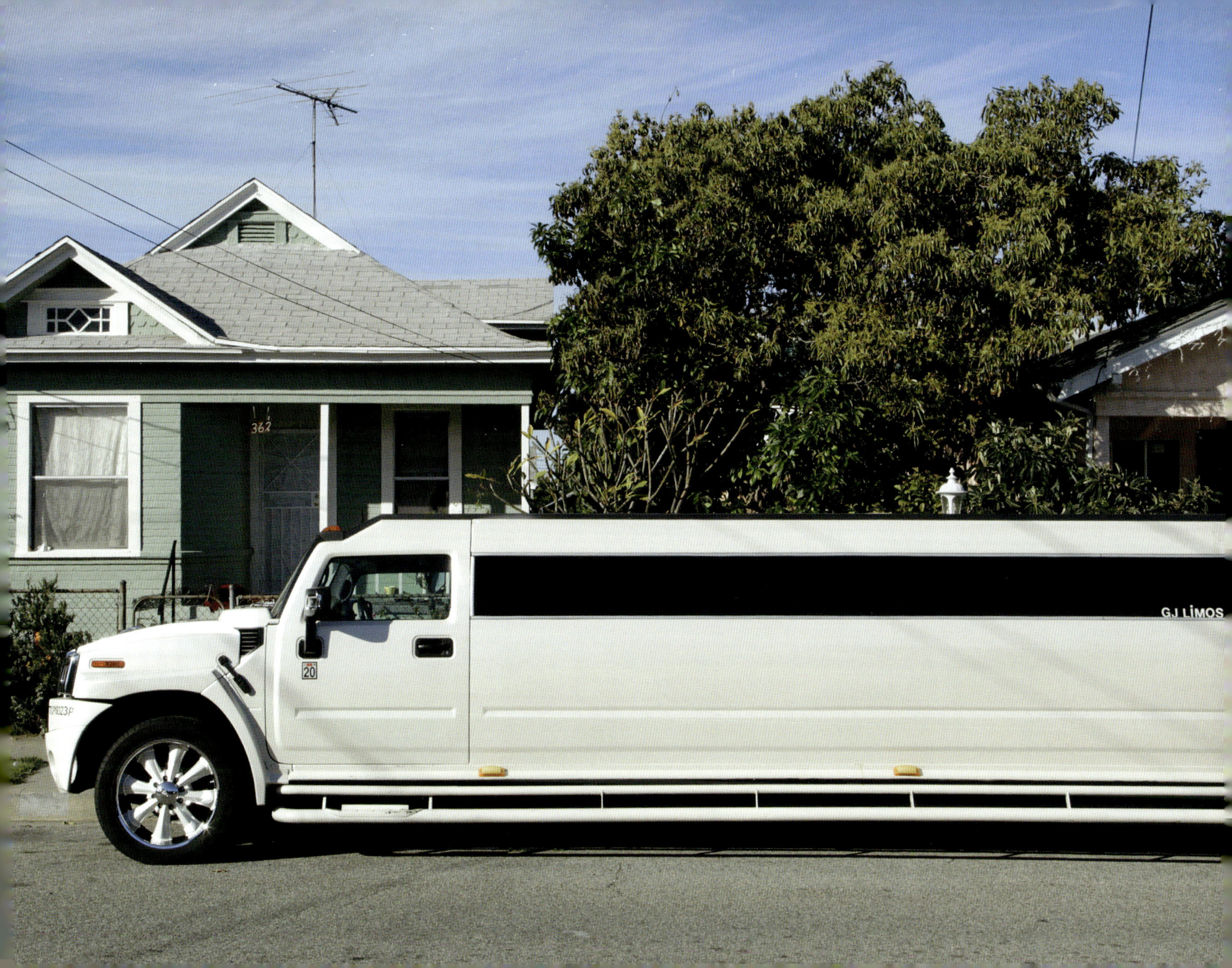
GJ LIMOS

008

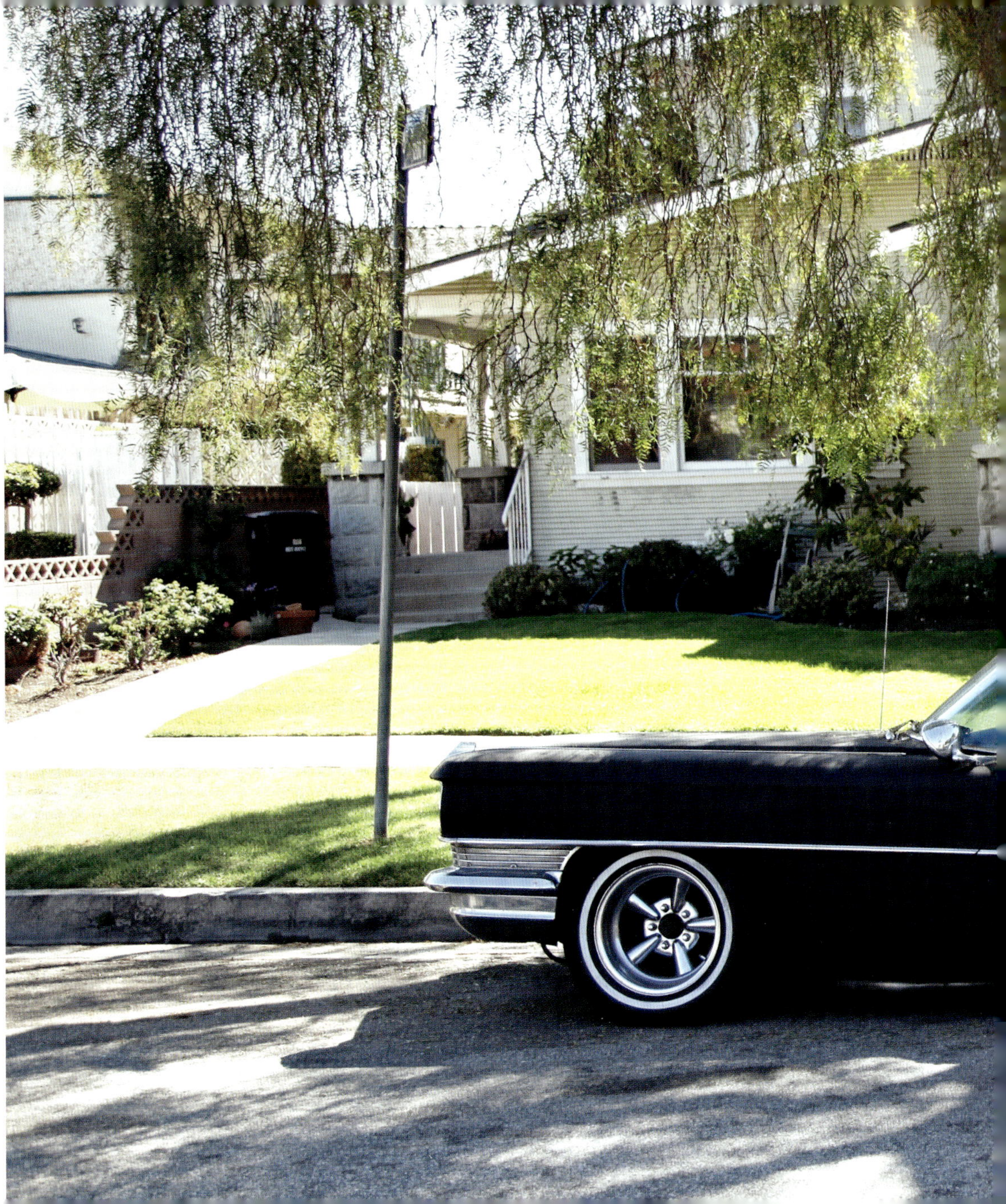

Cadillac Fleetwood von 1962 unter grüner Weide.
1962 Cadillac Fleetwood under a green willow tree.

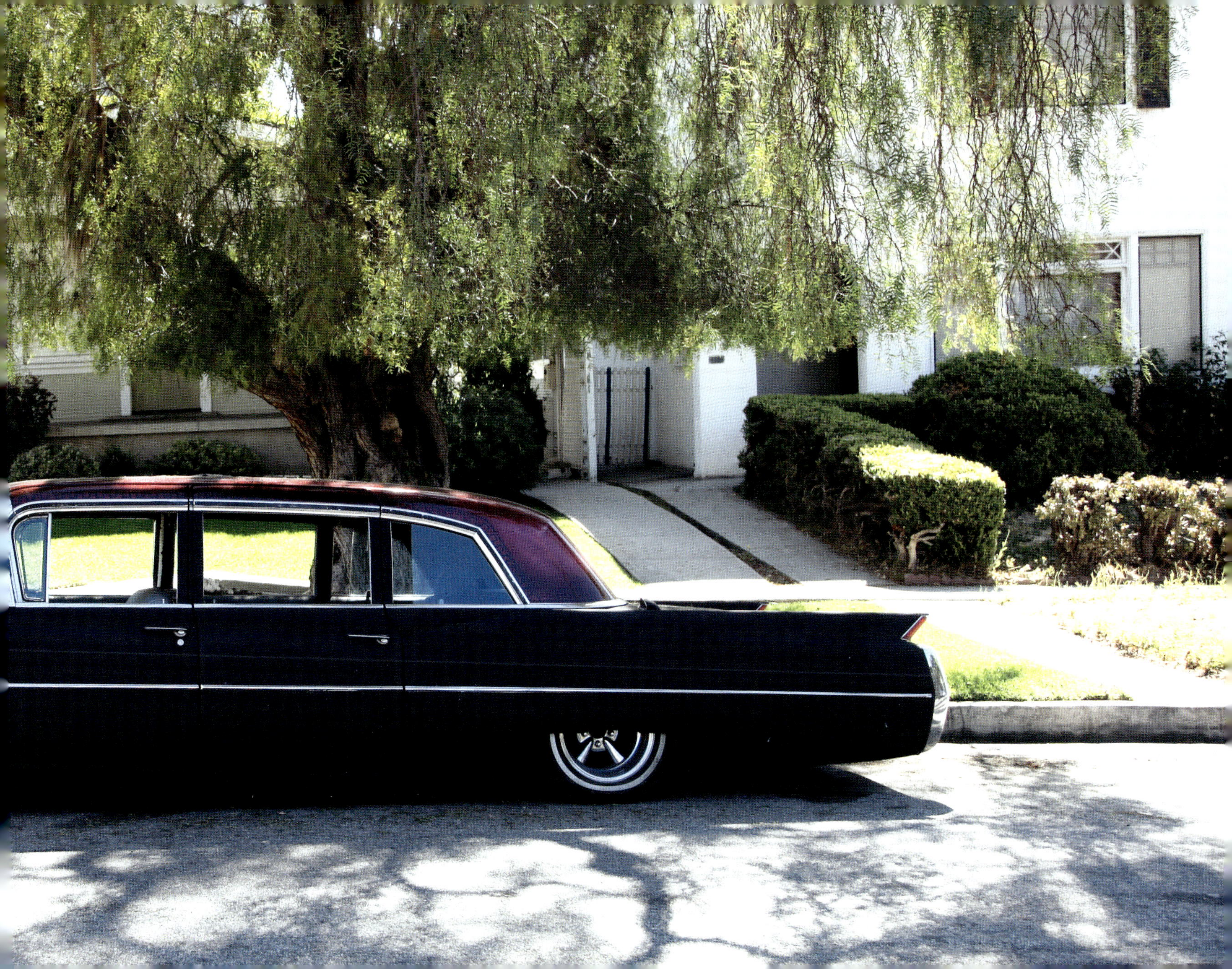

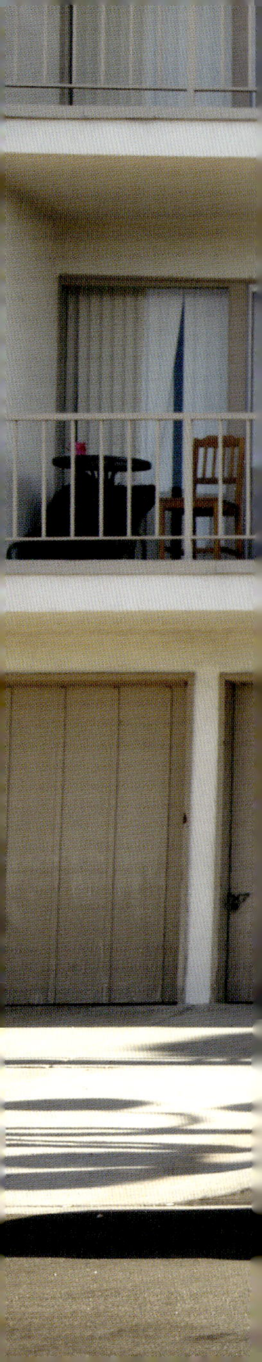

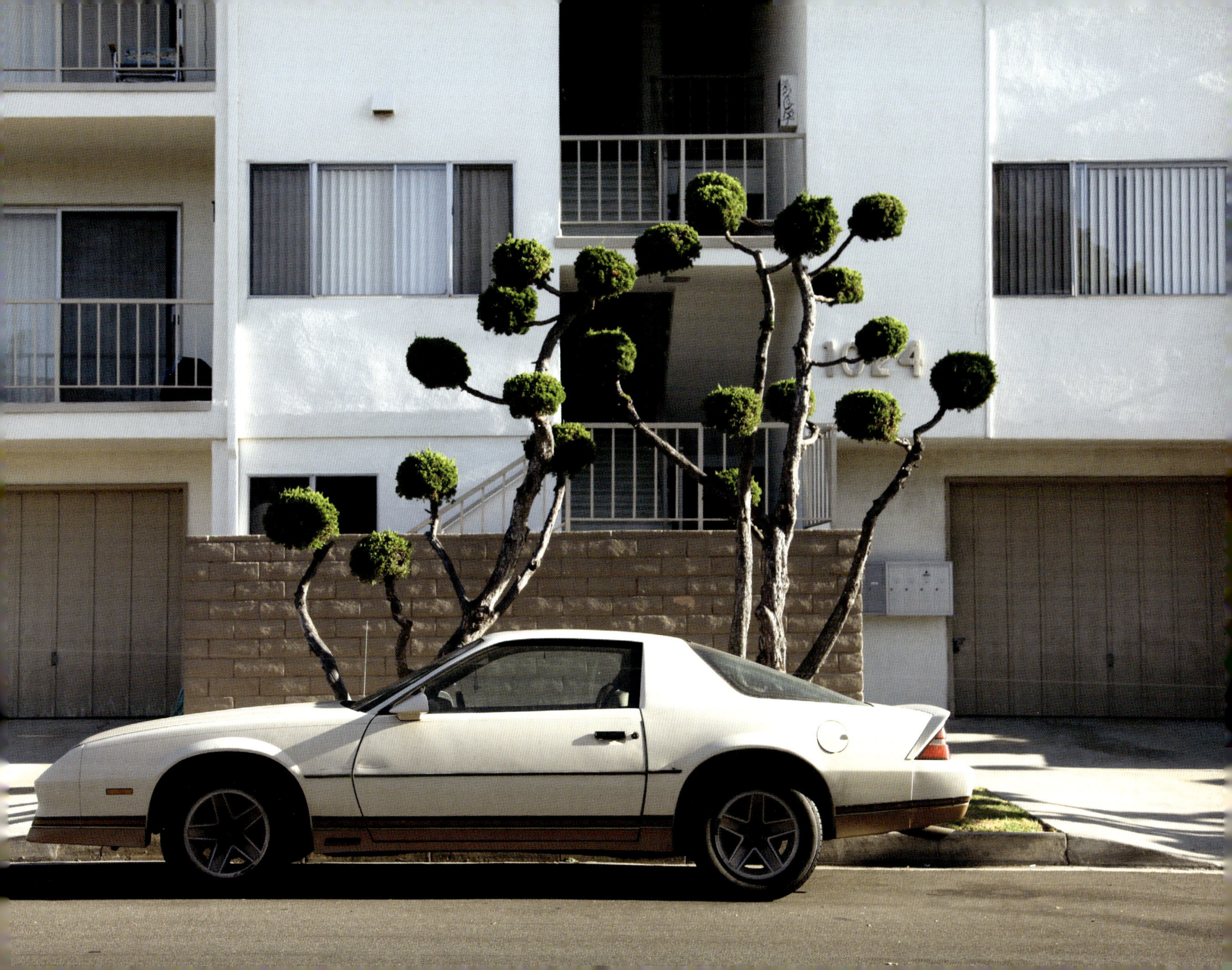
1024

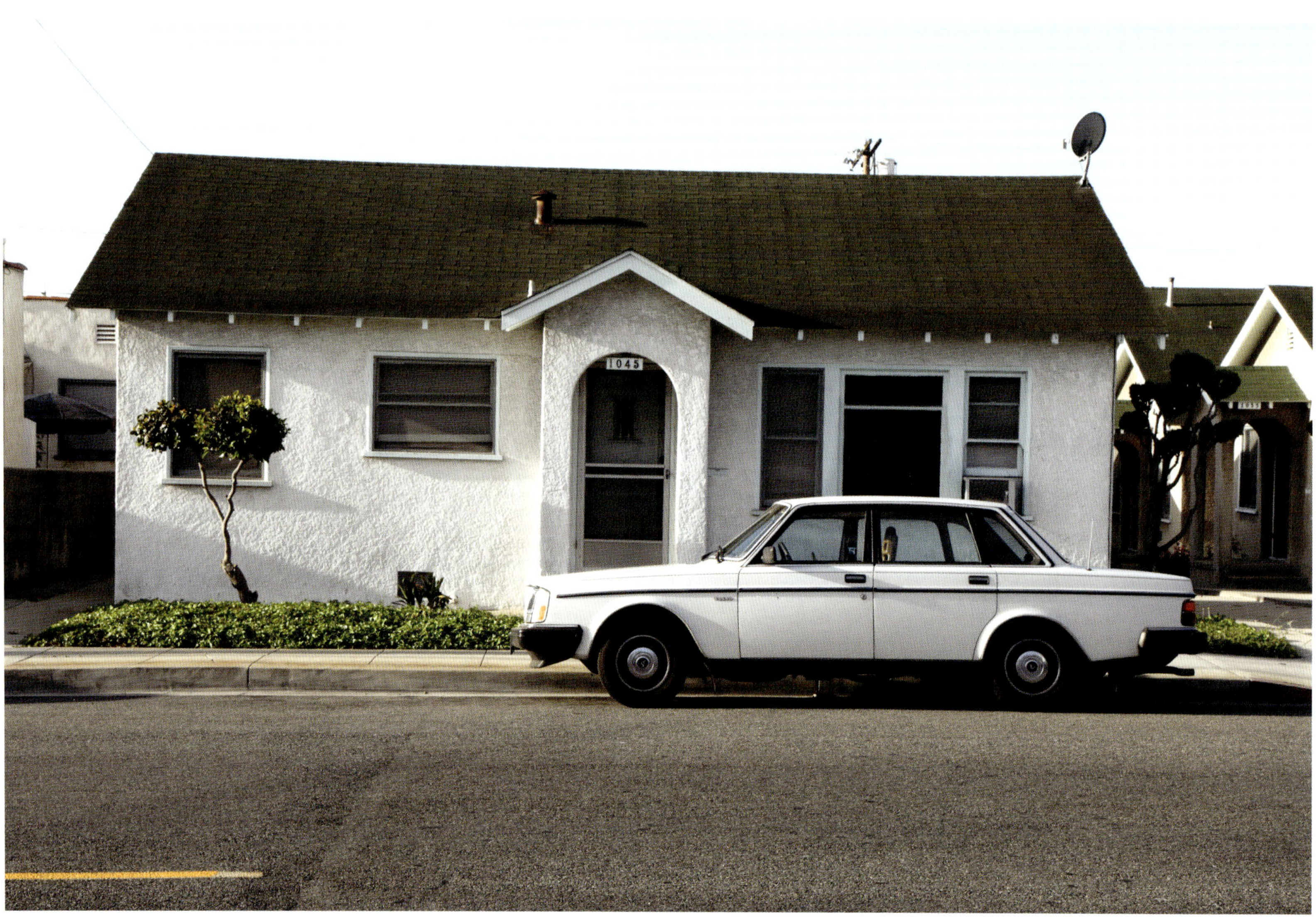

Haus und Auto in Schweden-Weiß. *House and car in Swedish white.*

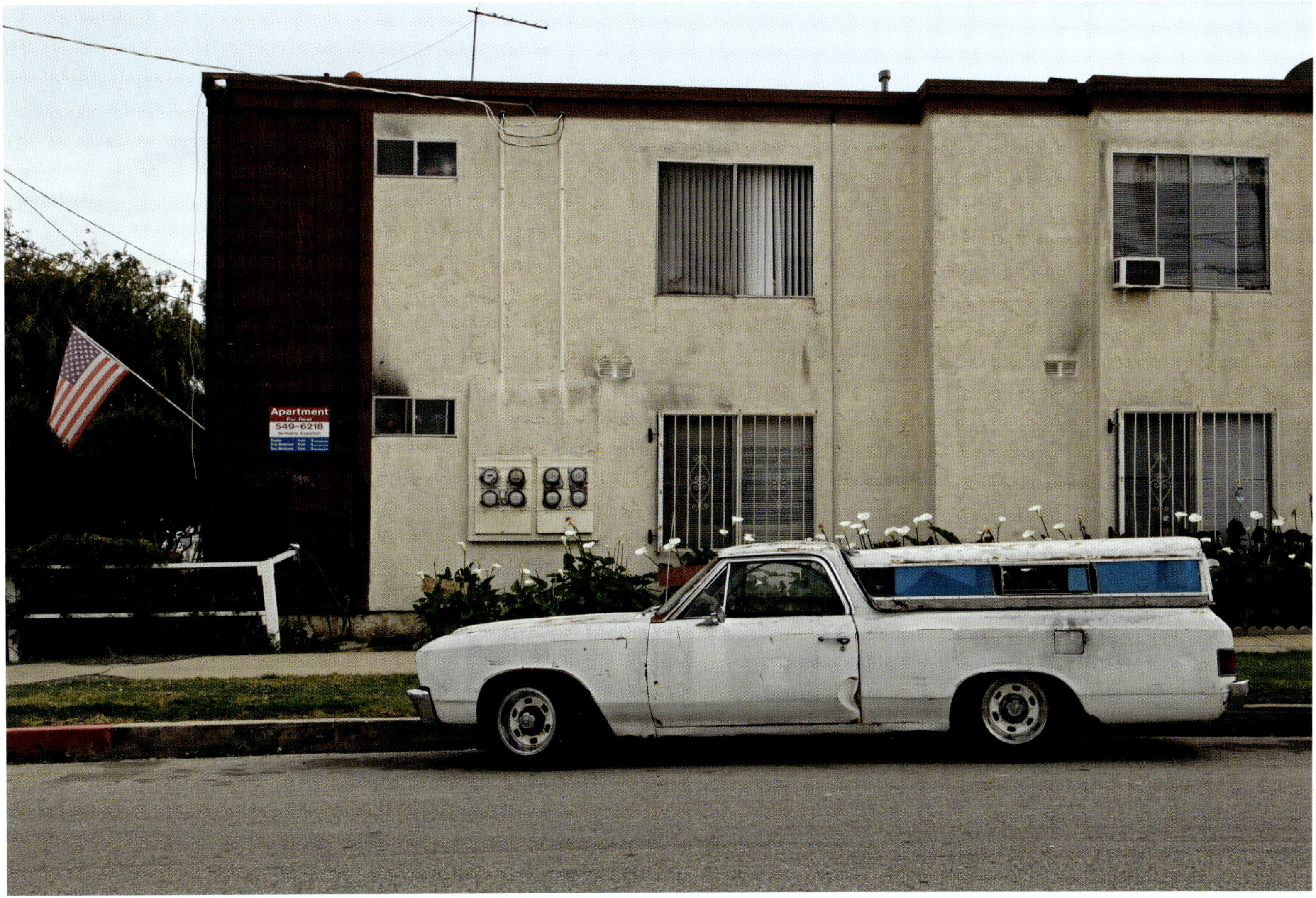

Patriotismus am und vor dem Haus. *Patriotism on and in front of the house.*

012 013

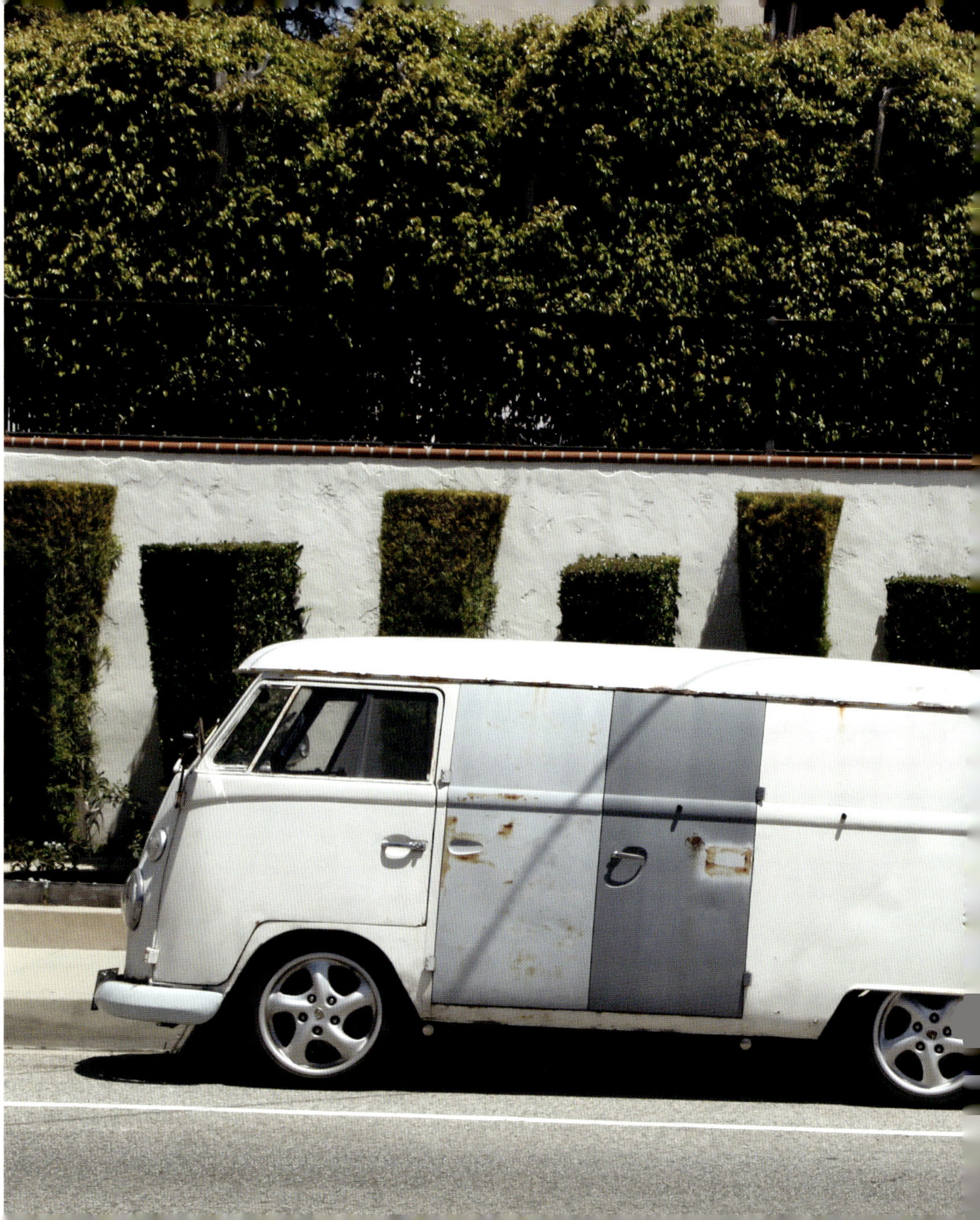

Deutsche Einwanderer,
gut assimiliert.
*German immigrants,
well-assimilated.*

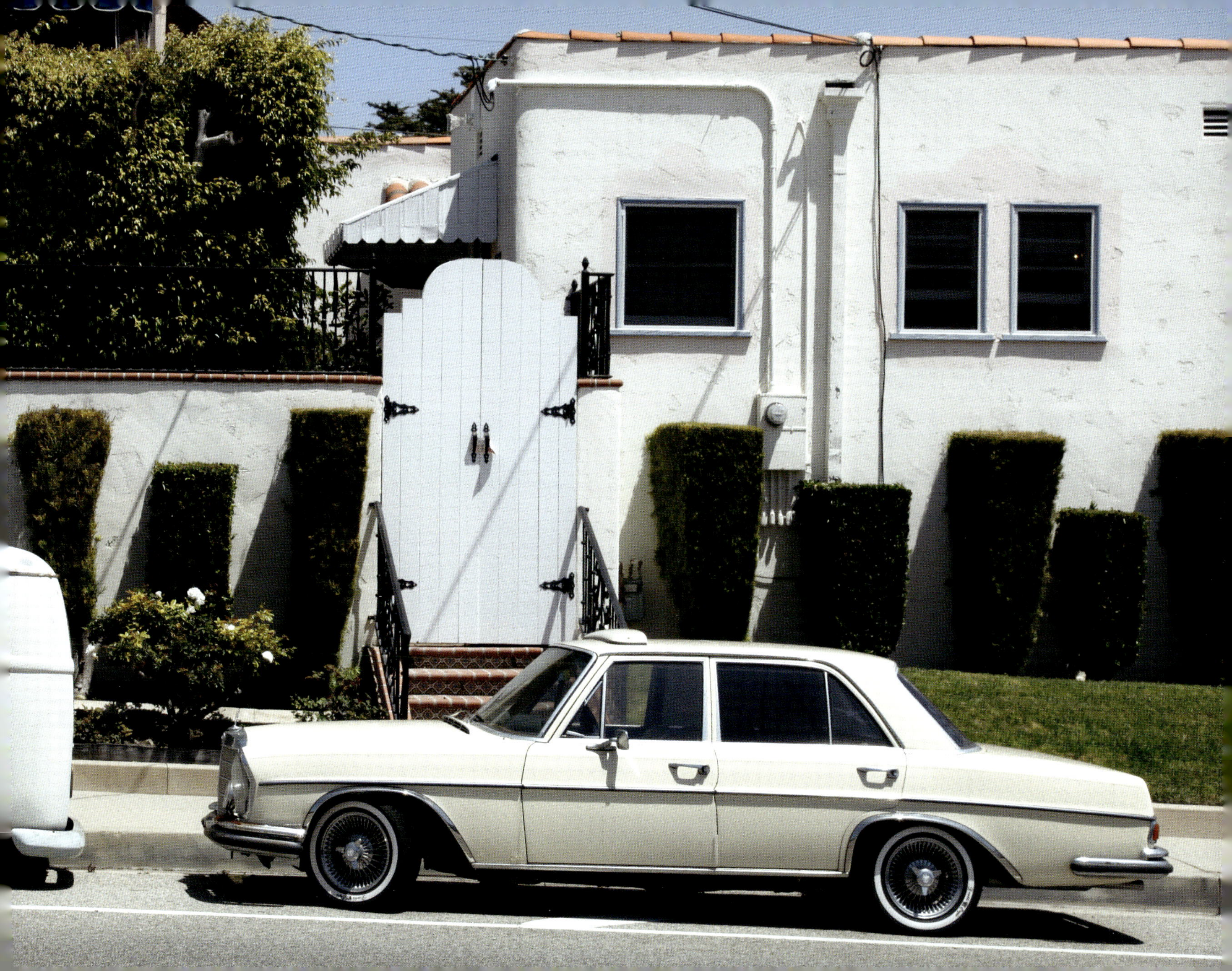

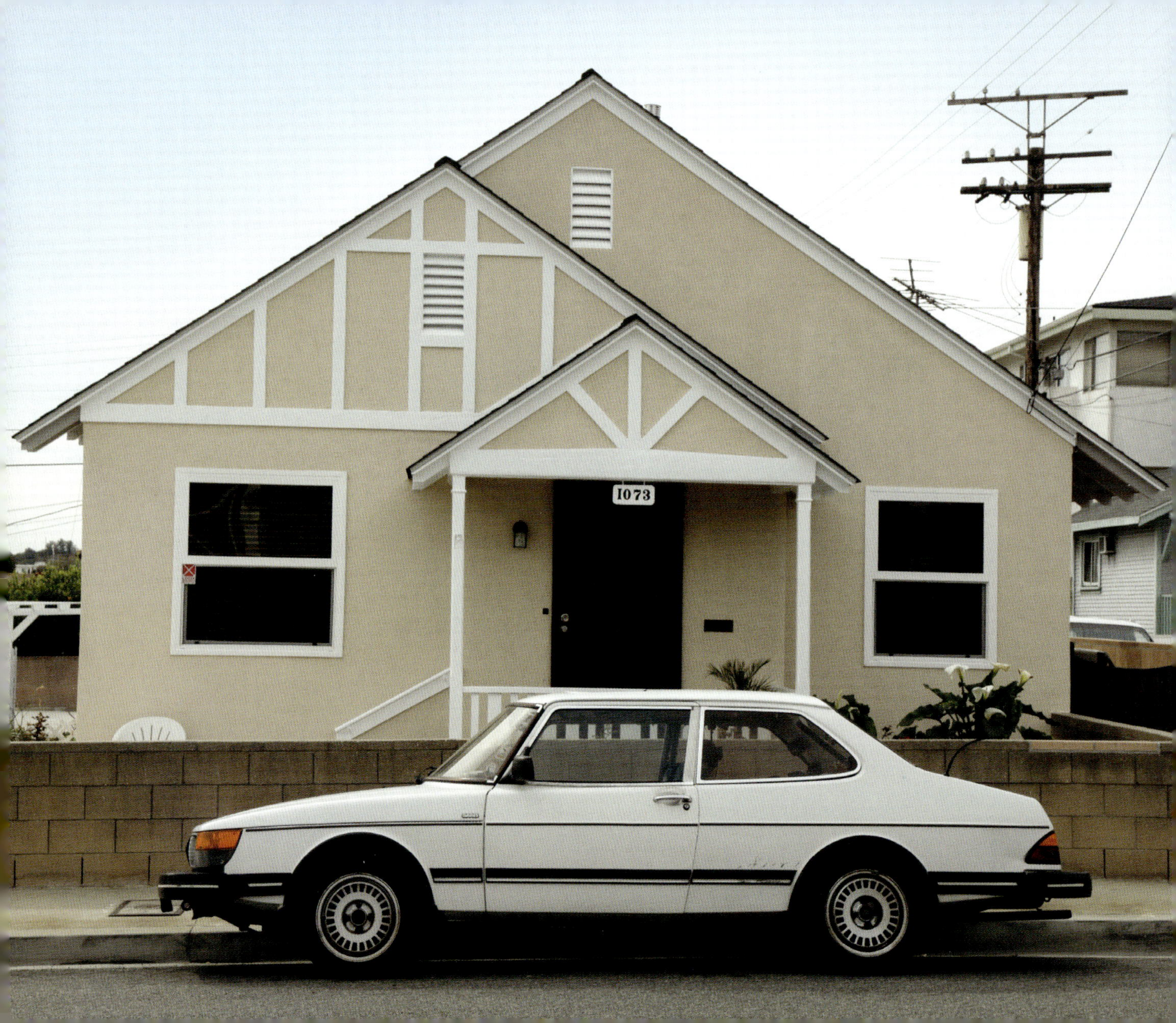
1073

014

Schnörkellose Zweck-
bauten unter sich.
*No frills. Functional
buildings amongst
themselves.*

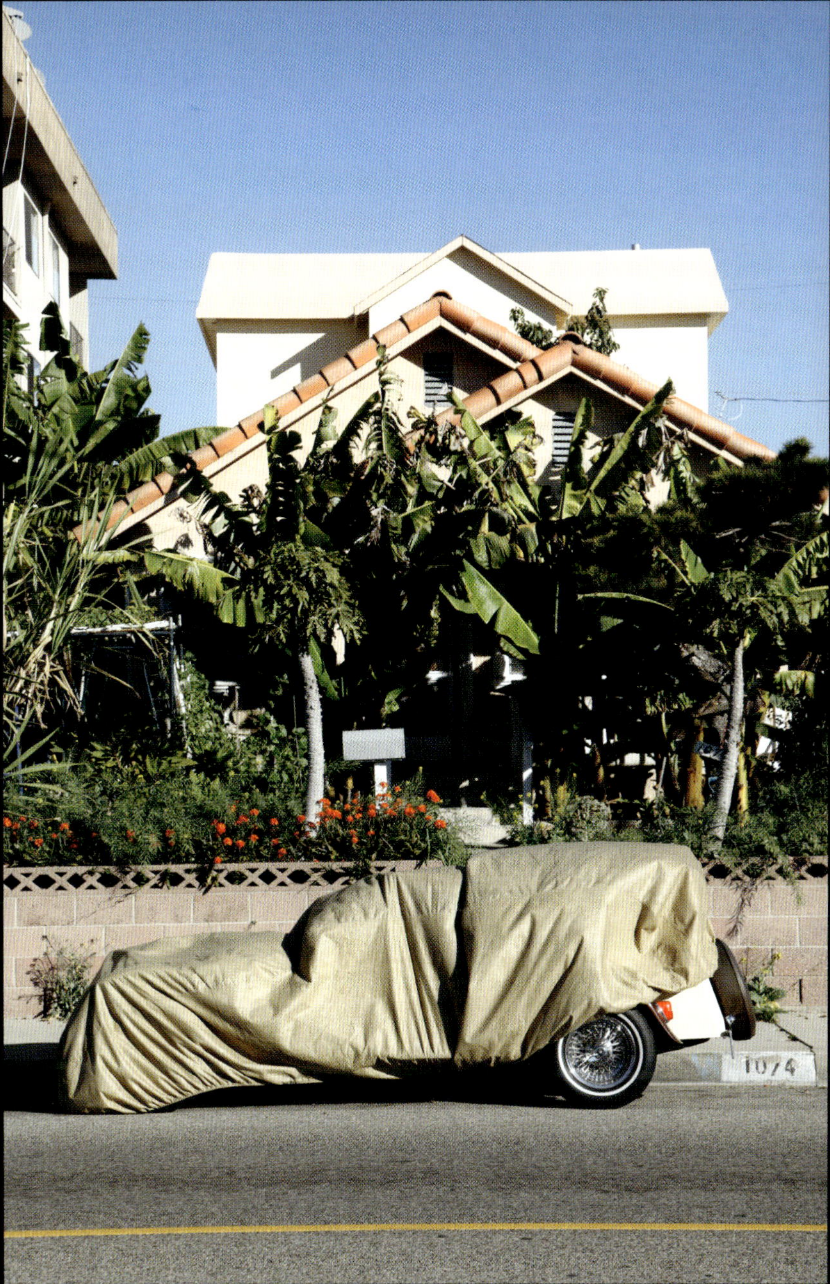

Plane und Palme: Nichts geht ohne Sonnenschutz.
Tarp and palm tree: nothing goes without protection from the sun.

015

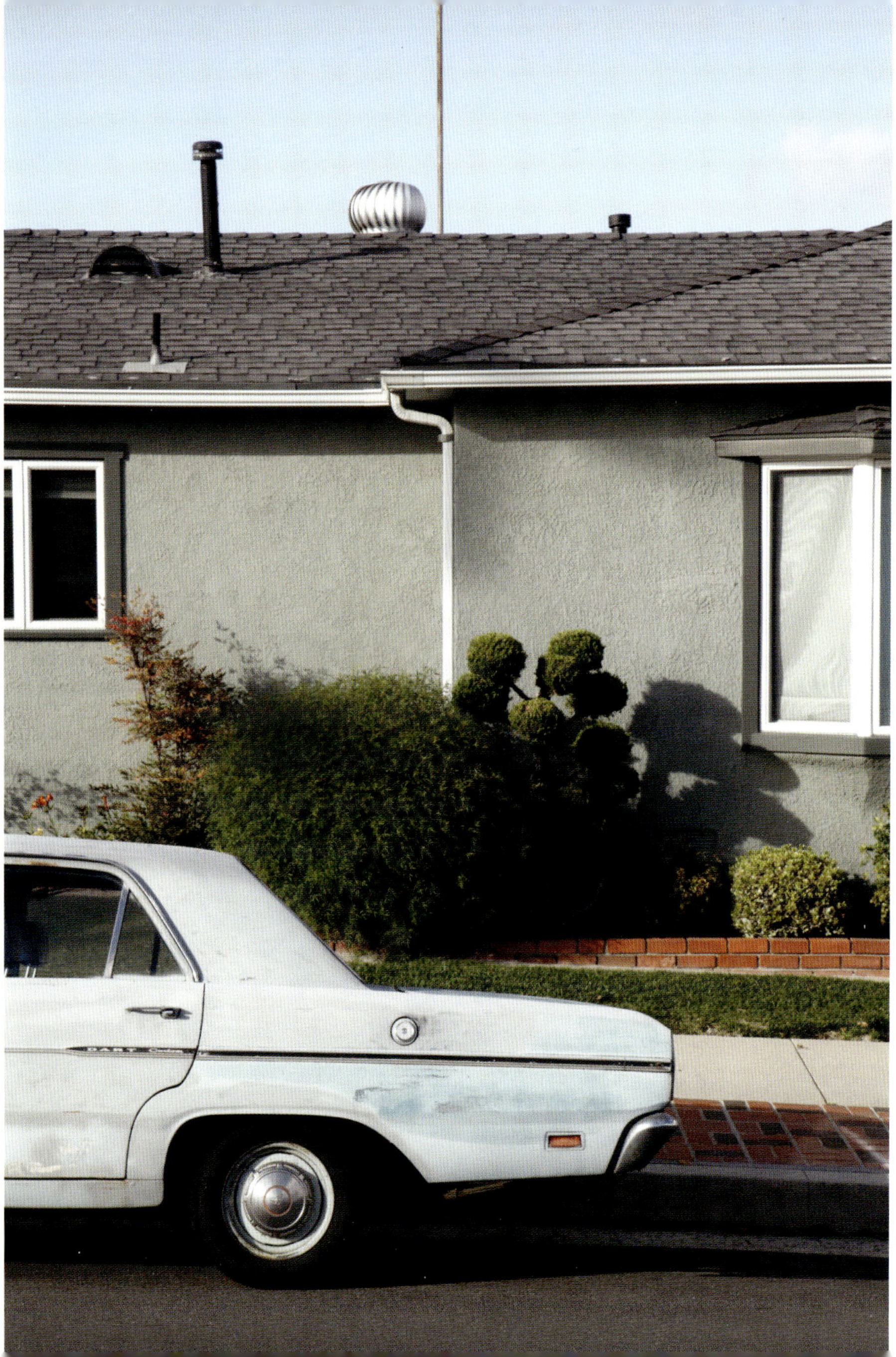

016

Ein klassischer Fall von Patina.
A classic case of patina.

017

Auto und Haus tauschen allmählich ihre Farben aus.
The car and the house will eventually trade colors.

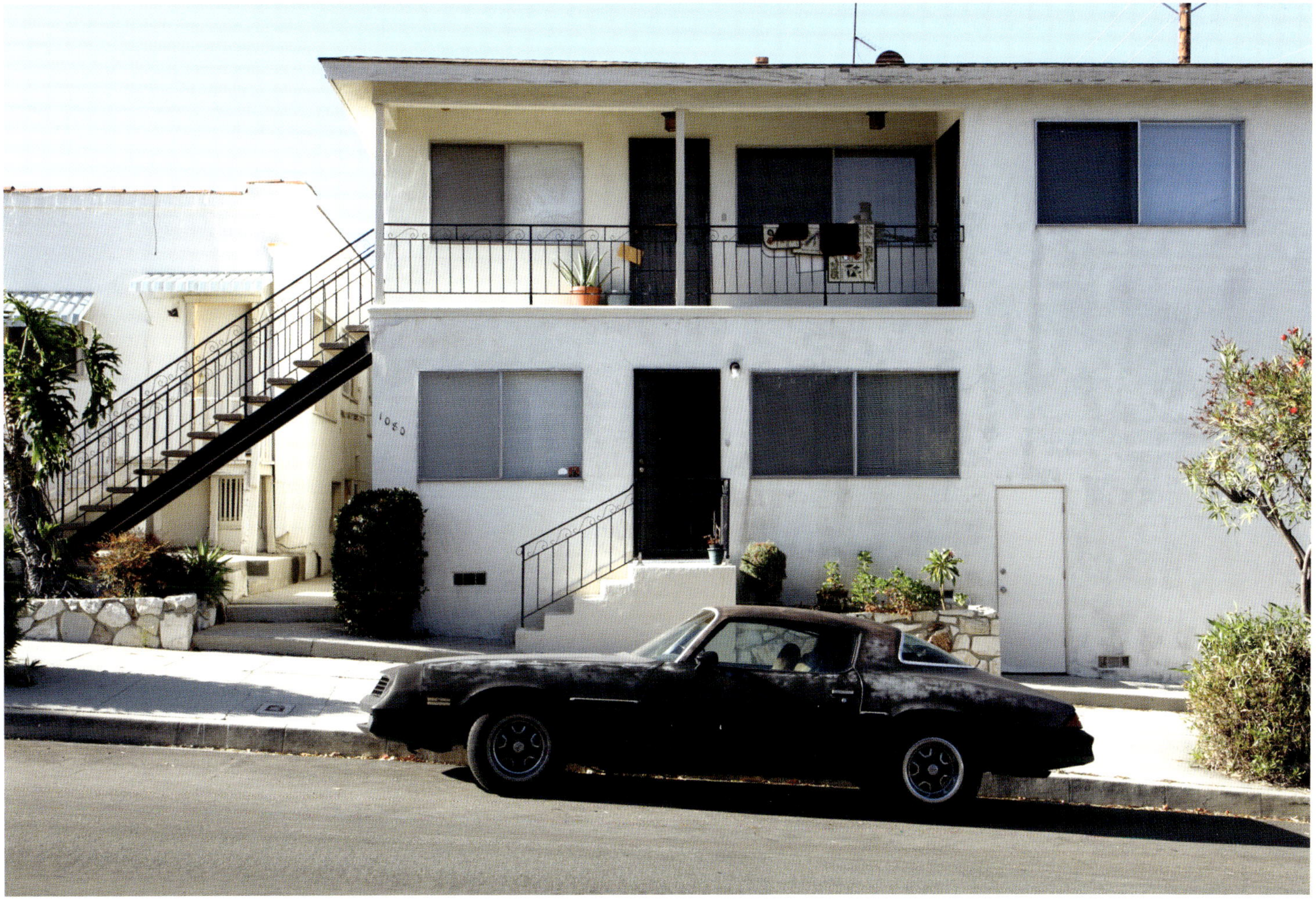

018

Käfer, beobachtet von unidentifizierten Objekten.
VW Bug being observed by an unidentified object.

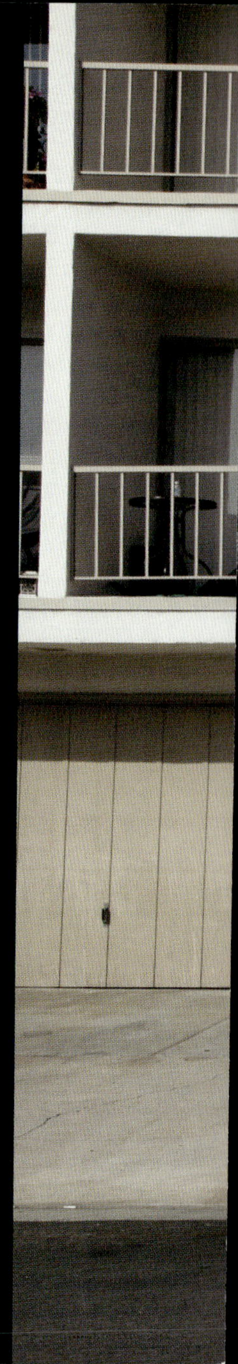

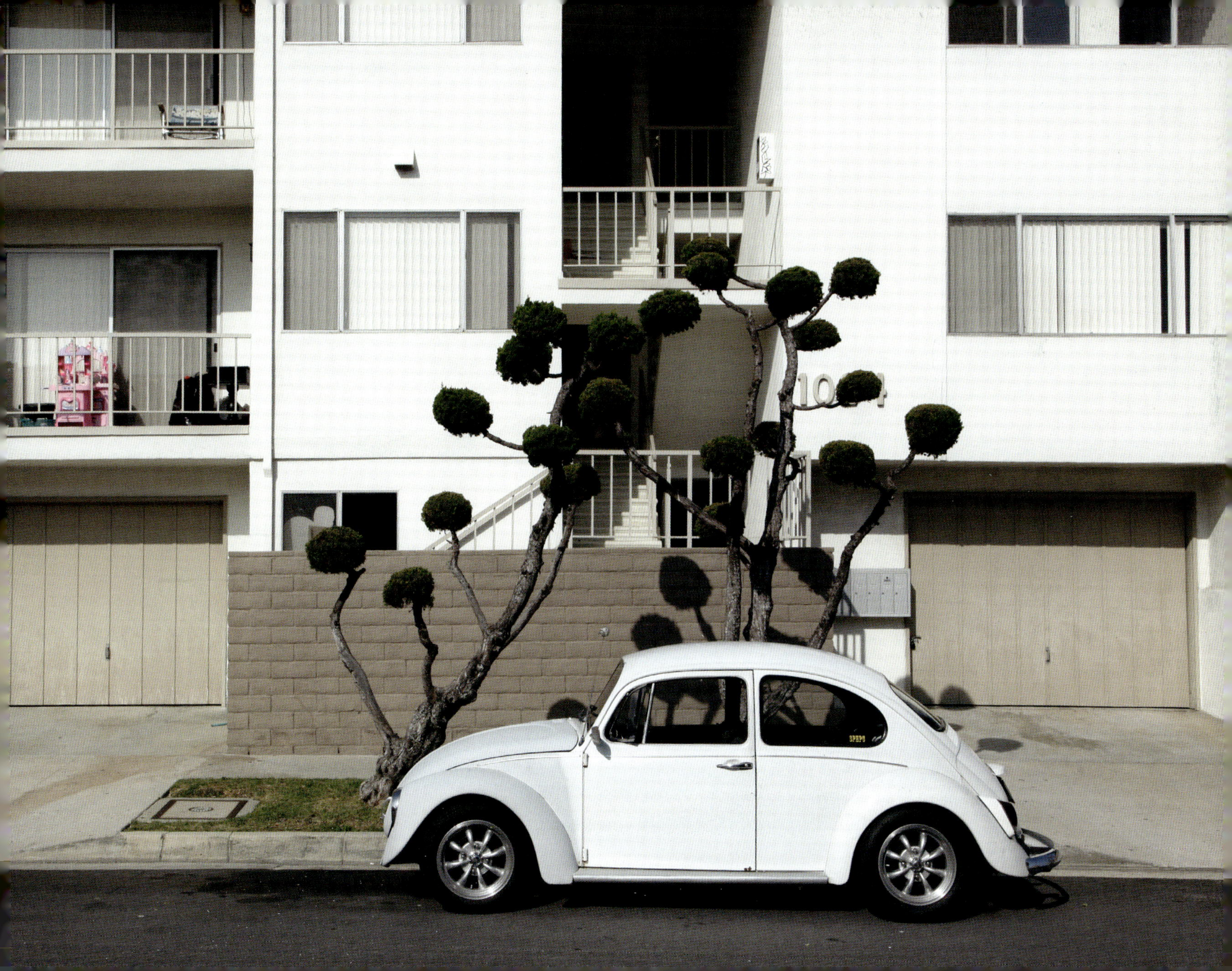

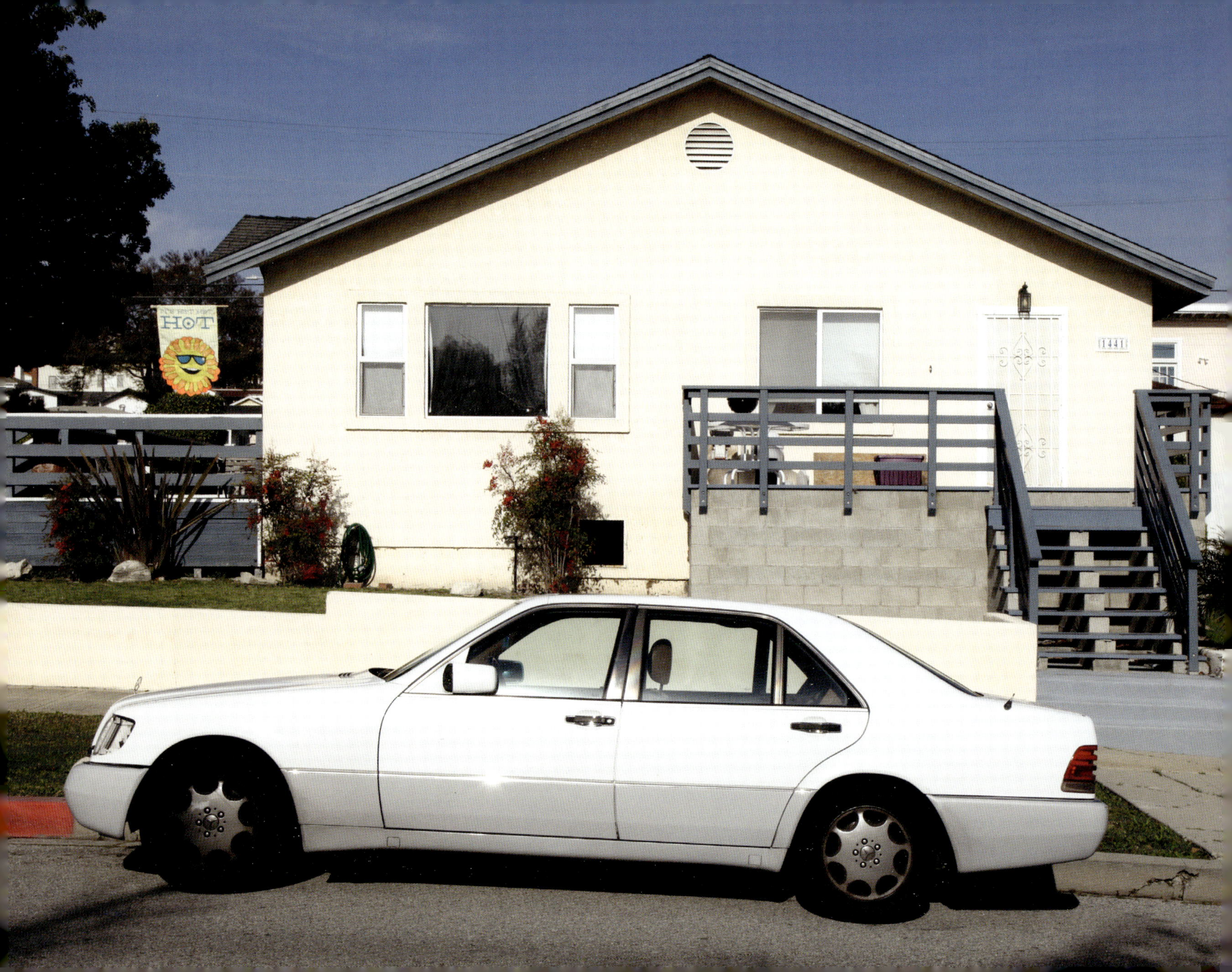
HOT
1441

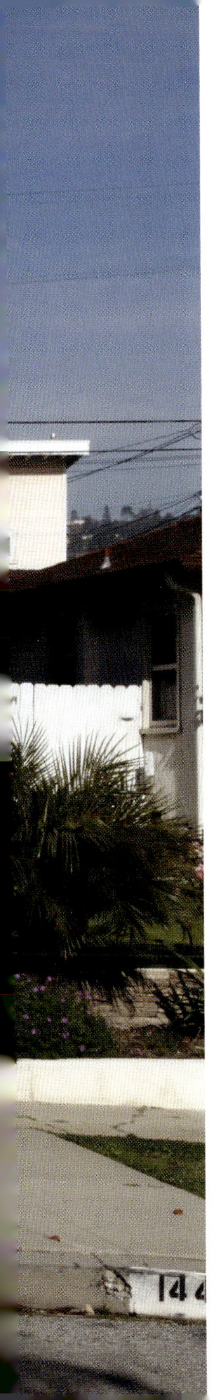

019

An diesem Tag ist
die Welt in Ordnung.
*On this day, the
world was alright.*

020

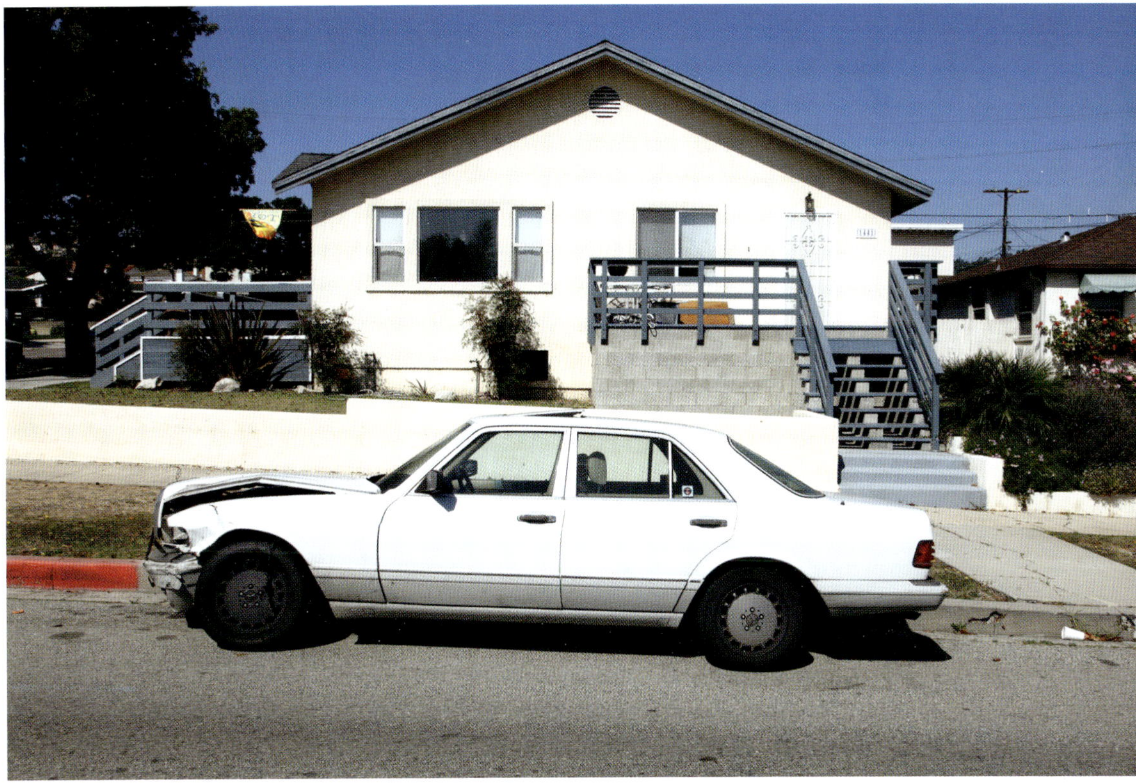

An diesem Tag ist etwas schiefgelaufen. *On this day, something went a little bit wrong.*

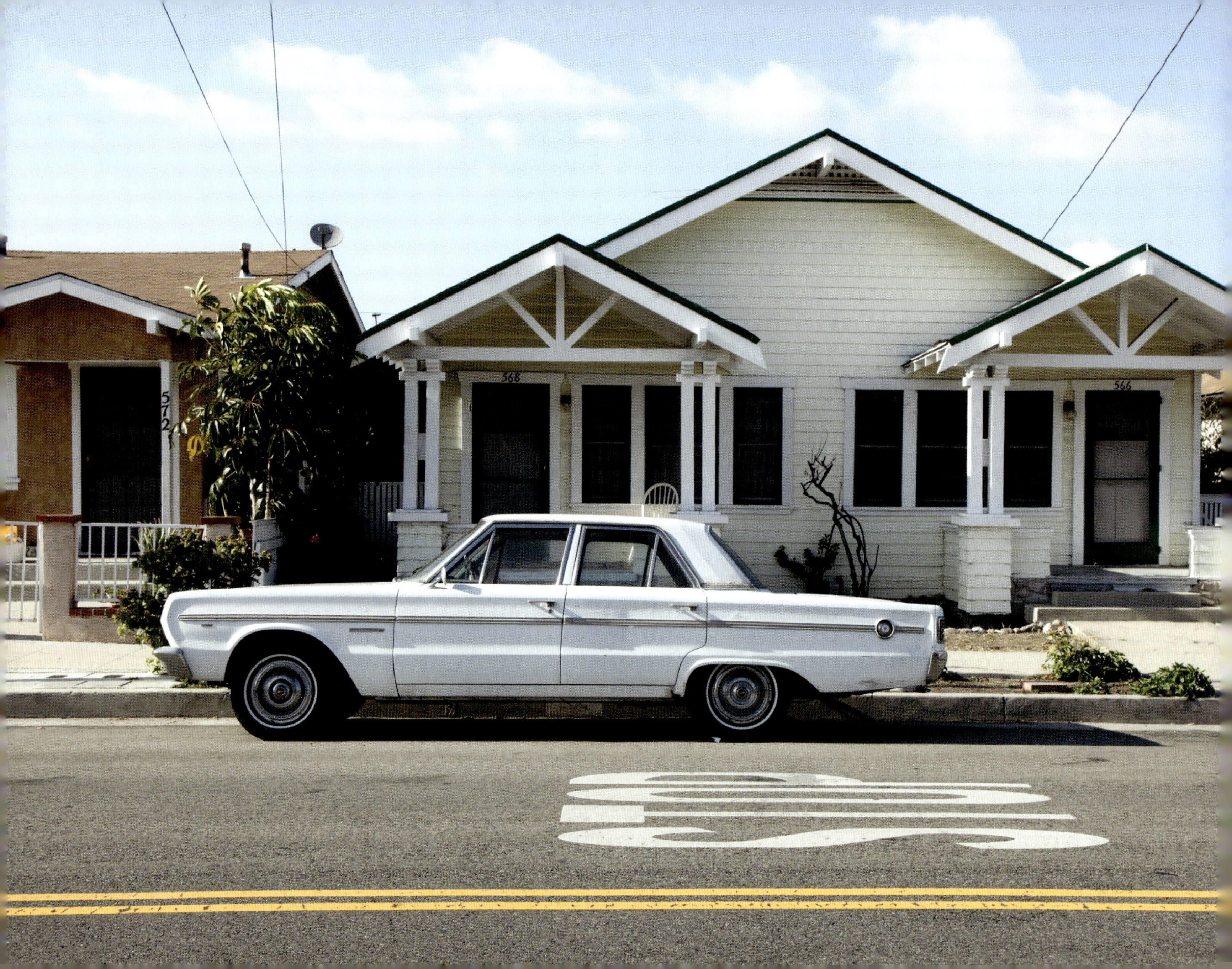
572
568
566
STOP

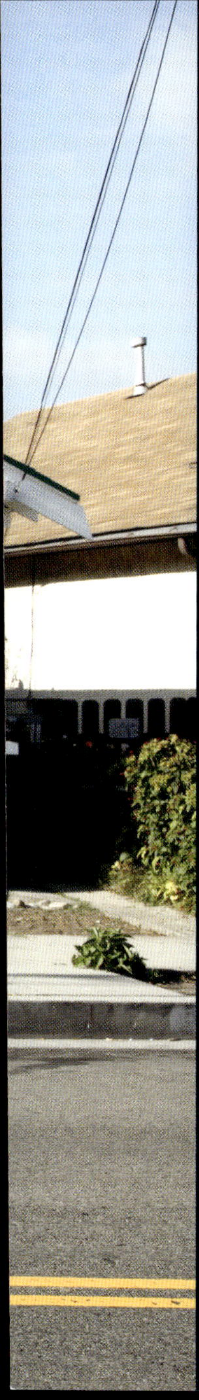

021

Zwei Schönheiten aus der Mitte der 1960er-Jahren. *Two beauties from the middle of the 1960s*

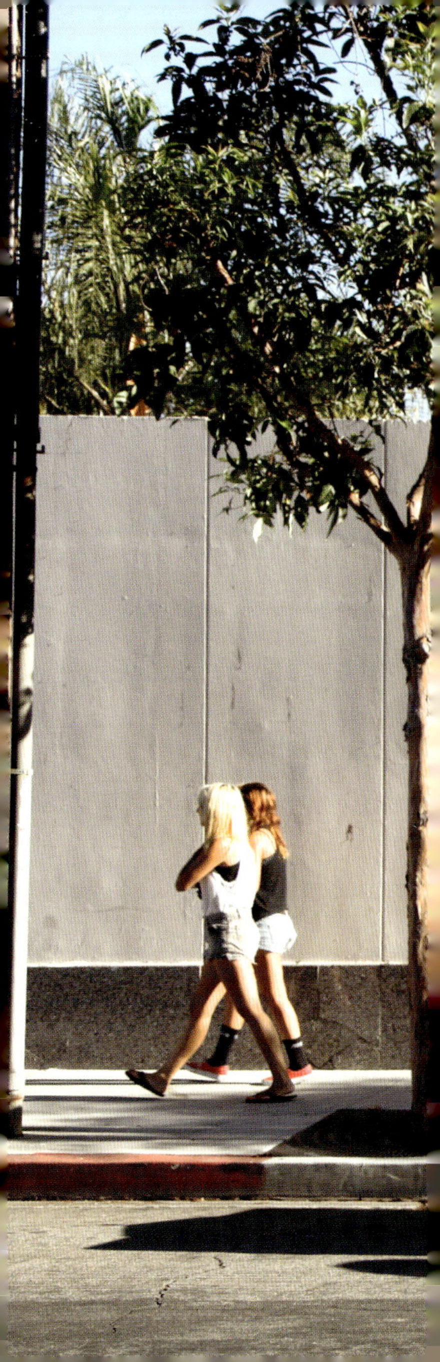

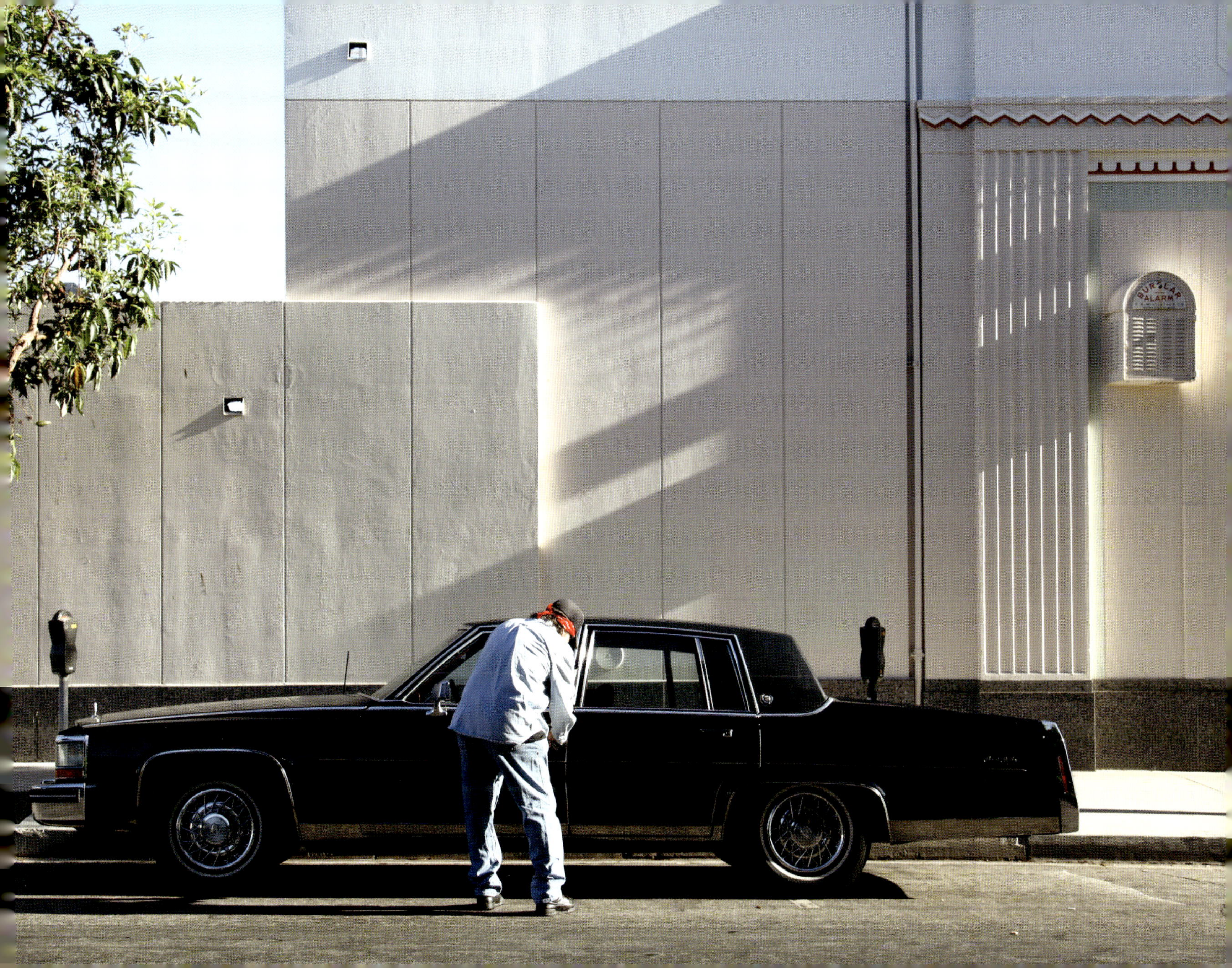
ALARM

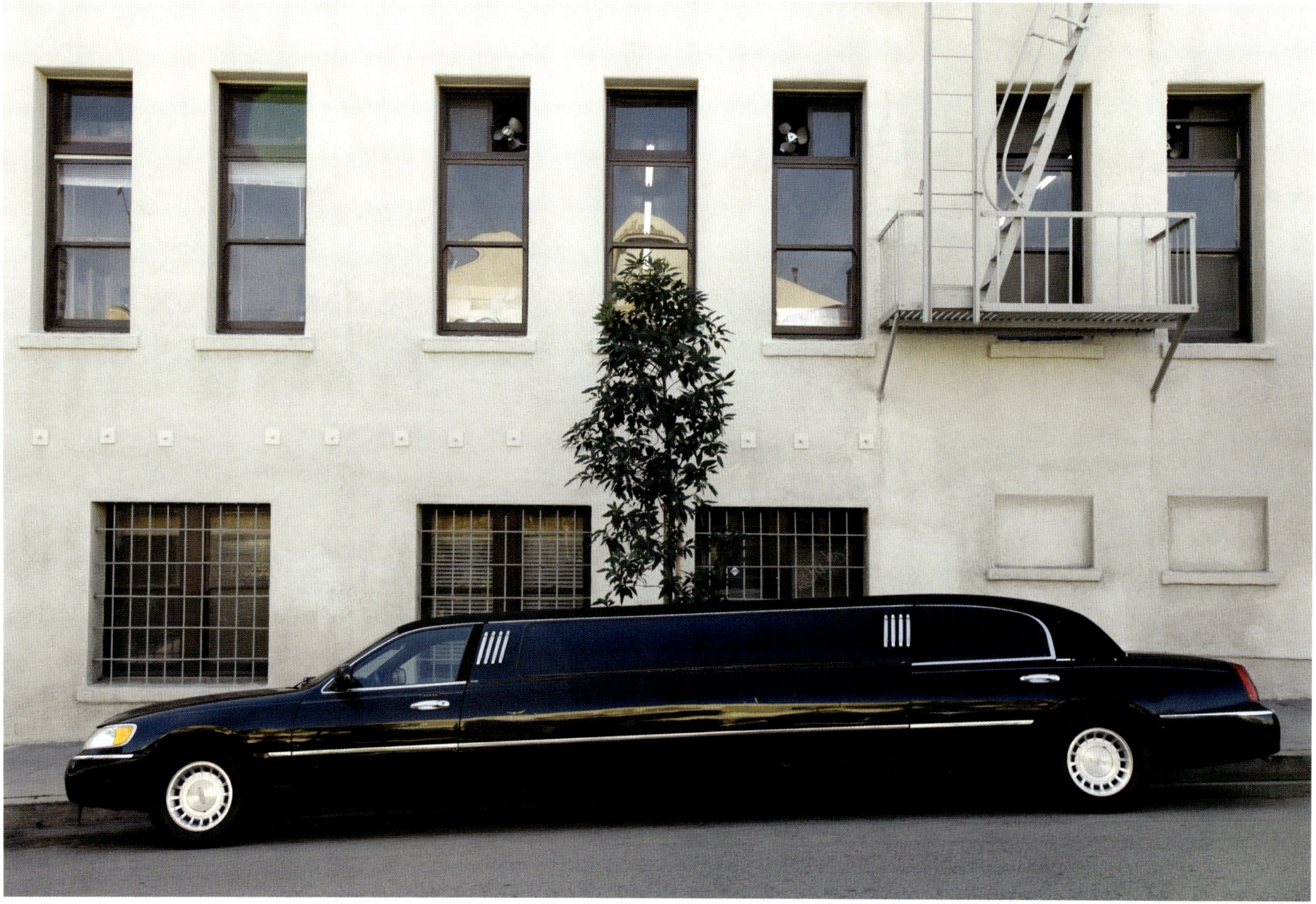

Strech-Limo mit Baum. Wächst er aus dem Schiebedach? *Stretch limo with tree. Is it growing out of the sunroof?*

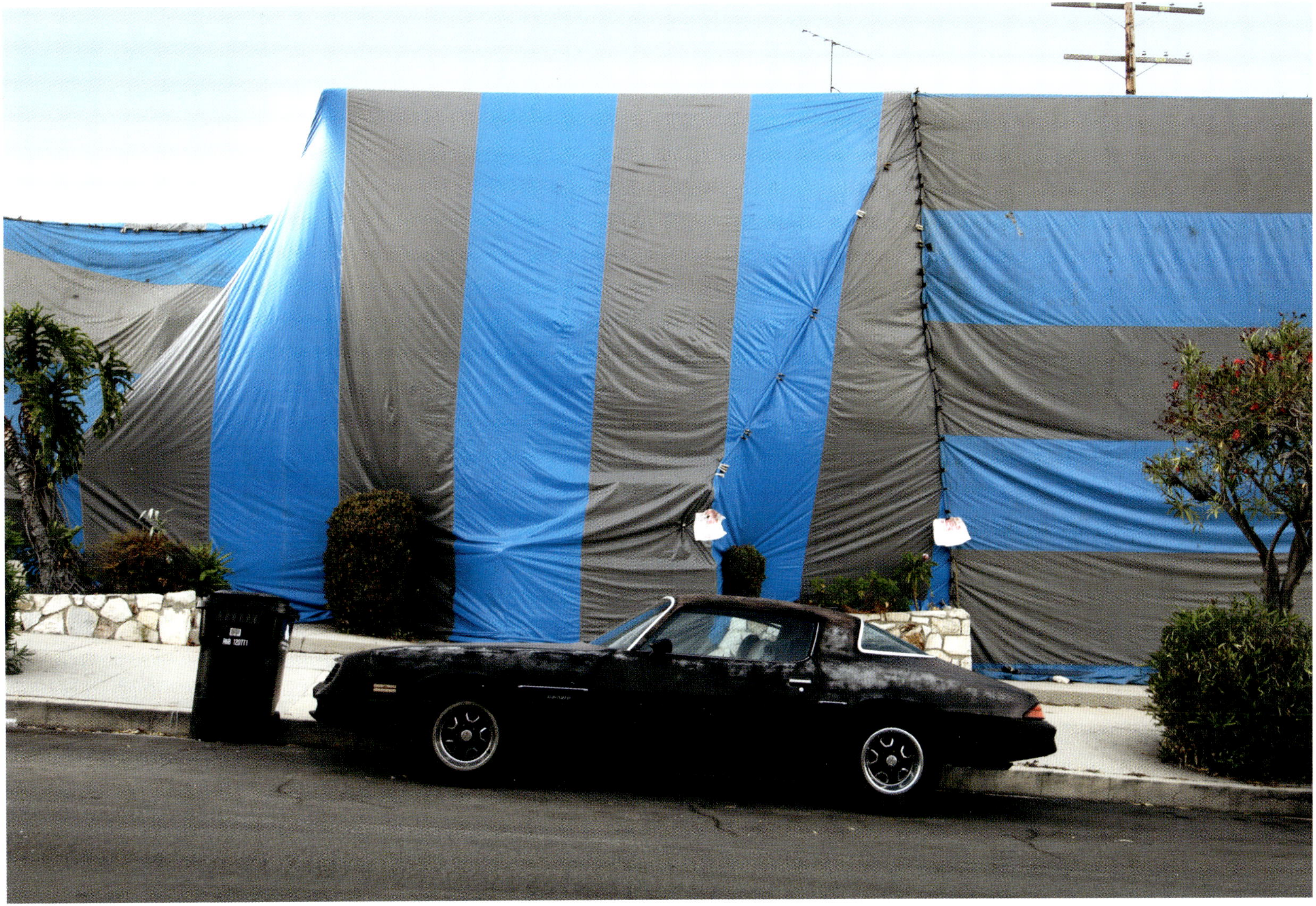

Haus vom Kammerjäger verhüllt. Das ist neu (siehe Seite 17). *The pest control operator's house under wraps. This is new (see page 17).*

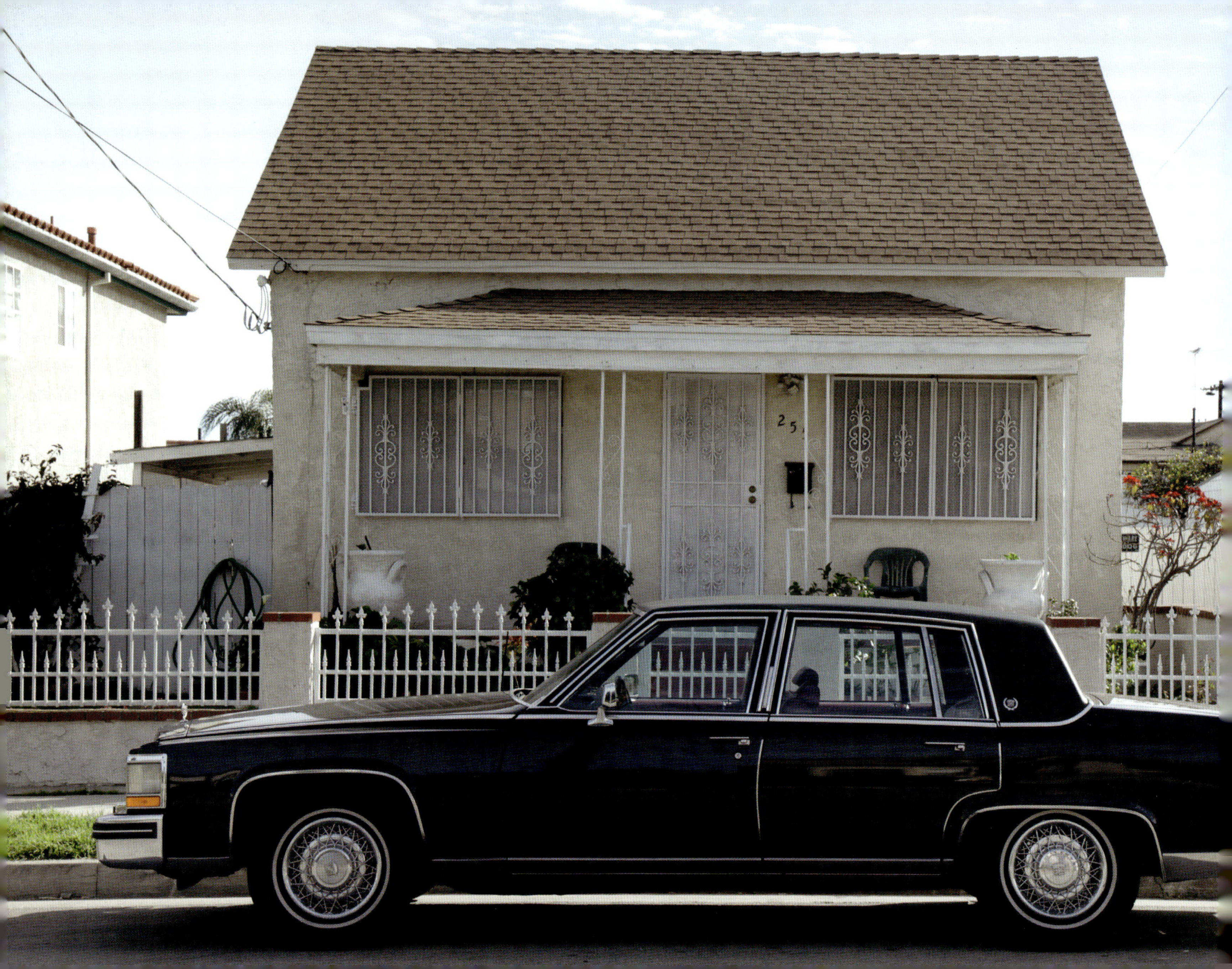

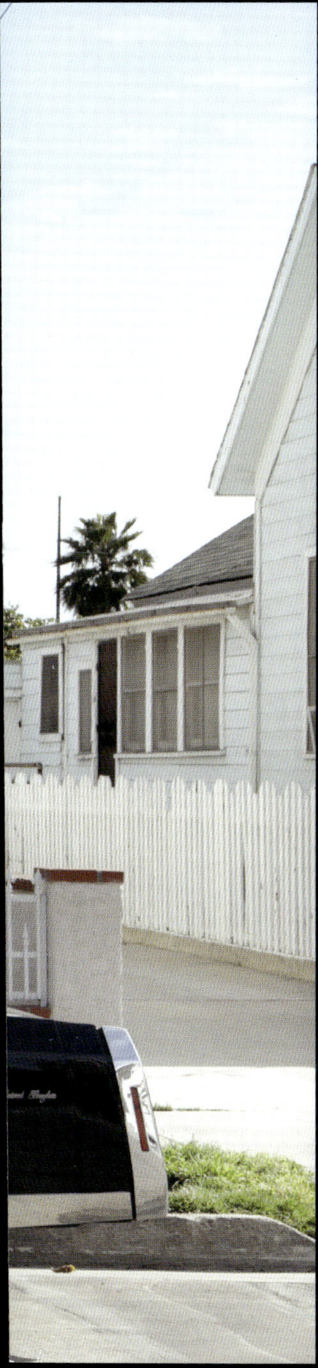

025

Schmiedeeiserne Ornamente zieren Tür und Fenster. *Wrought iron ornaments in front of door and windows*

026 027

Gleiche Straße, gleicher Geschmack.
Nachbarn, seelenverwandt motorisiert.
Same street, same taste.
Motorized neighbors, kindred spirits.

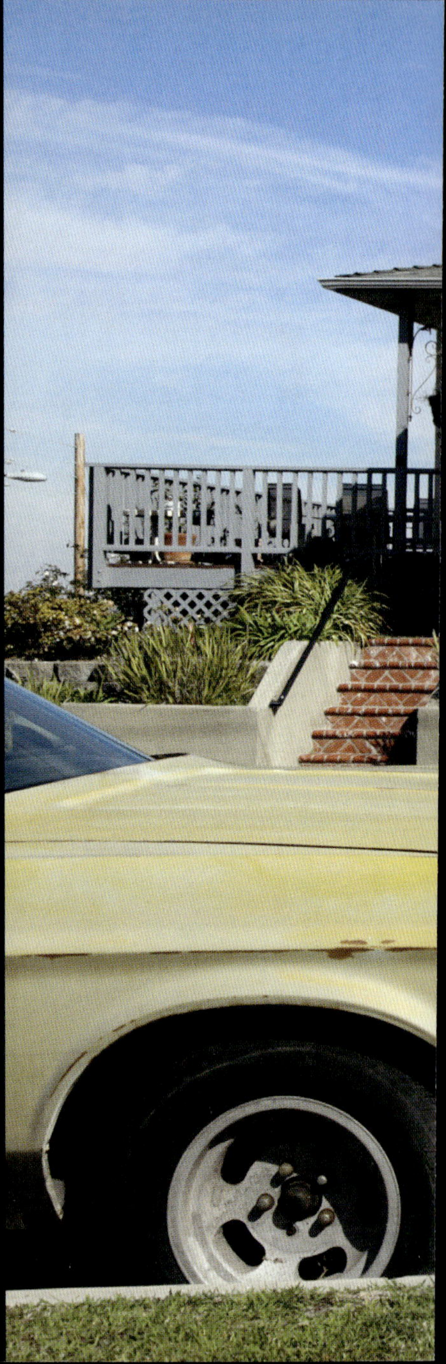

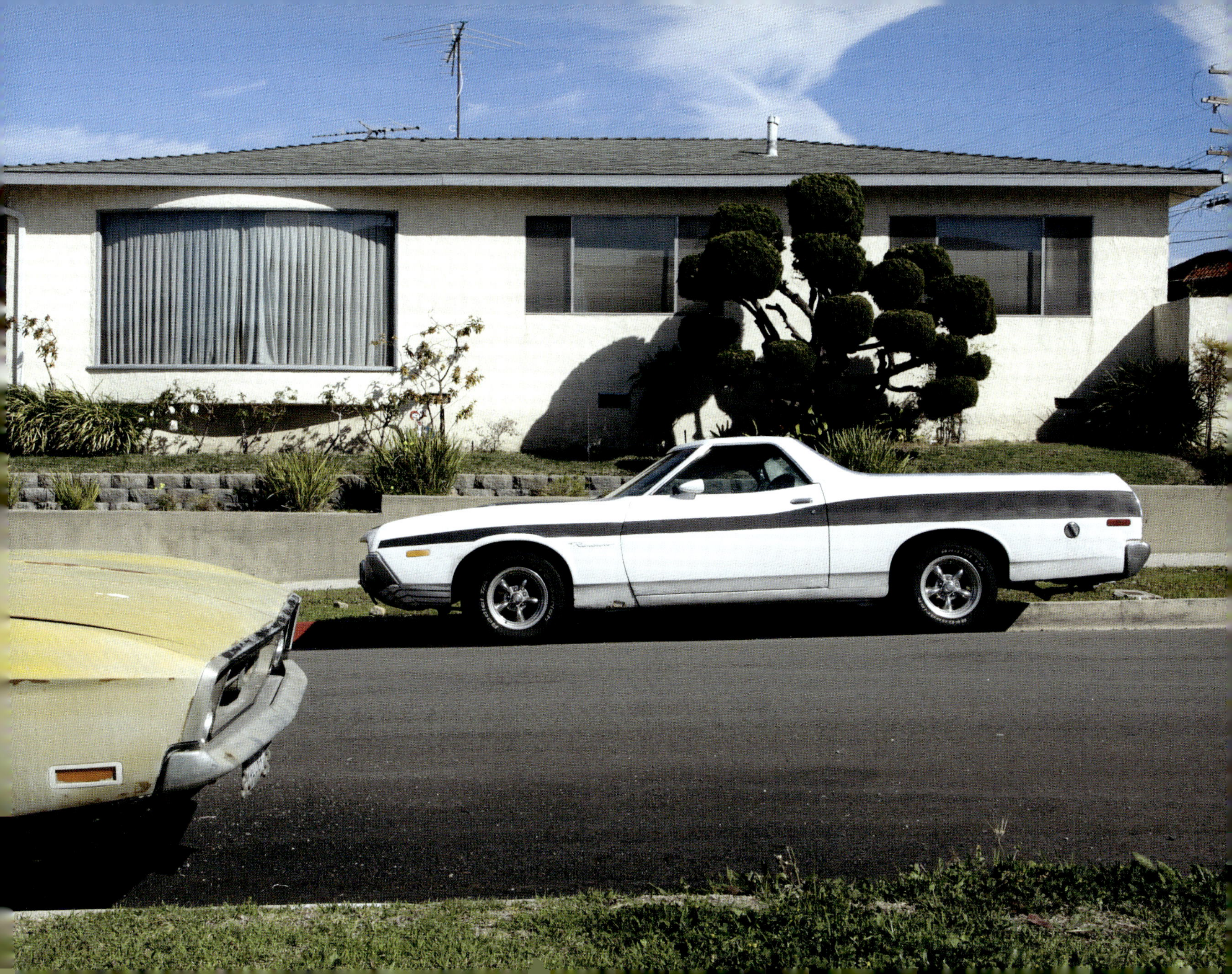

YELLOW. SUNSHINE AND OPTIMISM. YELLOW CARS ALWAYS SEEM TO COMPETE WITH THE SUN.

GELB. SONNE UND

OPTIMISMUS. GELBE AUTOS

KONKURRIEREN IMMER EIN BISSCHEN MIT DER SONNE.

»As we live a life of ease, everyone of us has all we need. Sky of blue and sea of green, in our yellow submarine.«
The Beatles

028

Wir sind ganz oben:
Mercedes S-Klasse vor
Villa am Hang.
At the very top:
Mercedes S-Class parked
in front of villa on a hill.

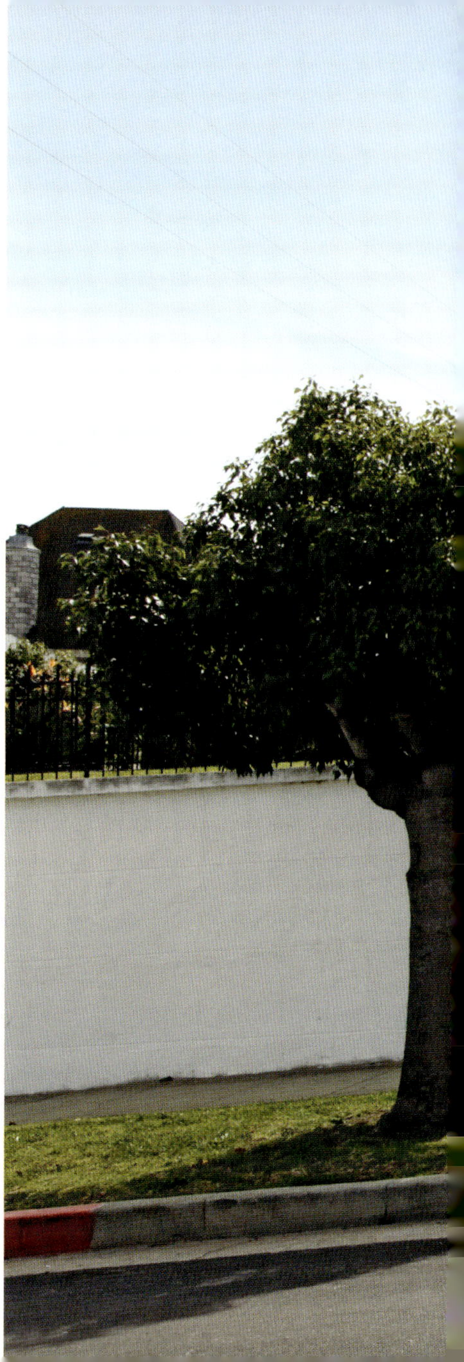

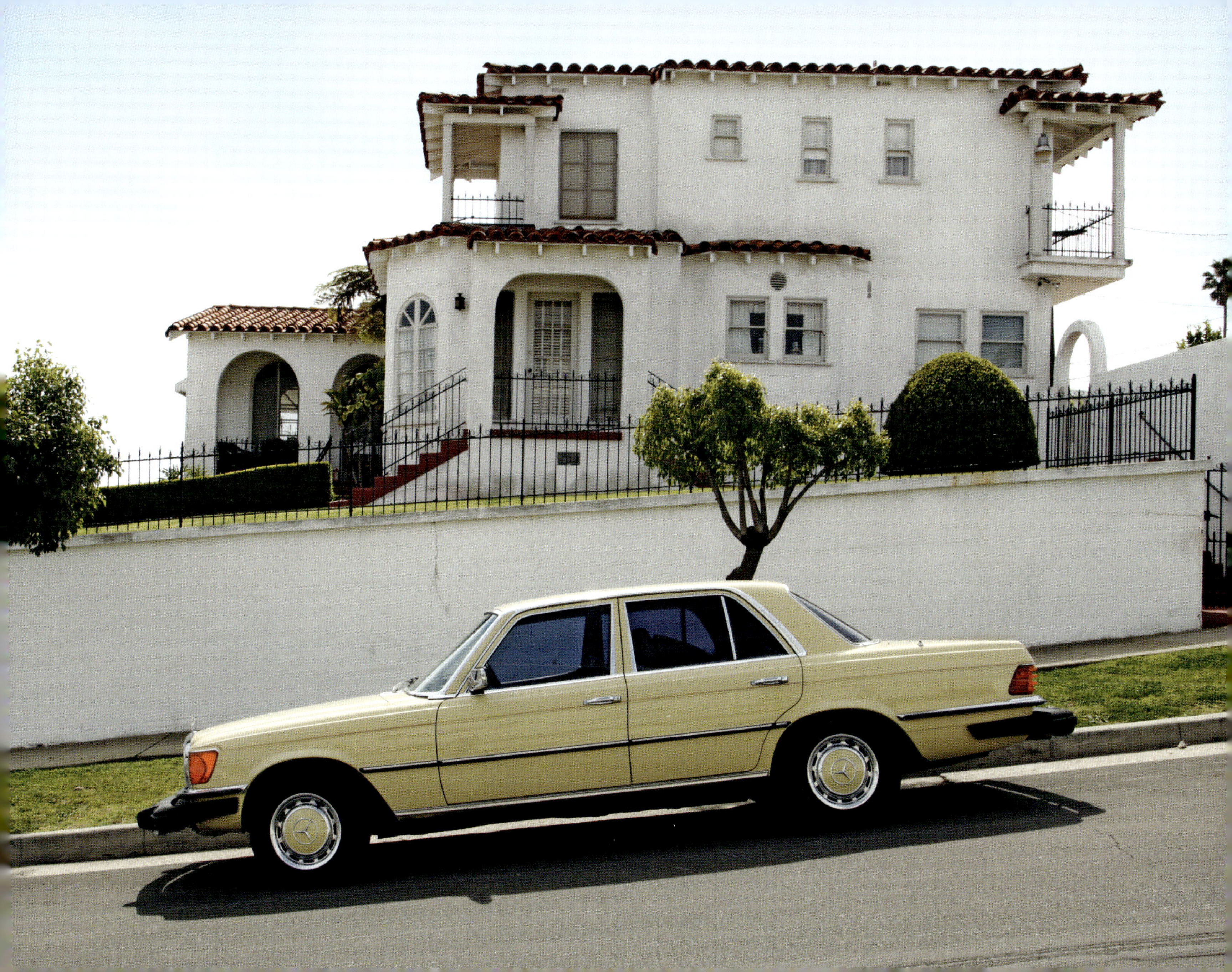

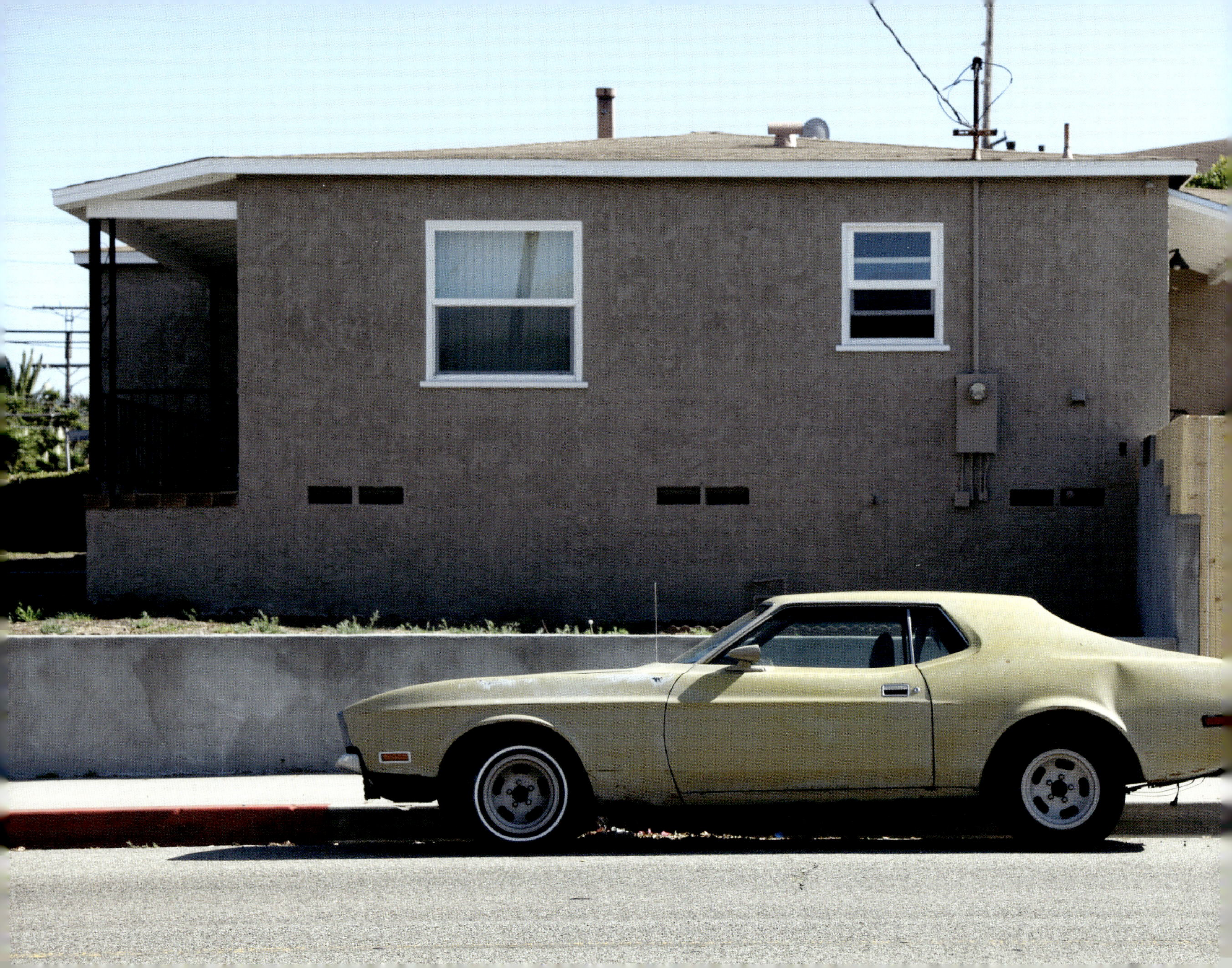

029

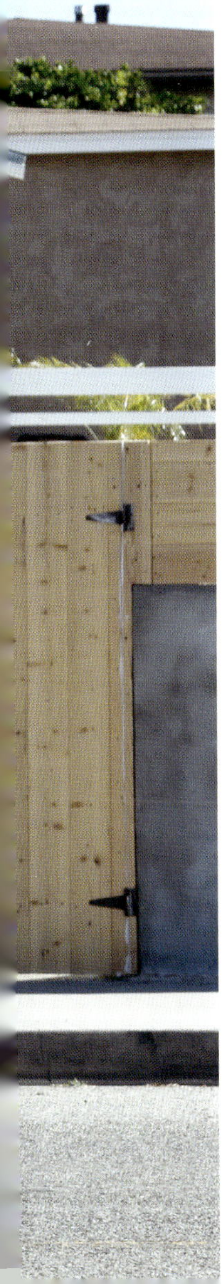

Mustang vor dem Haus – knackend in der Hitze abkühlend. *Mustang in front of the house, crackling as it cools in the heat.*

030

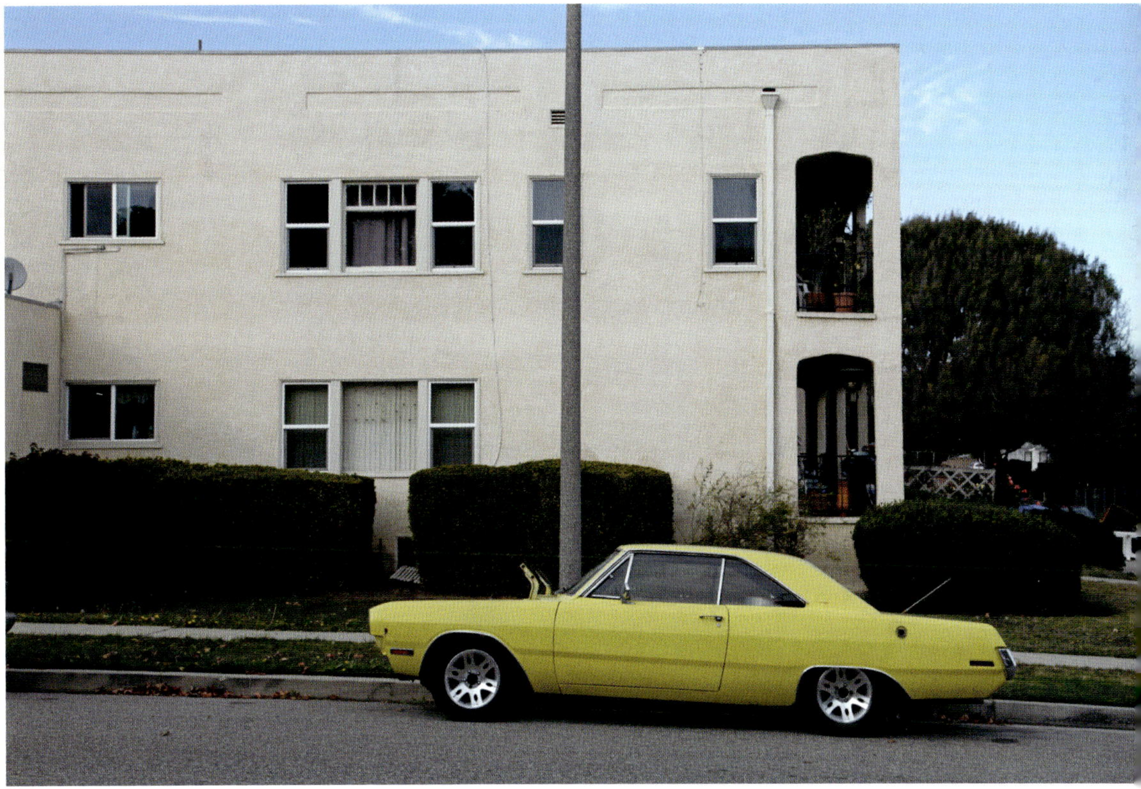

Giftgrüne Freizeitbeschäftigung für den versierten Mechaniker. *Toxic green: spare-time activity for the skilled mechanic.*

031 032

Wer zuerst kommt, kriegt den Platz im Schatten: Pontiac GTO und Chevrolet Camaro.
Whoever gets there first gets a spot in the shade: Pontiac GTO and Chevrolet Camaro.

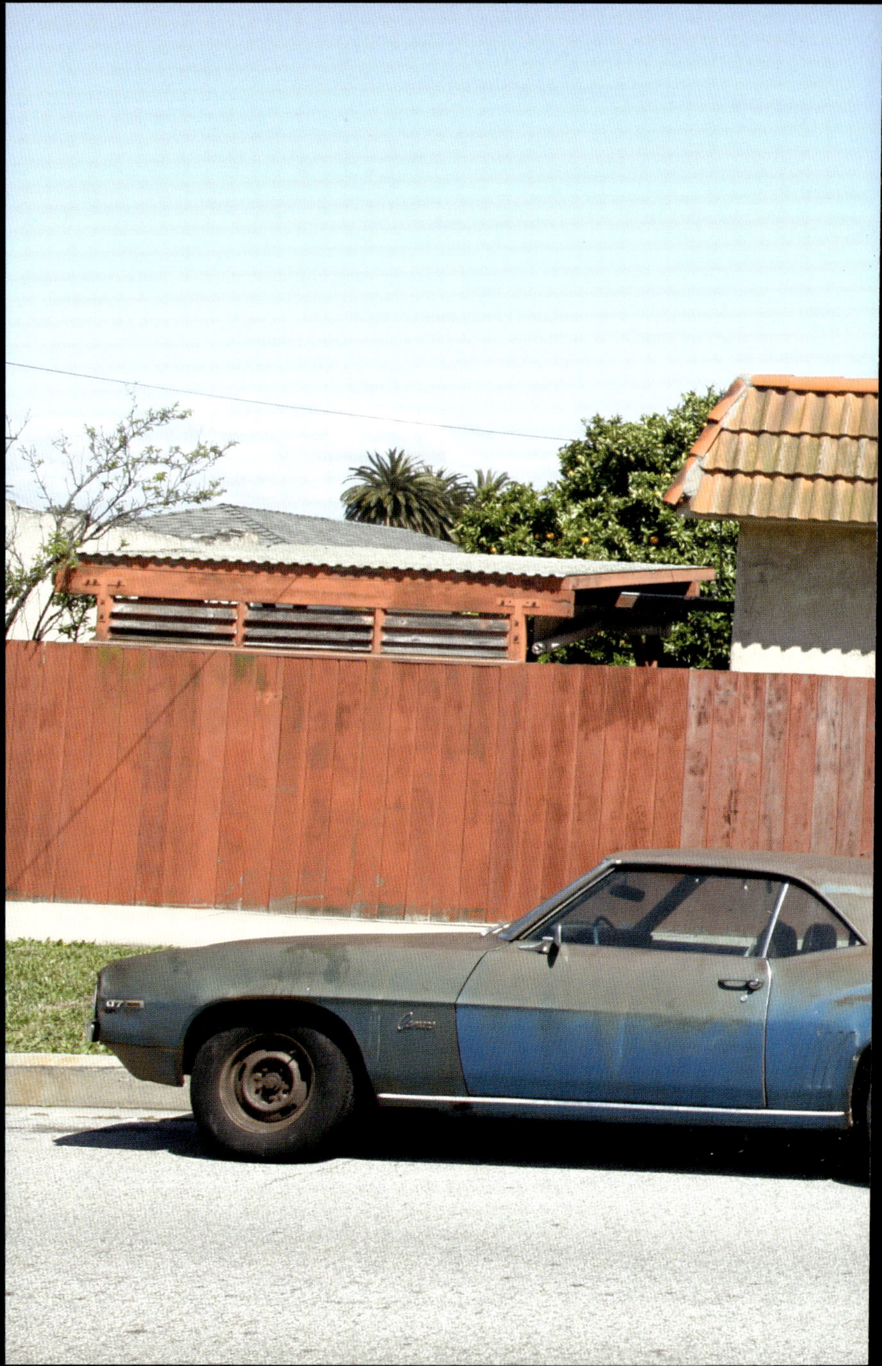

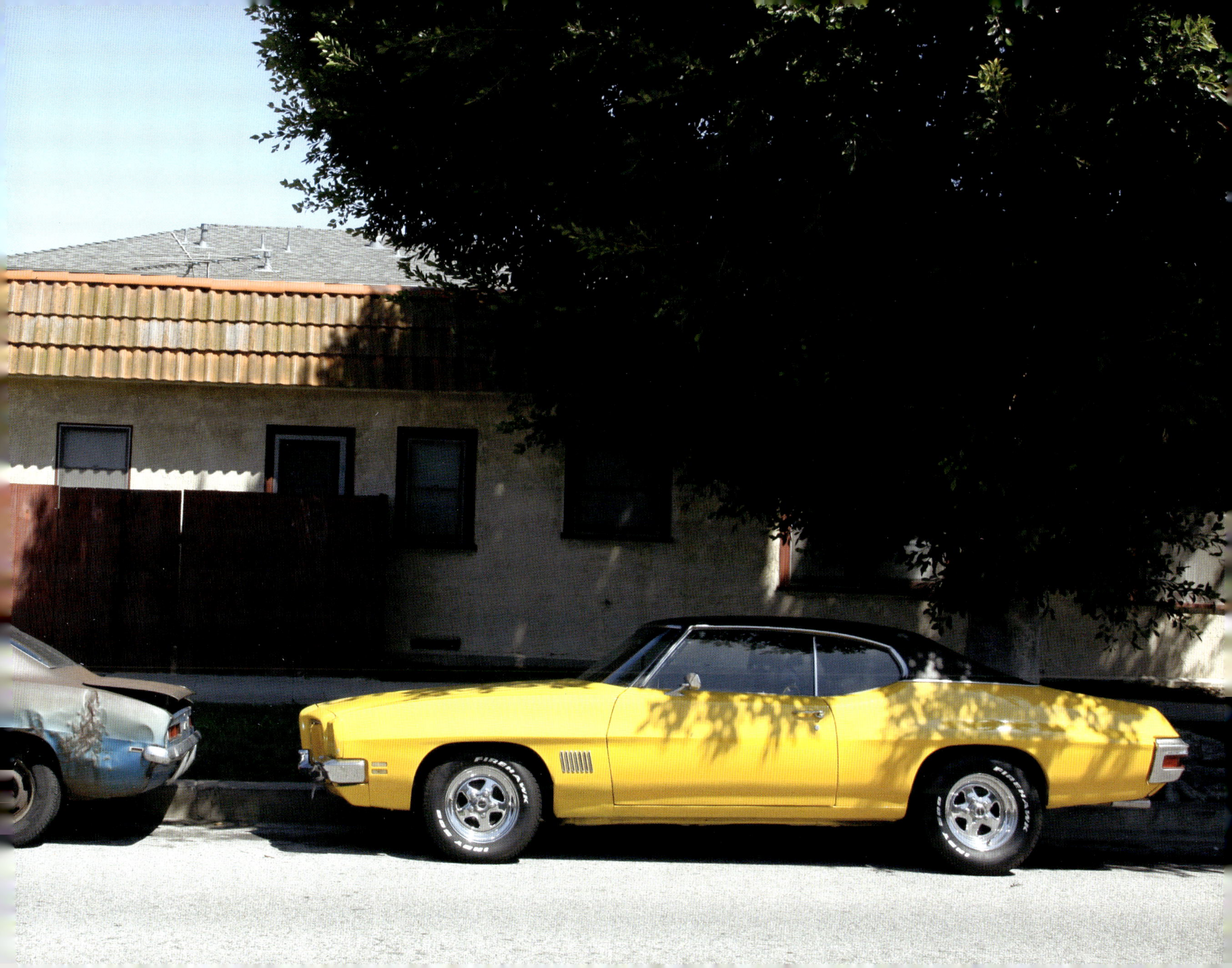
FIREHAWK
FIREHAWK

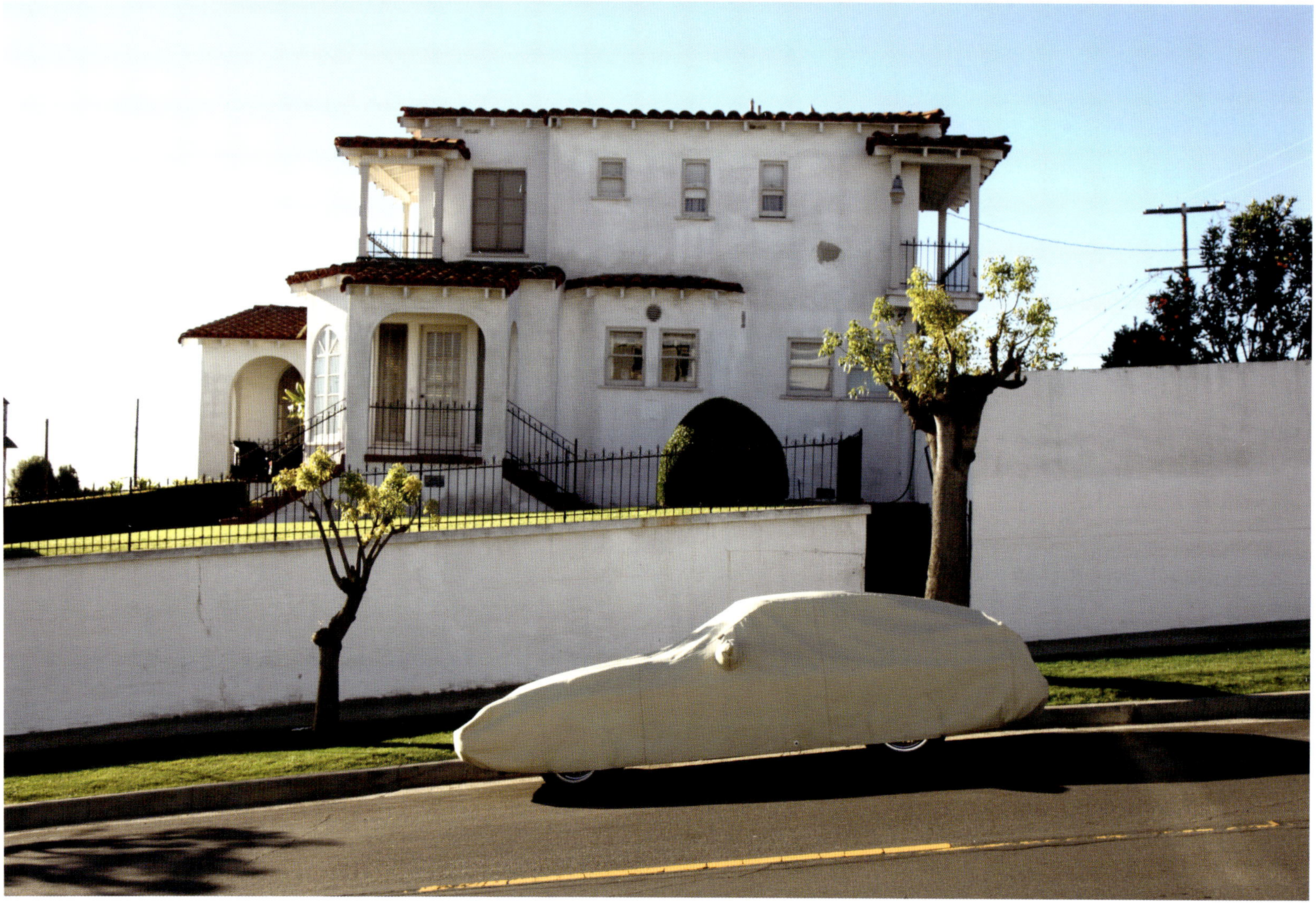

Wir sind immer noch oben. Villa mit Sonntagsauto, verhüllt. *We're still at the very top. Villa with veiled Sunday car.*

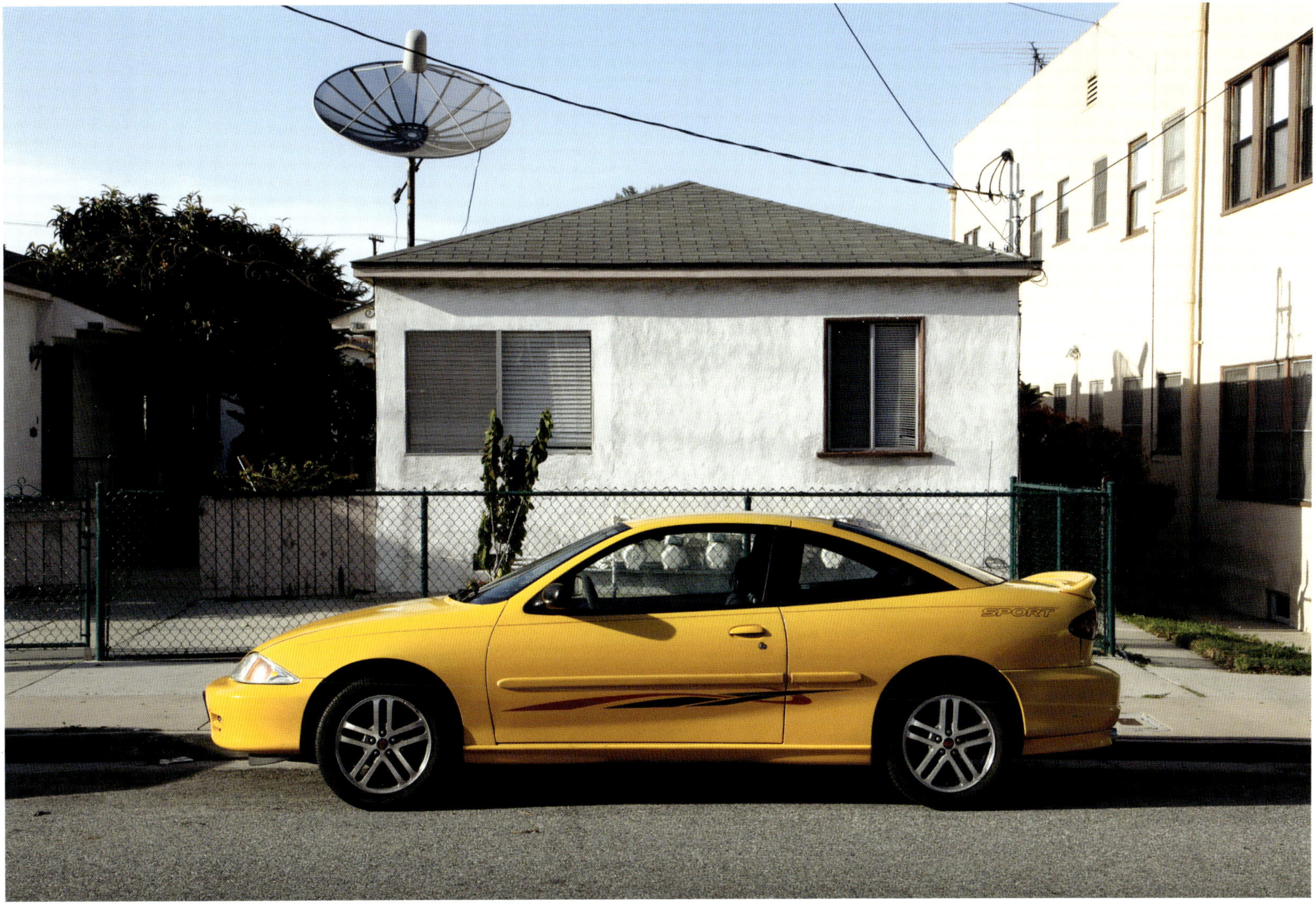

Ein Auto, zwei Zimmer, 200 Fernsehprogramme. *One car, two rooms and 200 television channels.*

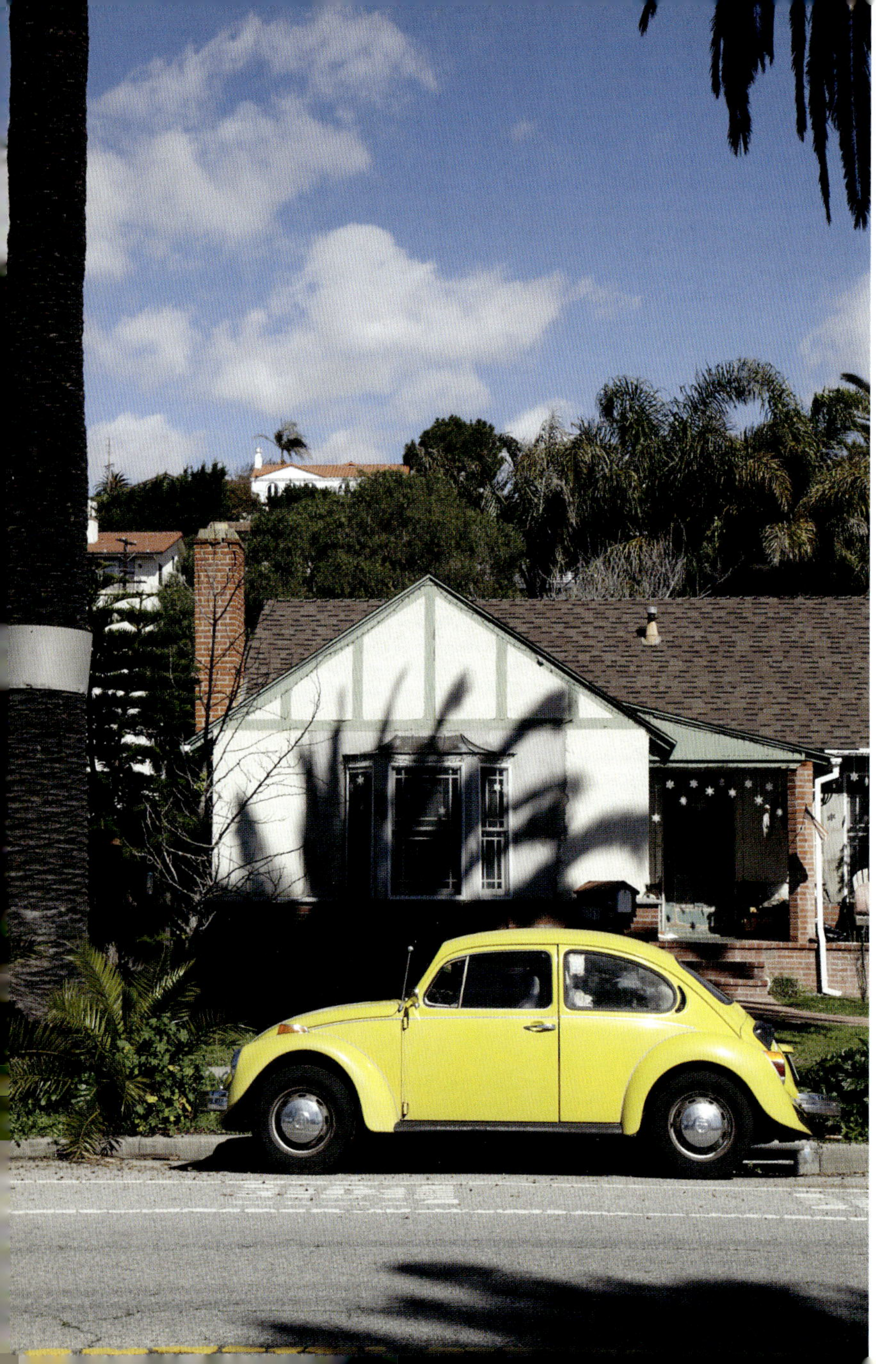

035

Bunte Tropenszene mit zitronengelbem Käfer.
Colorful, tropical scene with lemon-yellow Bug.

036

Hinter der Mauer liegt der Strand.
The beach might be right behind the wall.

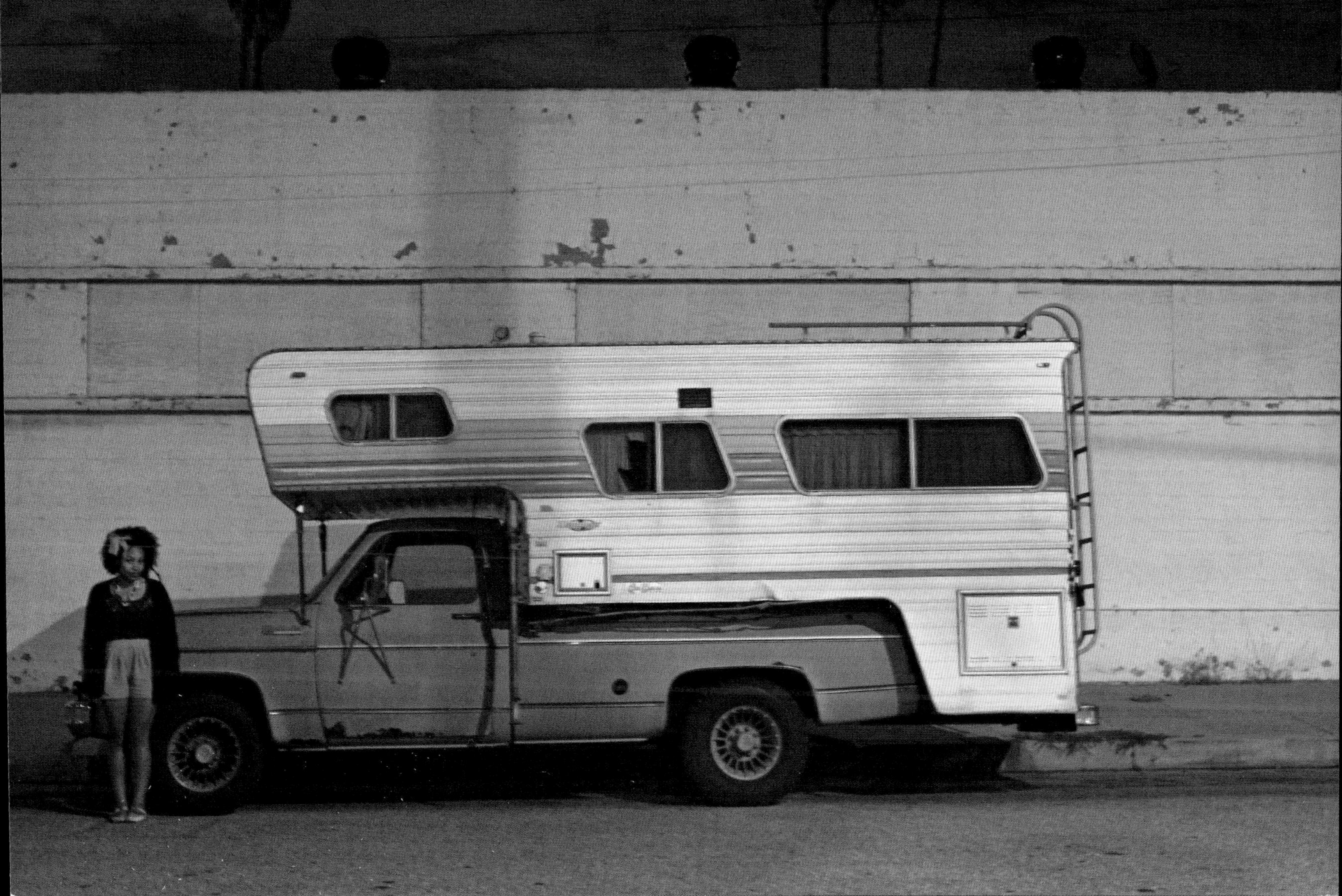

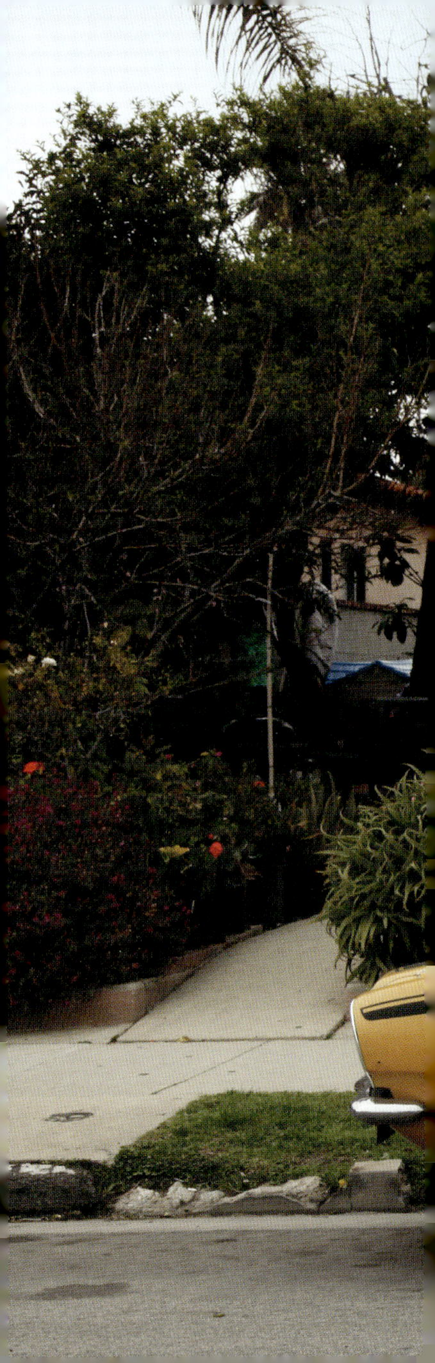

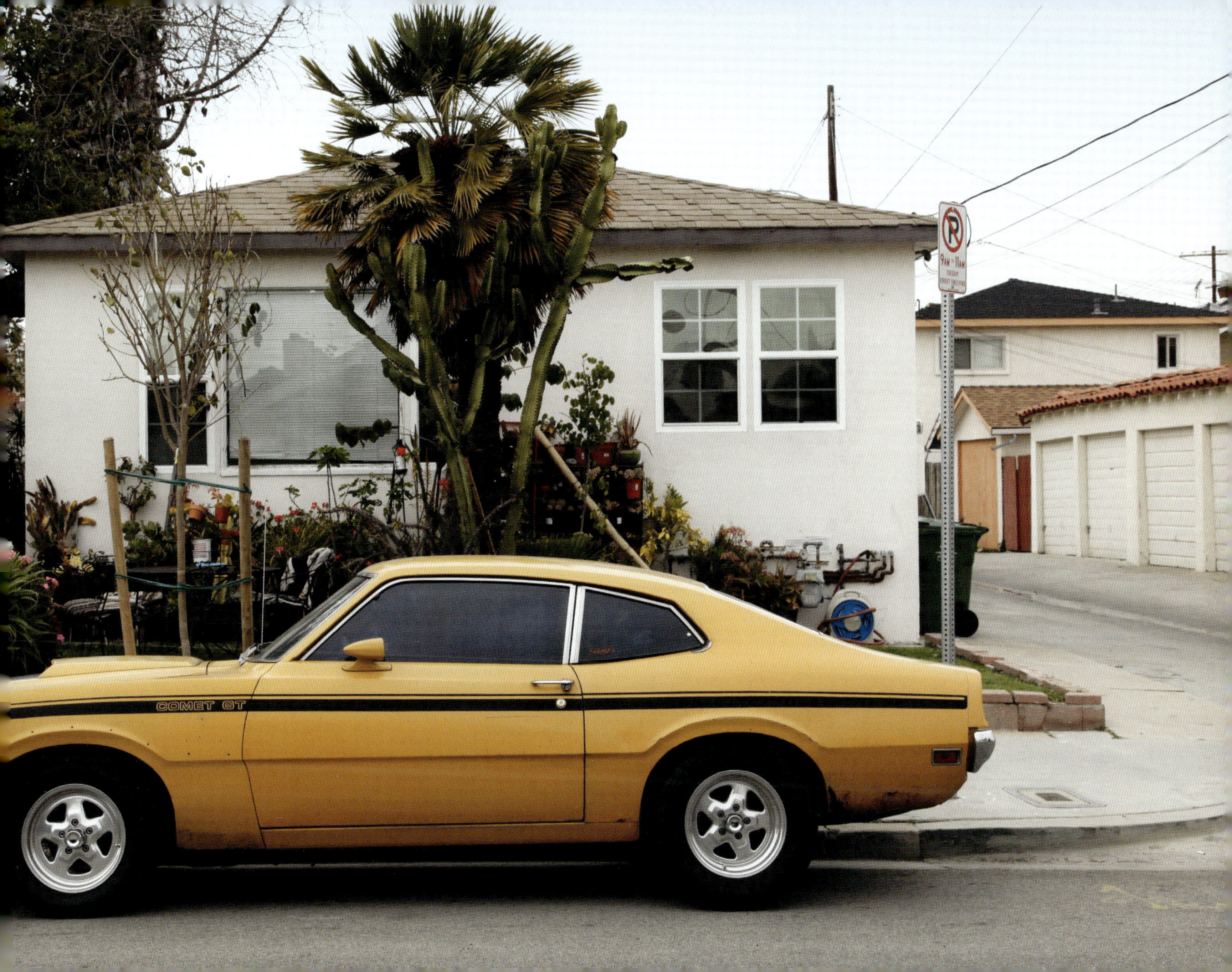
9AM 11AM
COMET GT

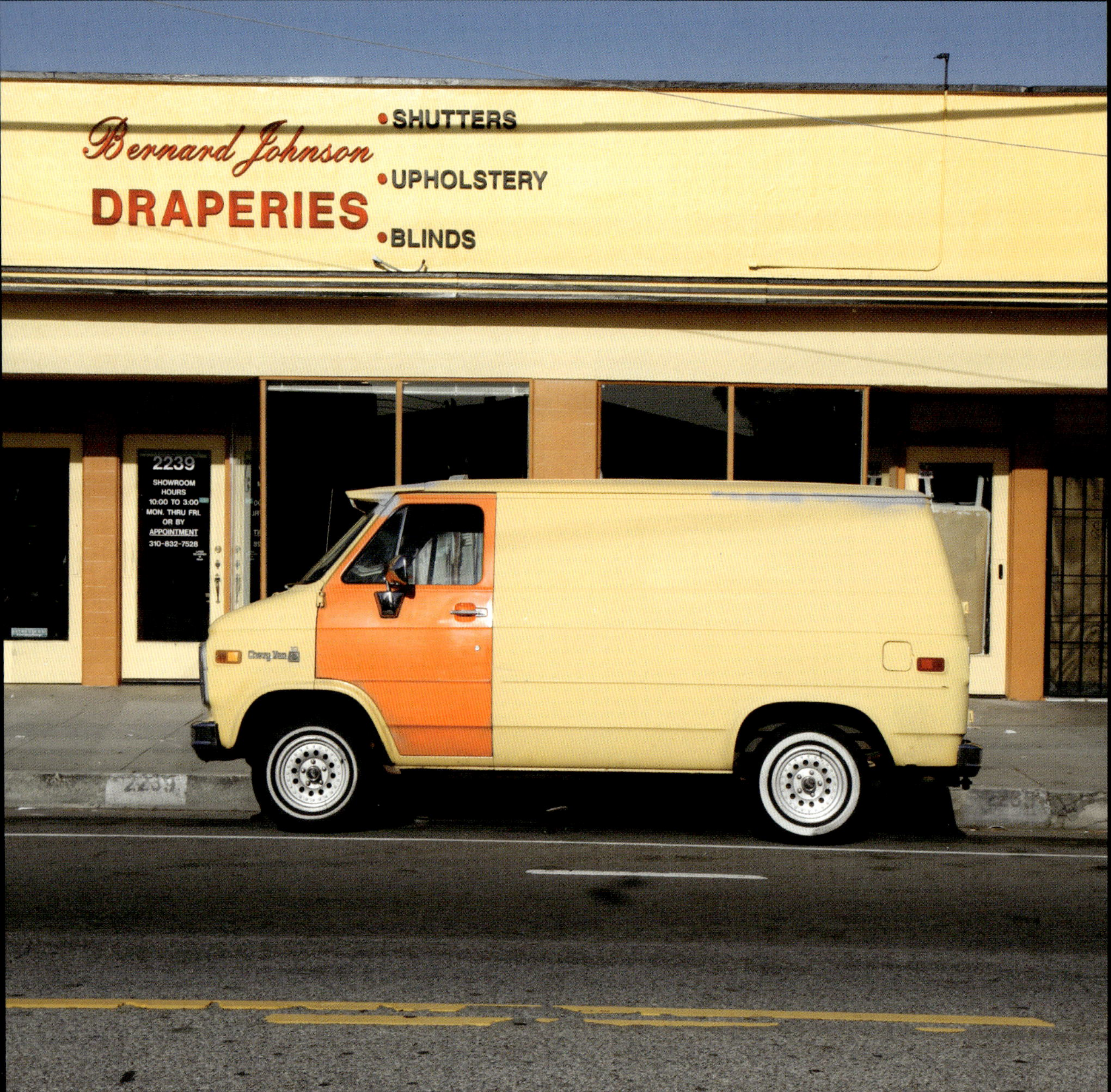

Polsterei mit Hang zu Pastellfarben.
Upholstery in pastel colors.

Hippie-Dienstwagen, im Ruhestand.
Company car for hippies now retired.

039

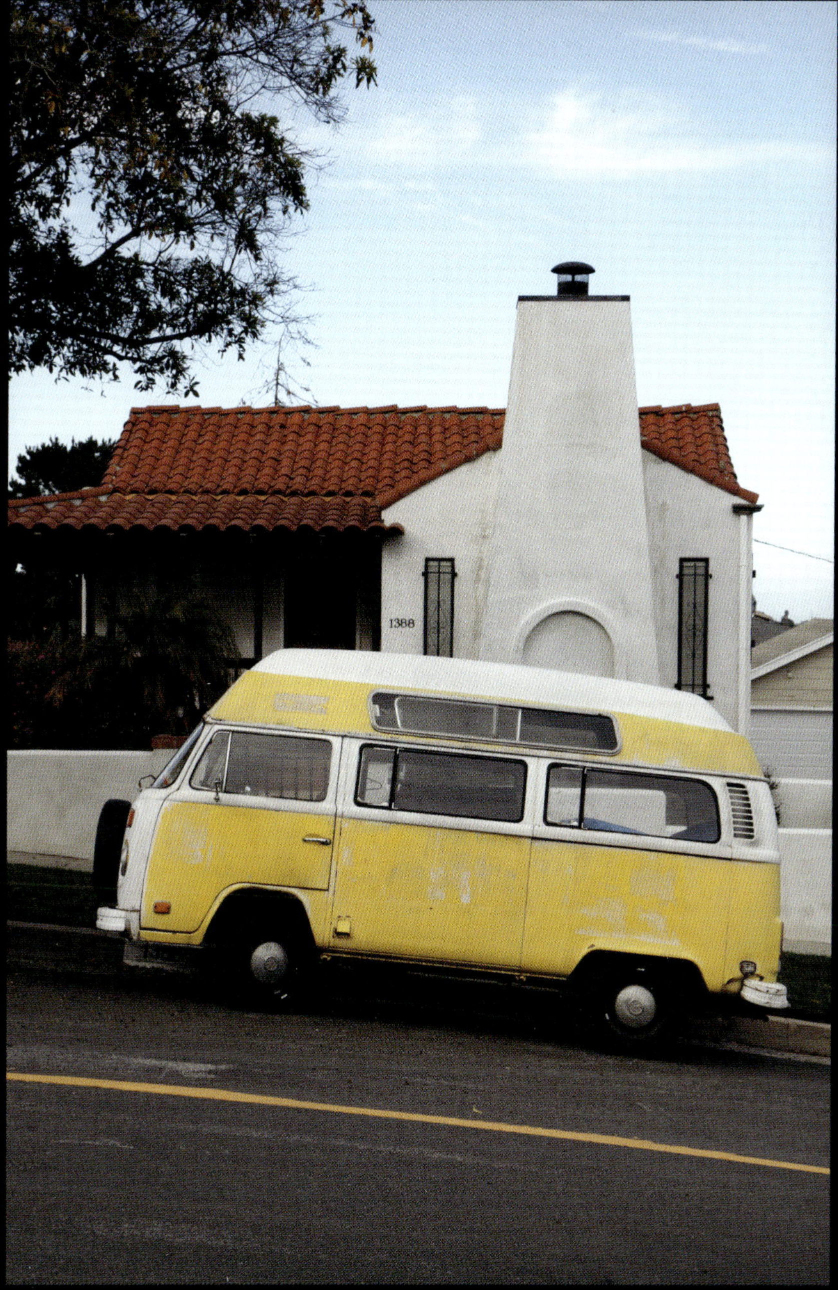

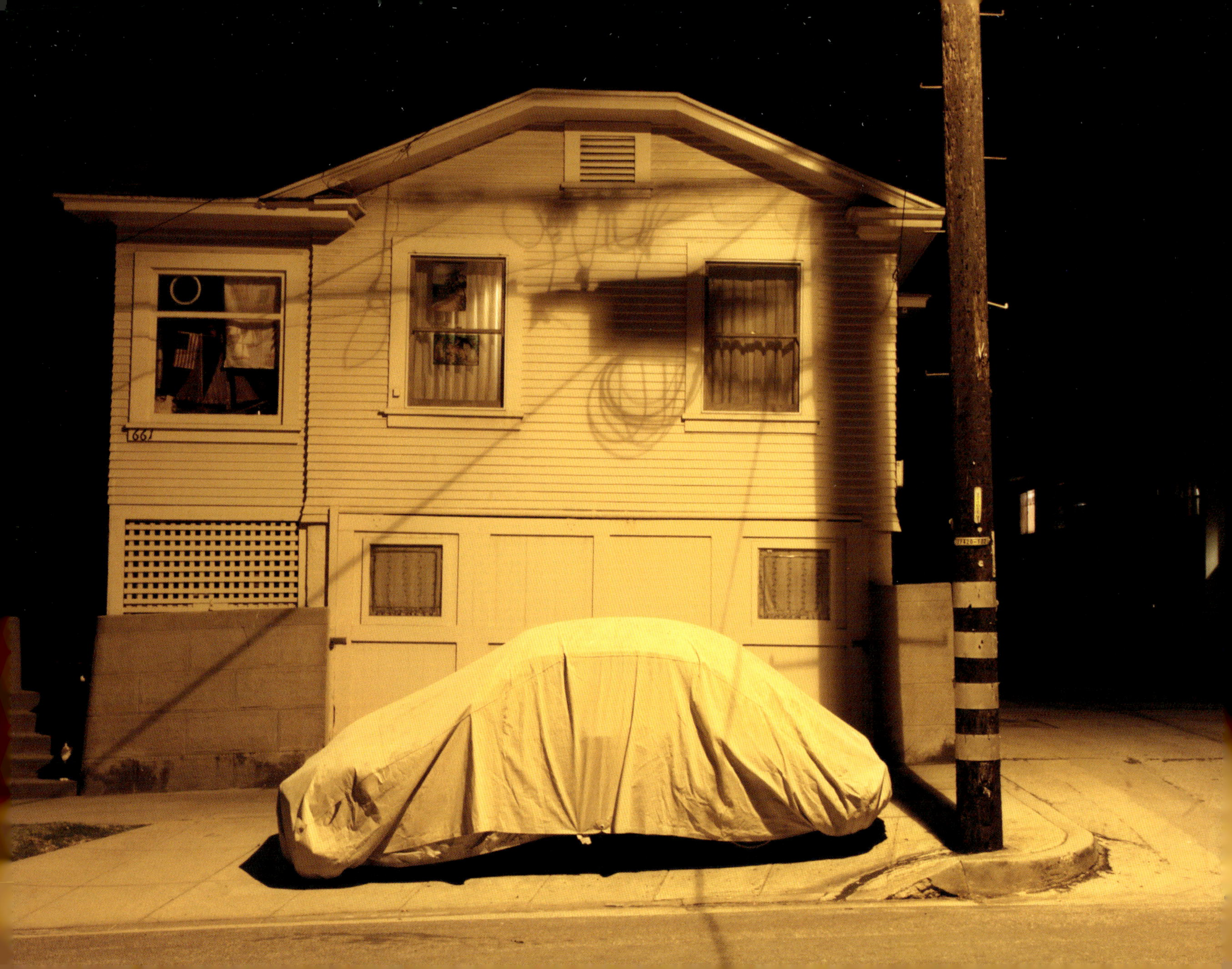

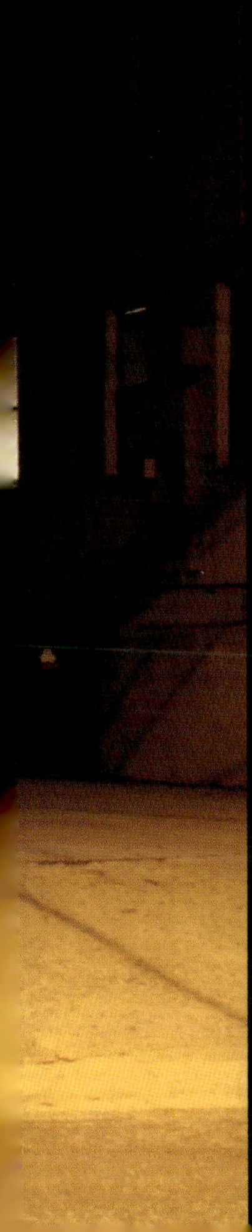

040

Midnight blues: Volkswagen mit Schlafmütze. *Midnight blues: Volkswagen with nightcap.*

ROT. LIEBE UND LEIDEN

RED. LOVE AND PASSION. WELCOME TO SAN PEDRO.

CHAFT. WILLKOMMEN IN SAN PEDRO

»I guess I should've known by the way you parked your car sideways, that it wouldn't last. And honey, I say, Little Red Corvette, baby, you're much too fast. (Oh) Little Red Corvette, you need a love that's gonna last.«

041

Dunkelroter Toyota, Mandelblüte in San Pedro. *Dark-red Toyota, almond blossoms in San Pedro.*

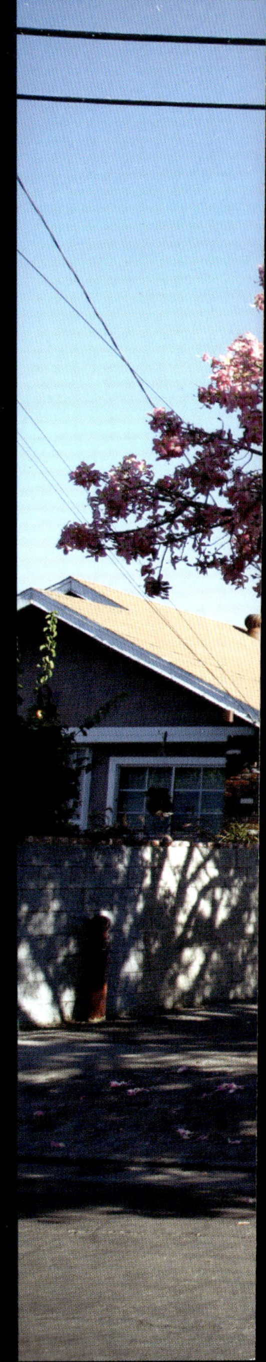

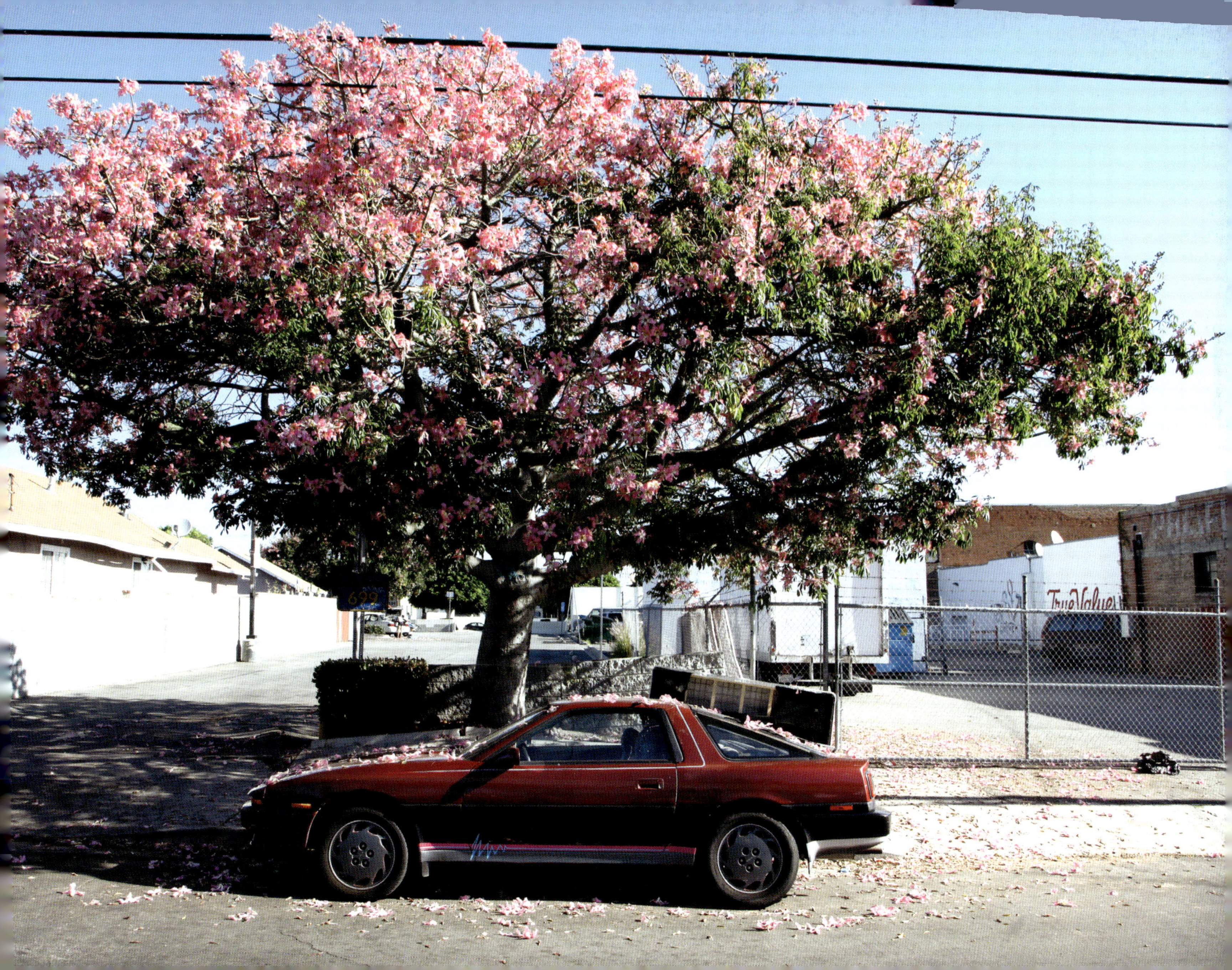
True Value

042

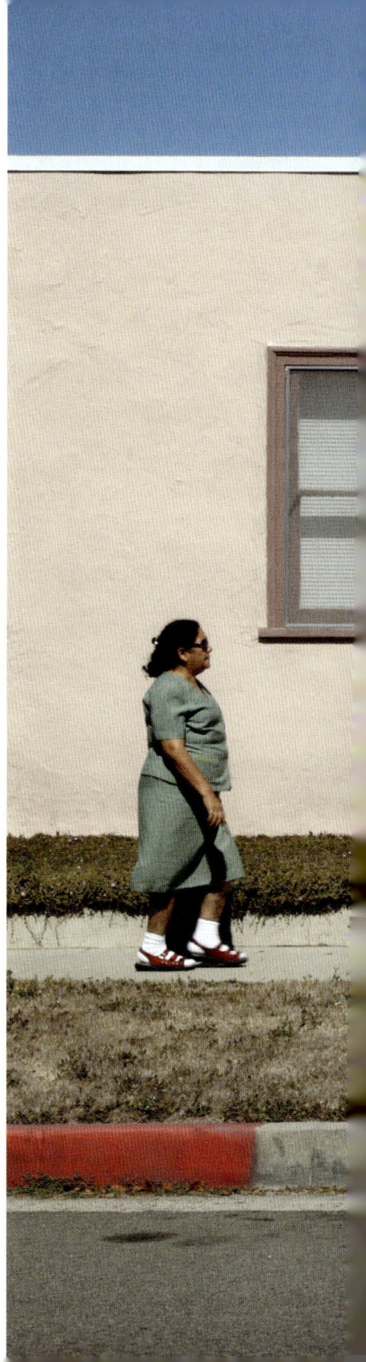

Komposition in Rot –
sogar die Schuhe der
Dame passen dazu.
*Composition in red: even
this lady's shoes match.*

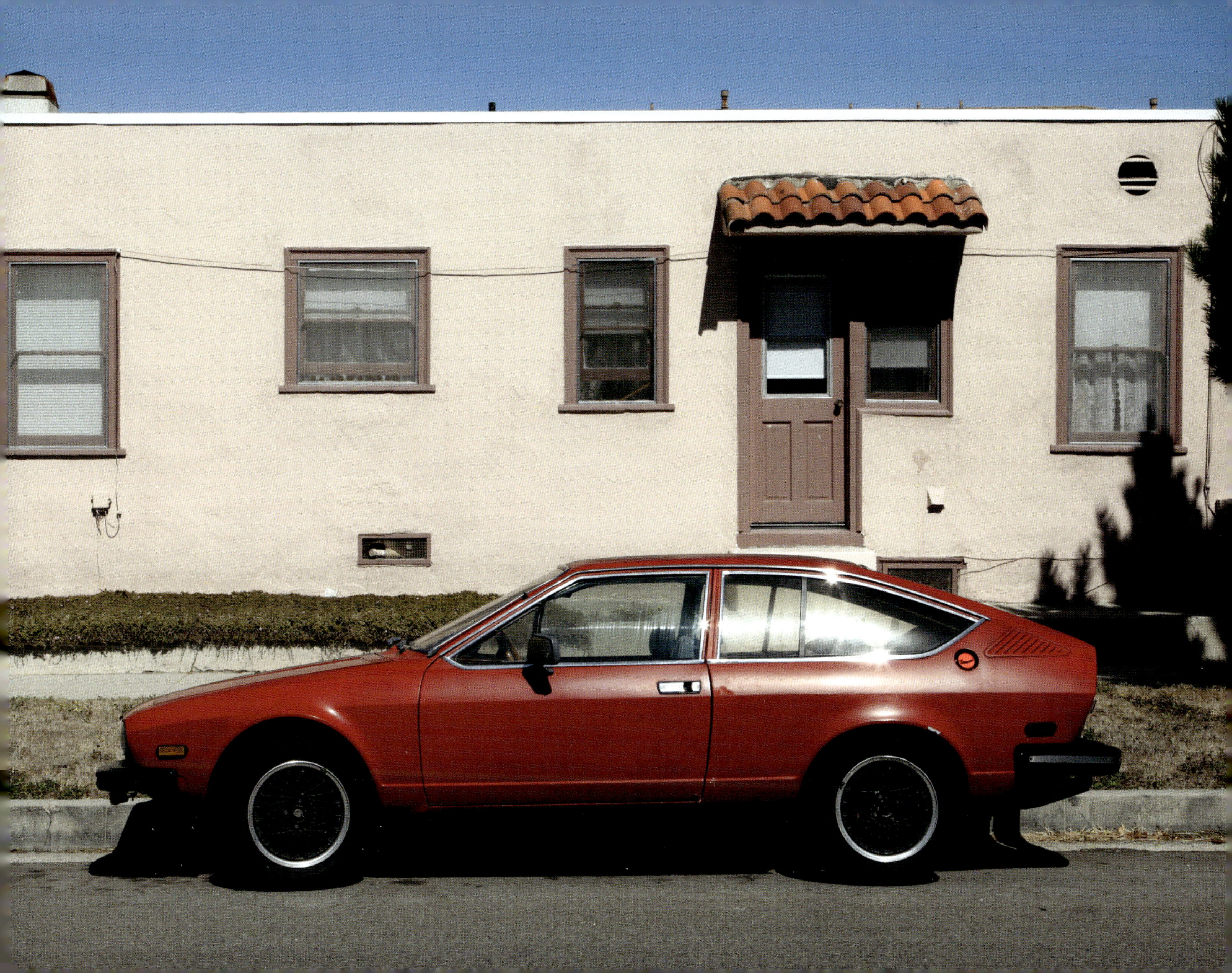

043

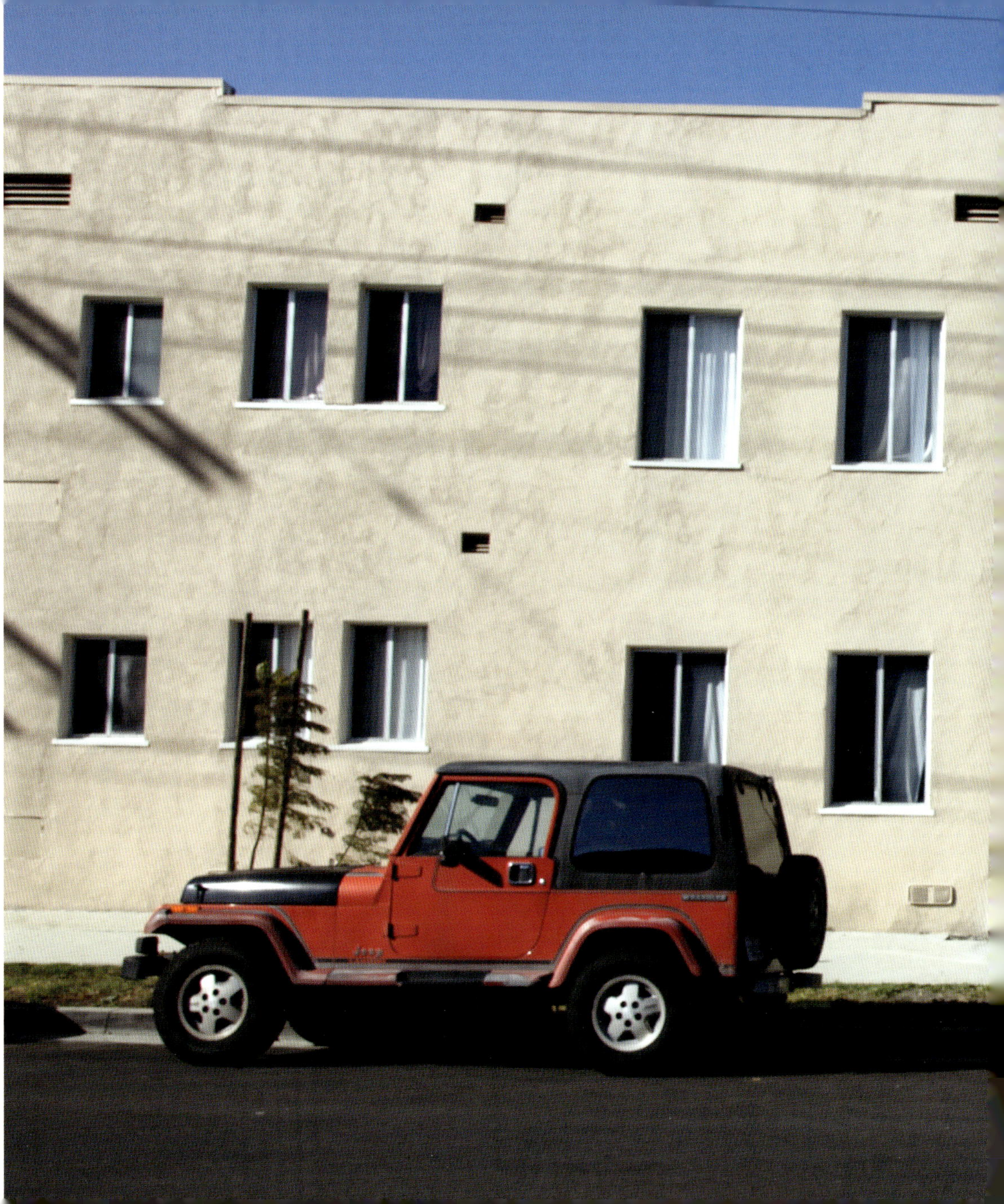

Zwei Jeep CJ, nach der Geburt getrennt.
Civilian Jeeps separated at birth.

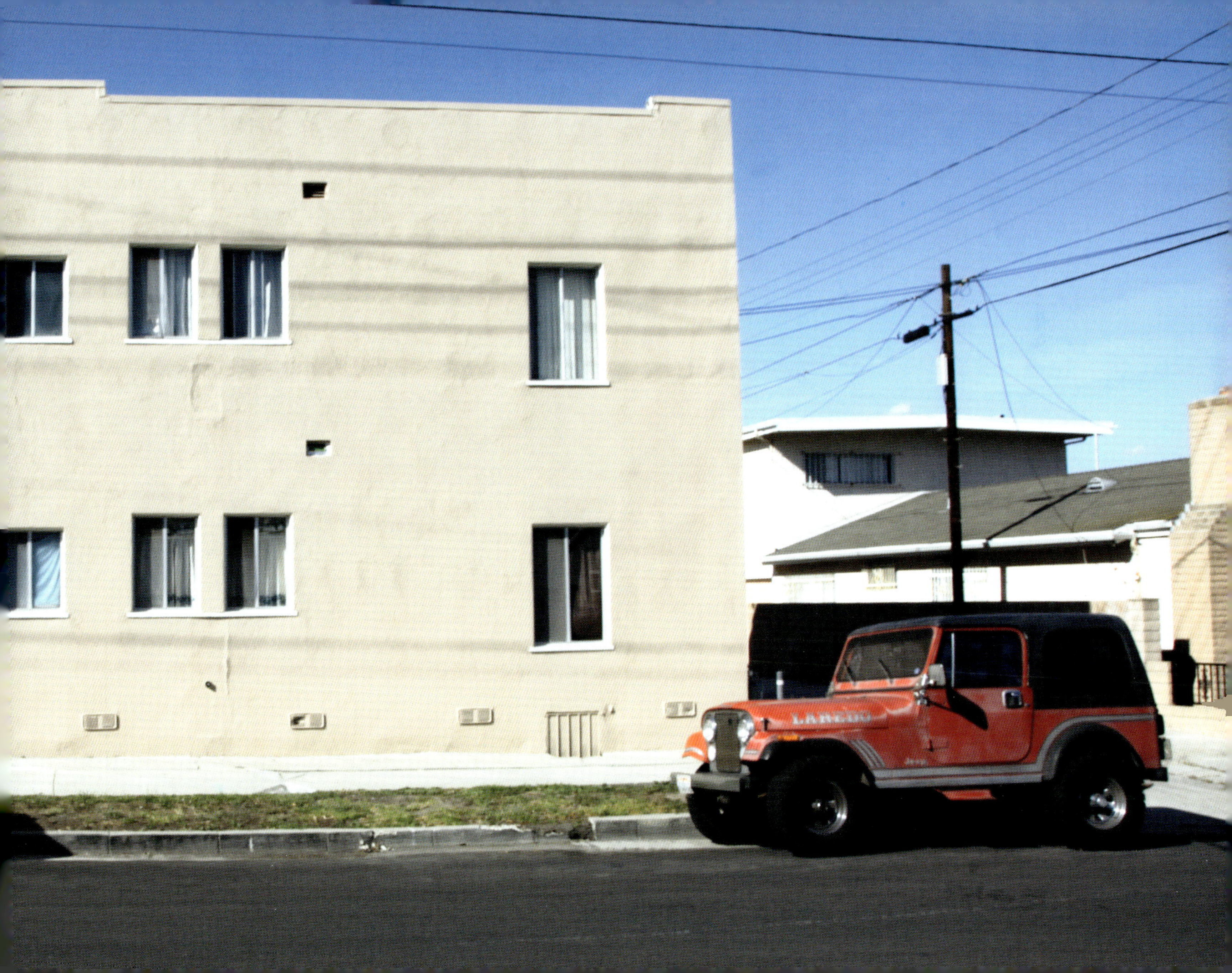

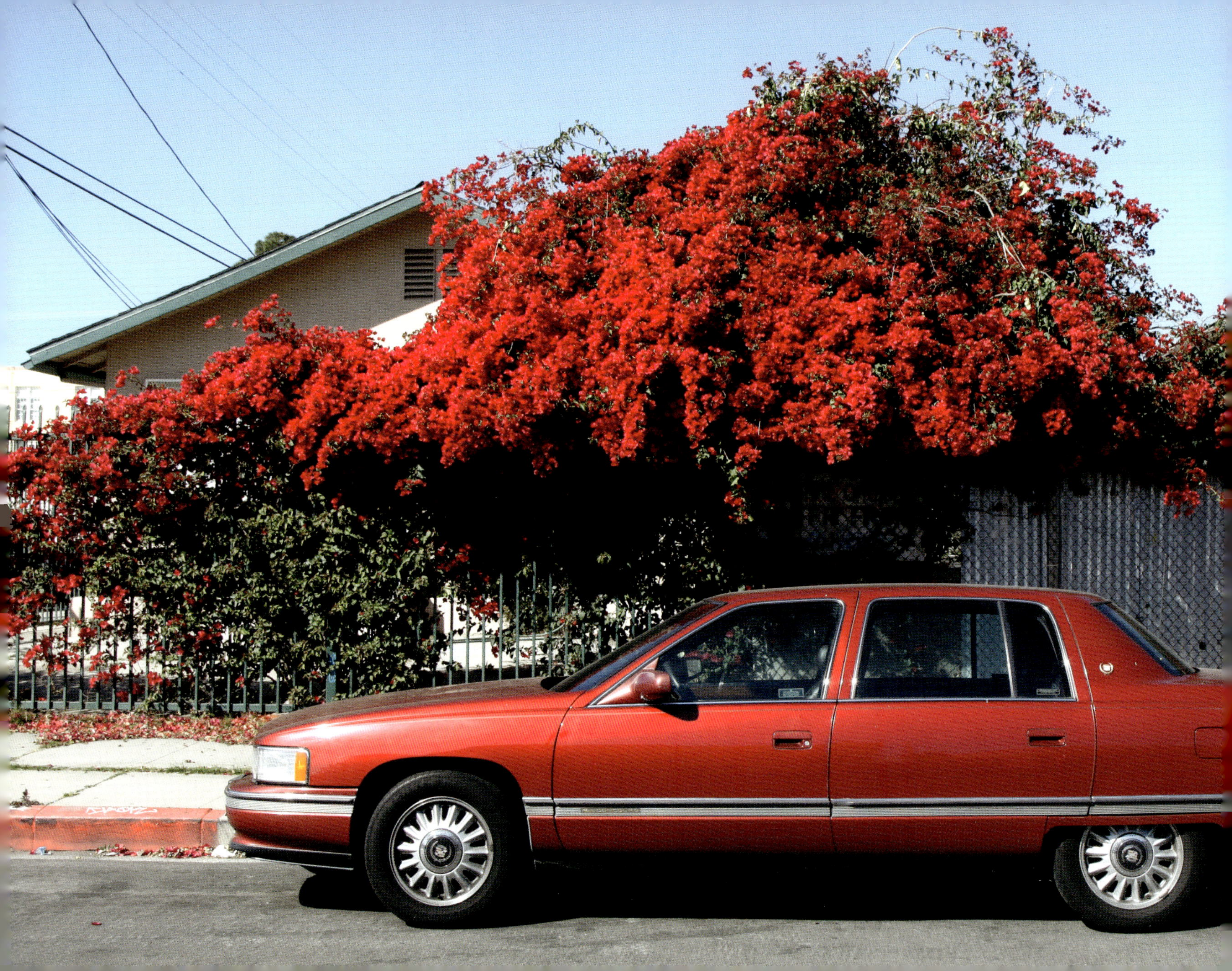

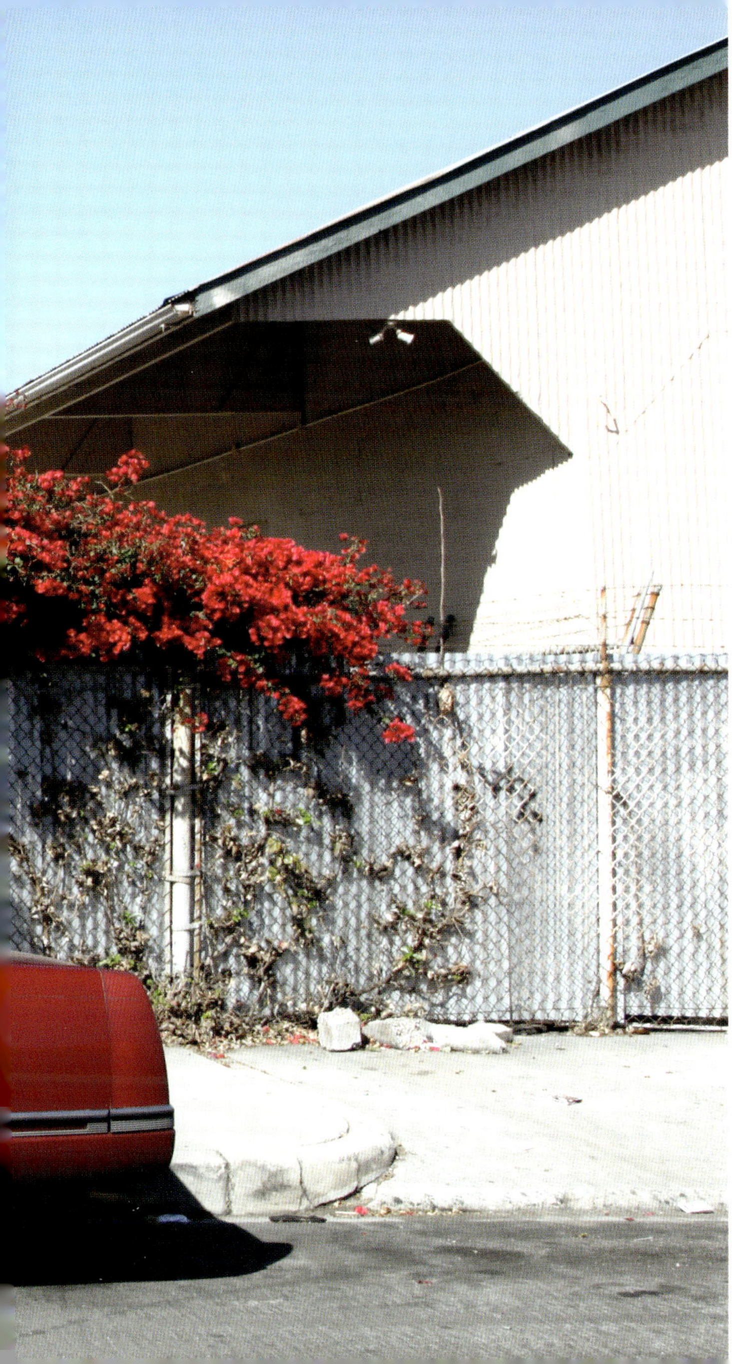

Land Art mit Cadillac.
Land art with Cadillac.

Was für ein Tag: Auto kaputt, TV kaputt.
What a day: broken car, broken television.

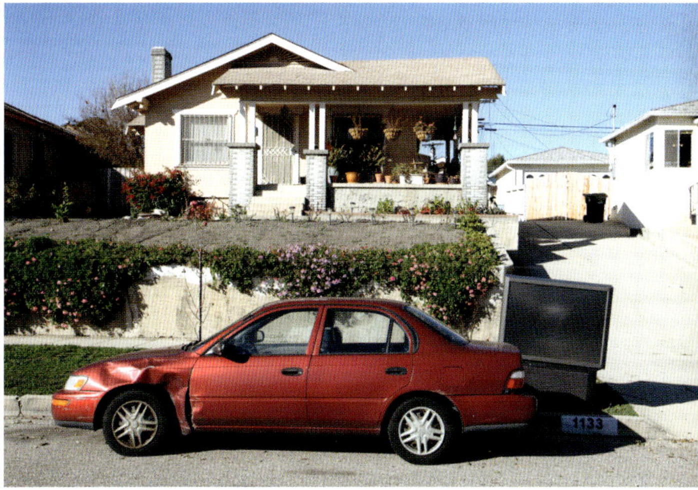

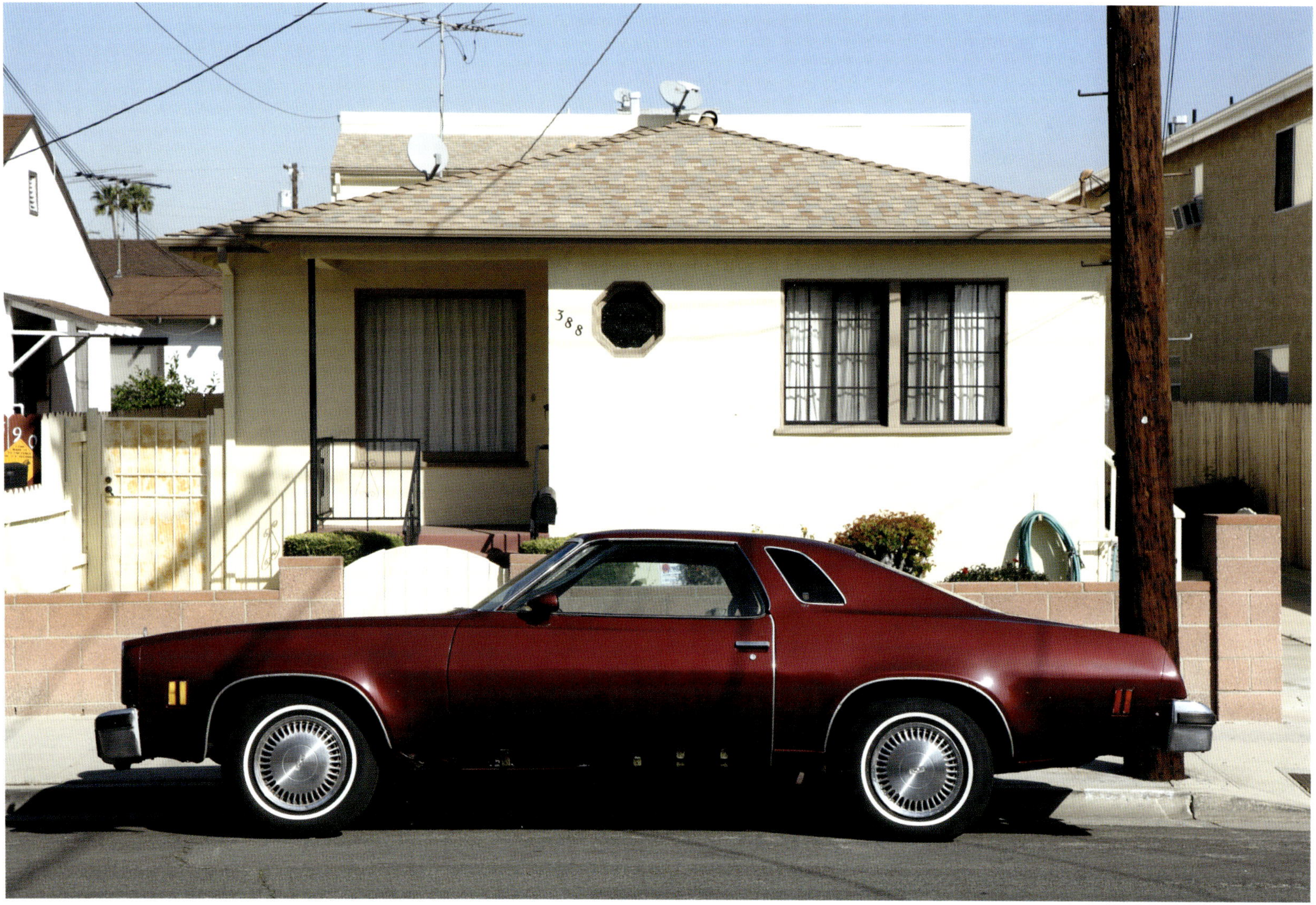

Oldsmobile, zu Hause in Hausnummer 388. *Oldsmobile at home at No. 388.*

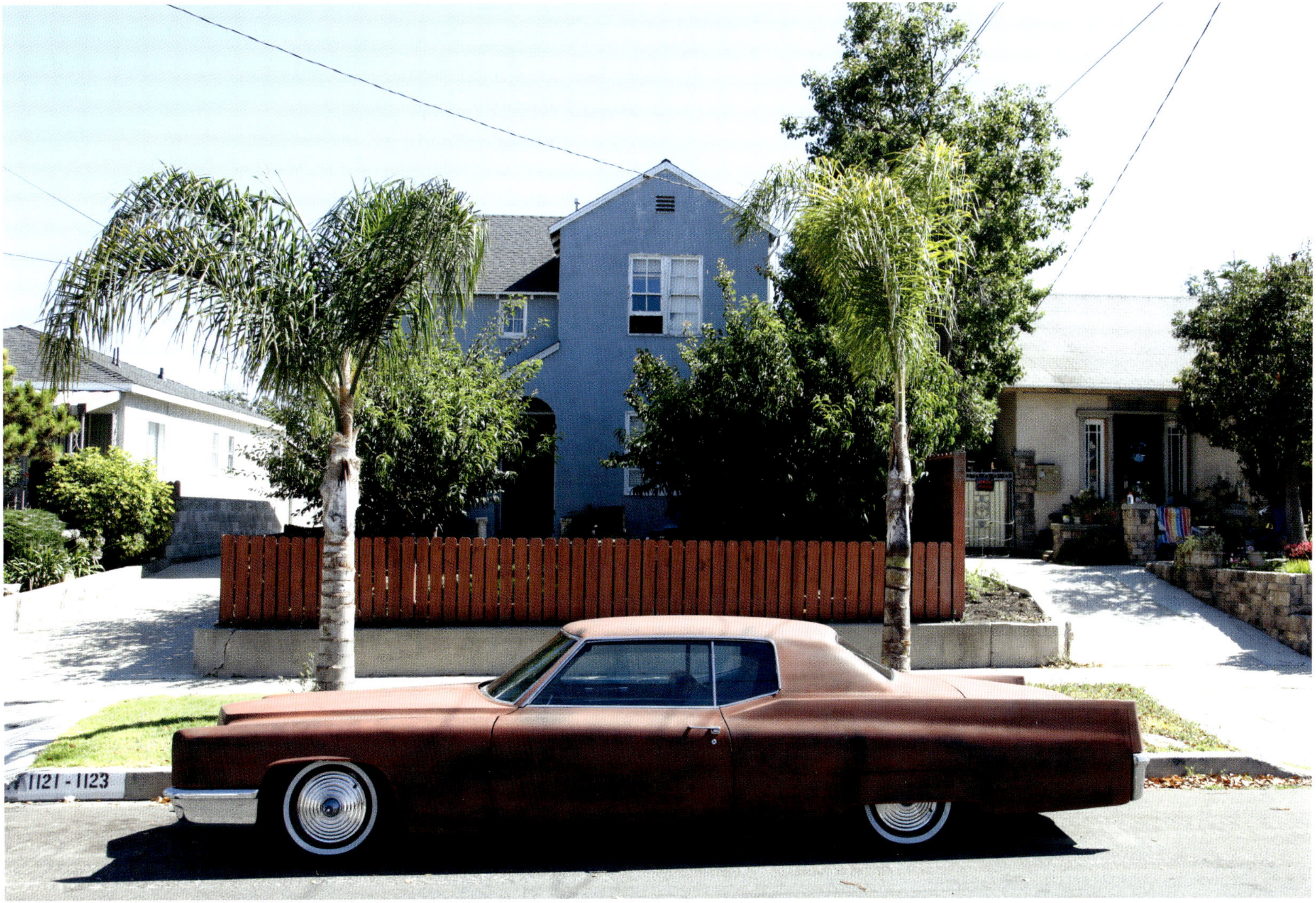

Sinn für Symmetrie: Lowrider-Cadillac zwischen Palmen. *A sense for symmetry: lowrider Cadillac between two palm trees.*

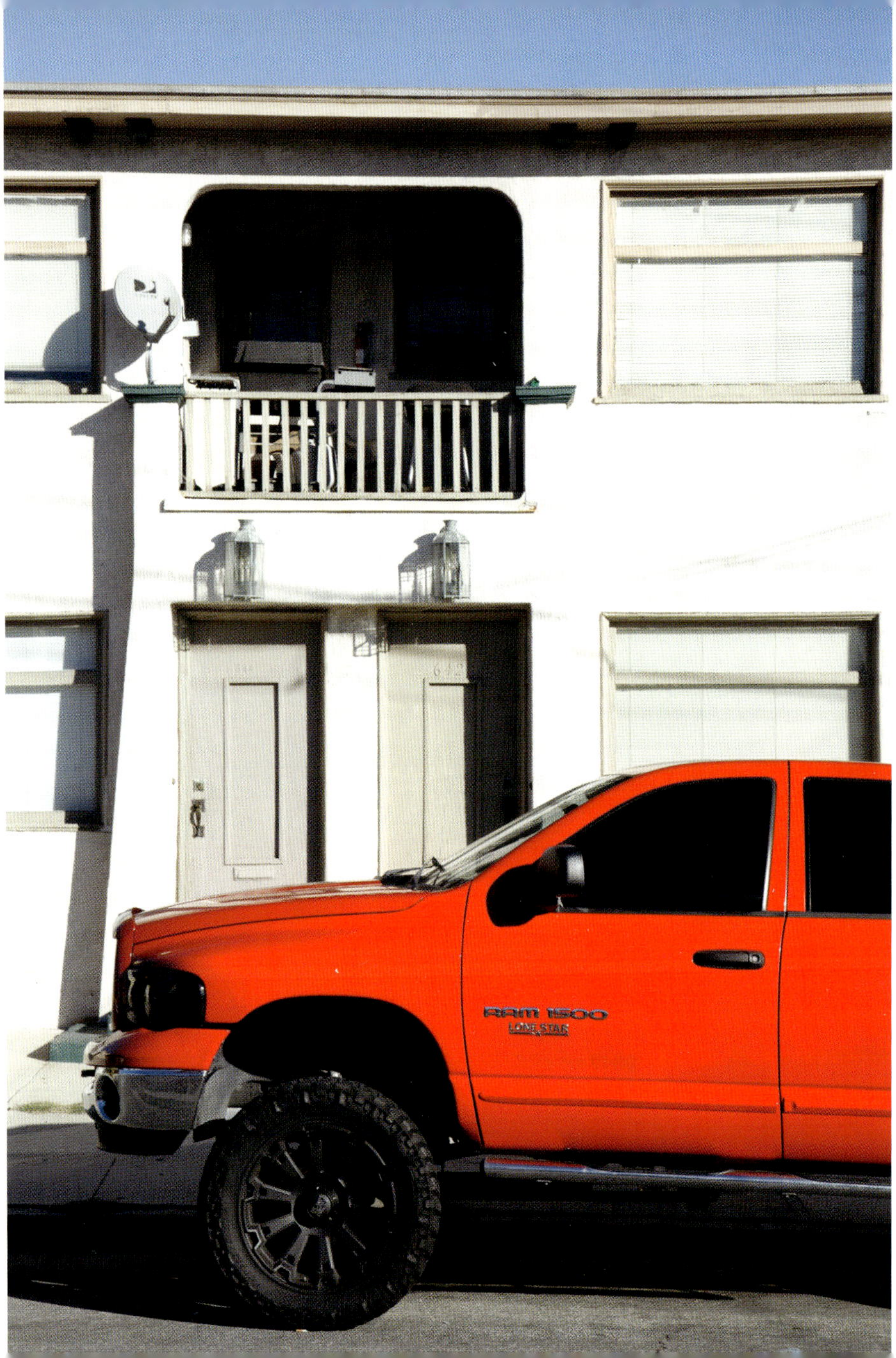

048

Fahrersitz in der ersten Etage, Balkon auch.
Second-story driver's seat and balcony.

049

Heißer Käfer vor cooler Kachelwand.
Hot Bug in front of cool, tiled wall.

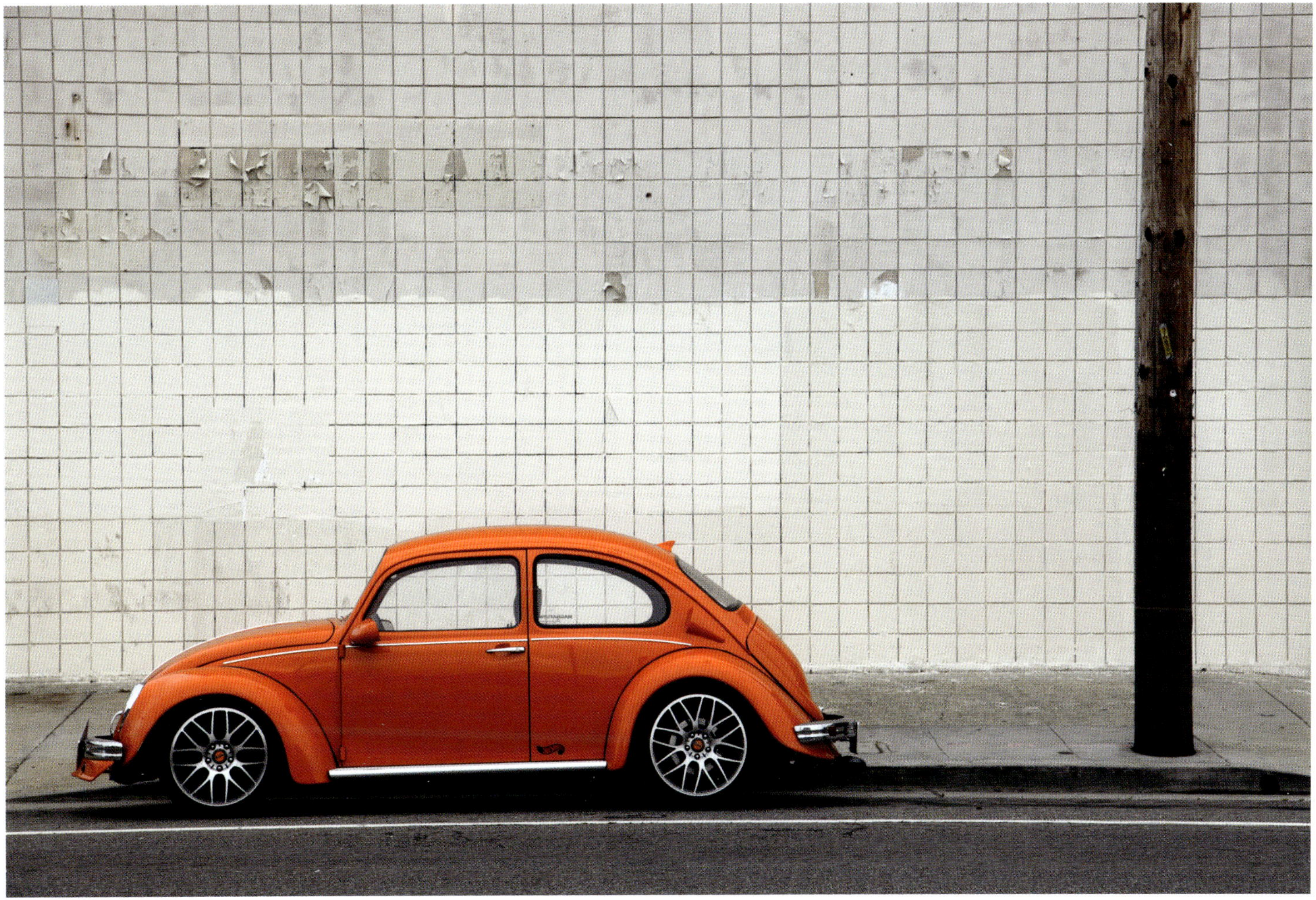

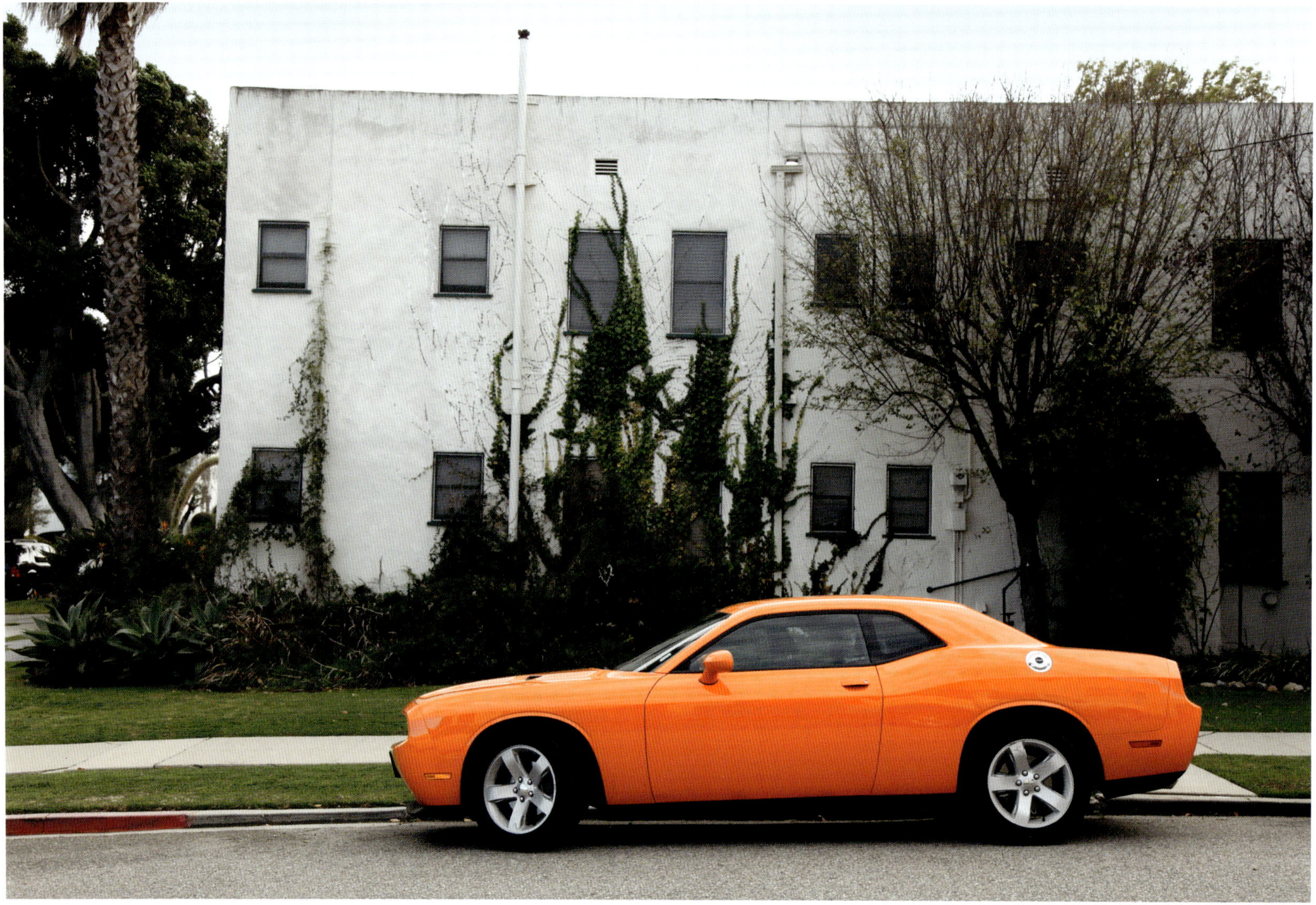

Fluchtauto vor Wohnschachtel. *Getaway car in front of housing unit.*

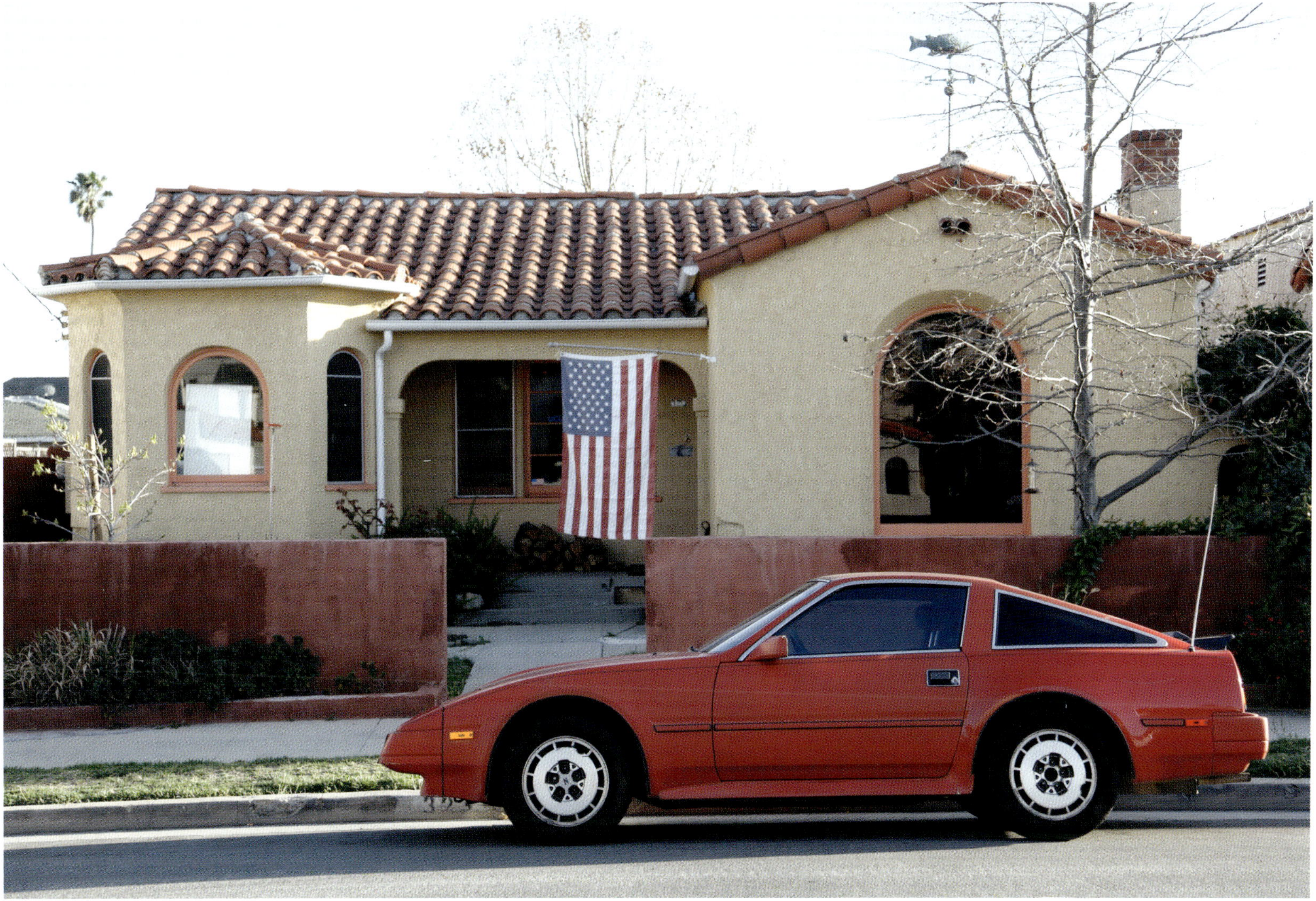

Haus spanisch, Flagge amerikanisch, Auto japanisch. *Spanish house, American flag, Japanese car.*

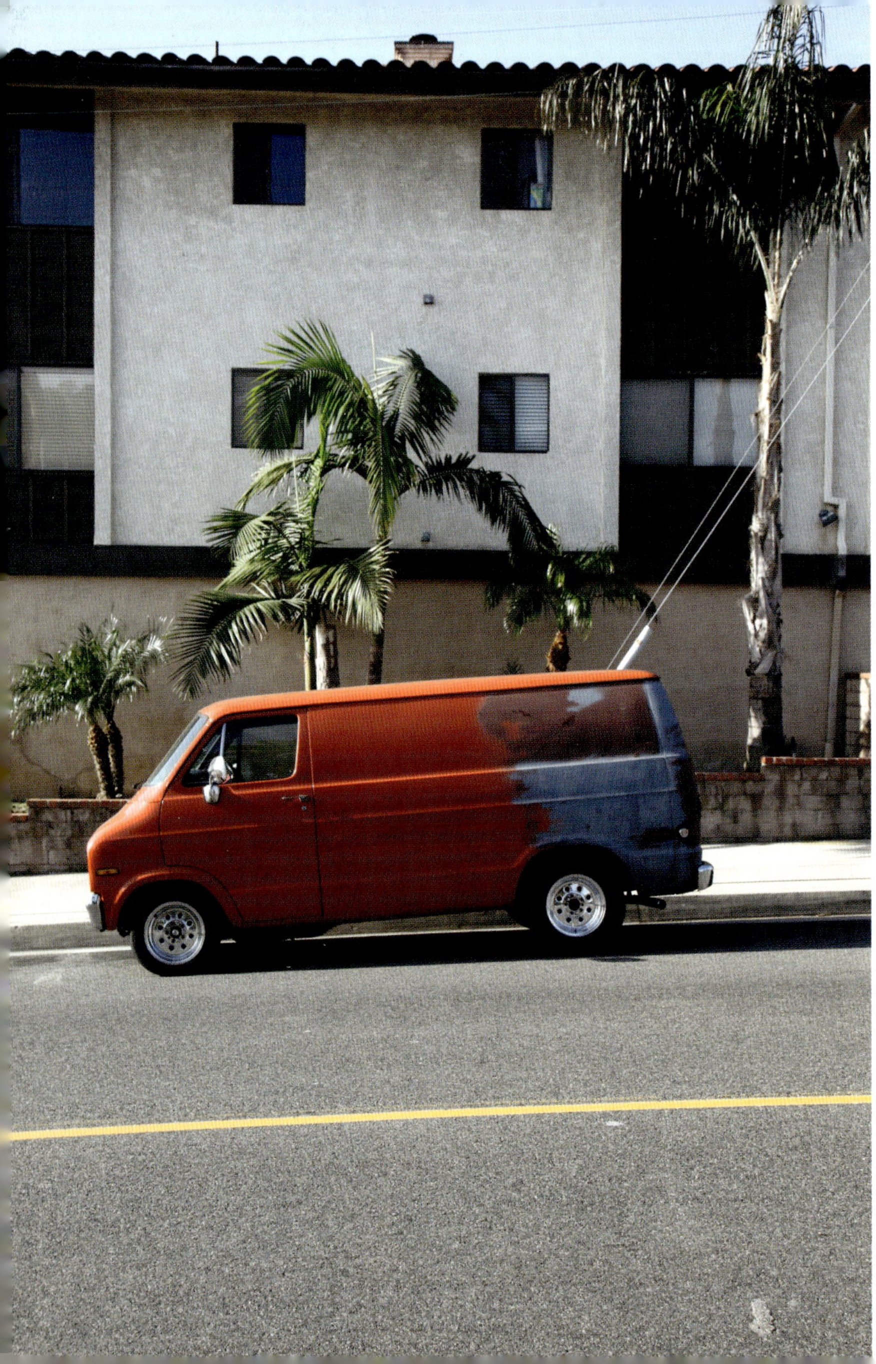

052

053

Wenn unterwegs die Farbe ausgeht, dann sieht das Ergebnis so aus.
When the paint runs out halfway through, the result looks like this.

Alternder Pontiac Trans Am vor verwaschener Kulisse.
Aging Pontiac Trans Am in front of washed out back-drop.

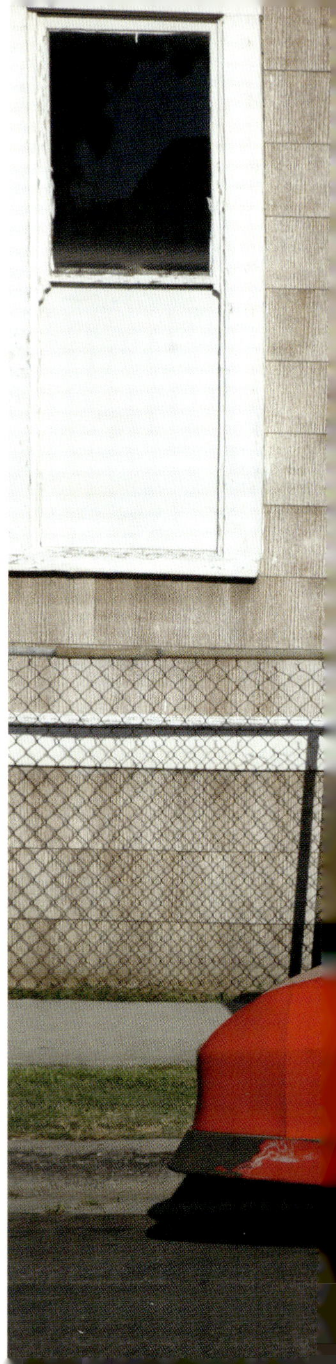

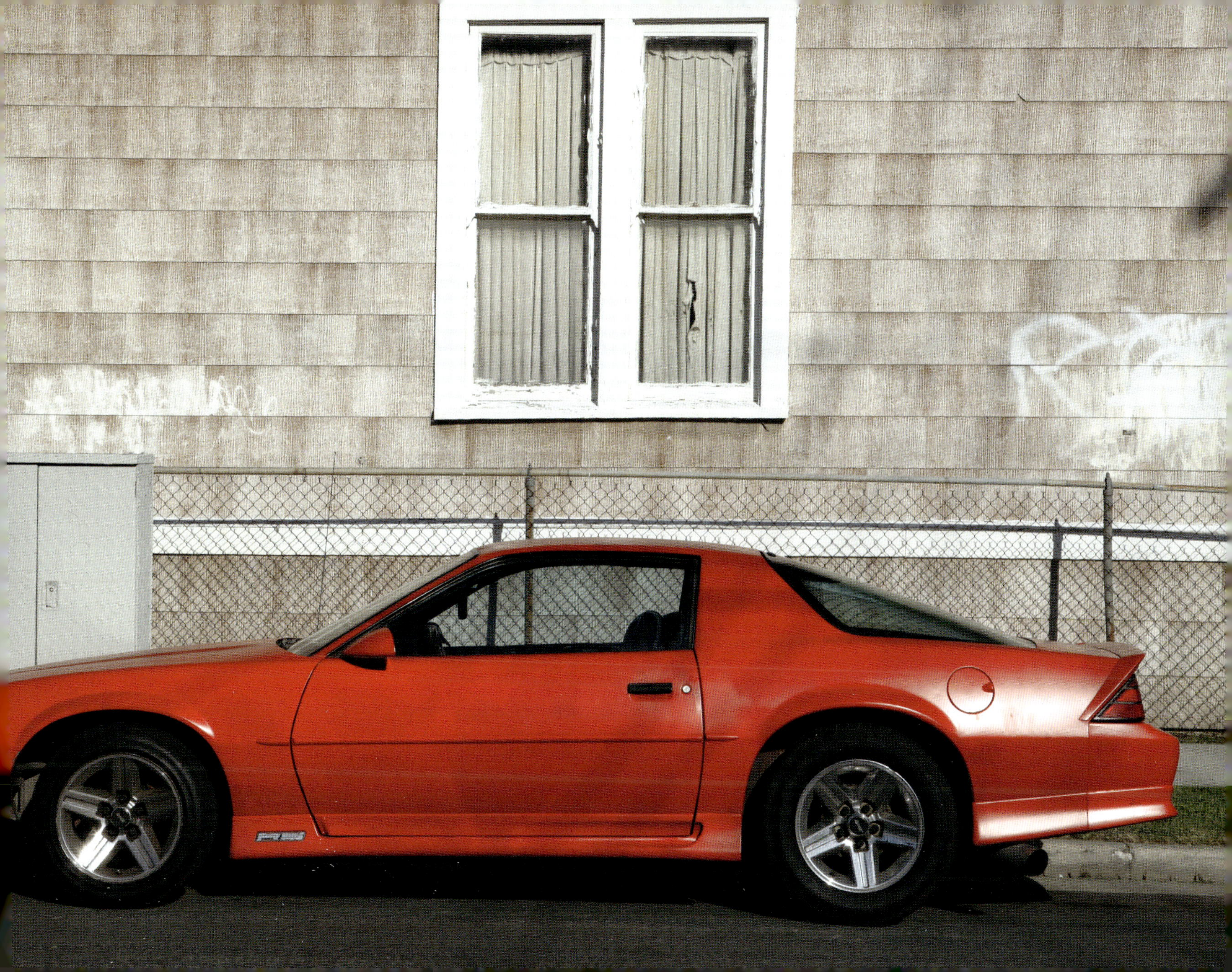

054 055 056

Dreimal Buick, einmal Graffiti im Schatten einer Supermarkt-Wand.
Three times Buick and one time graffiti in the shade of a supermarket wall.

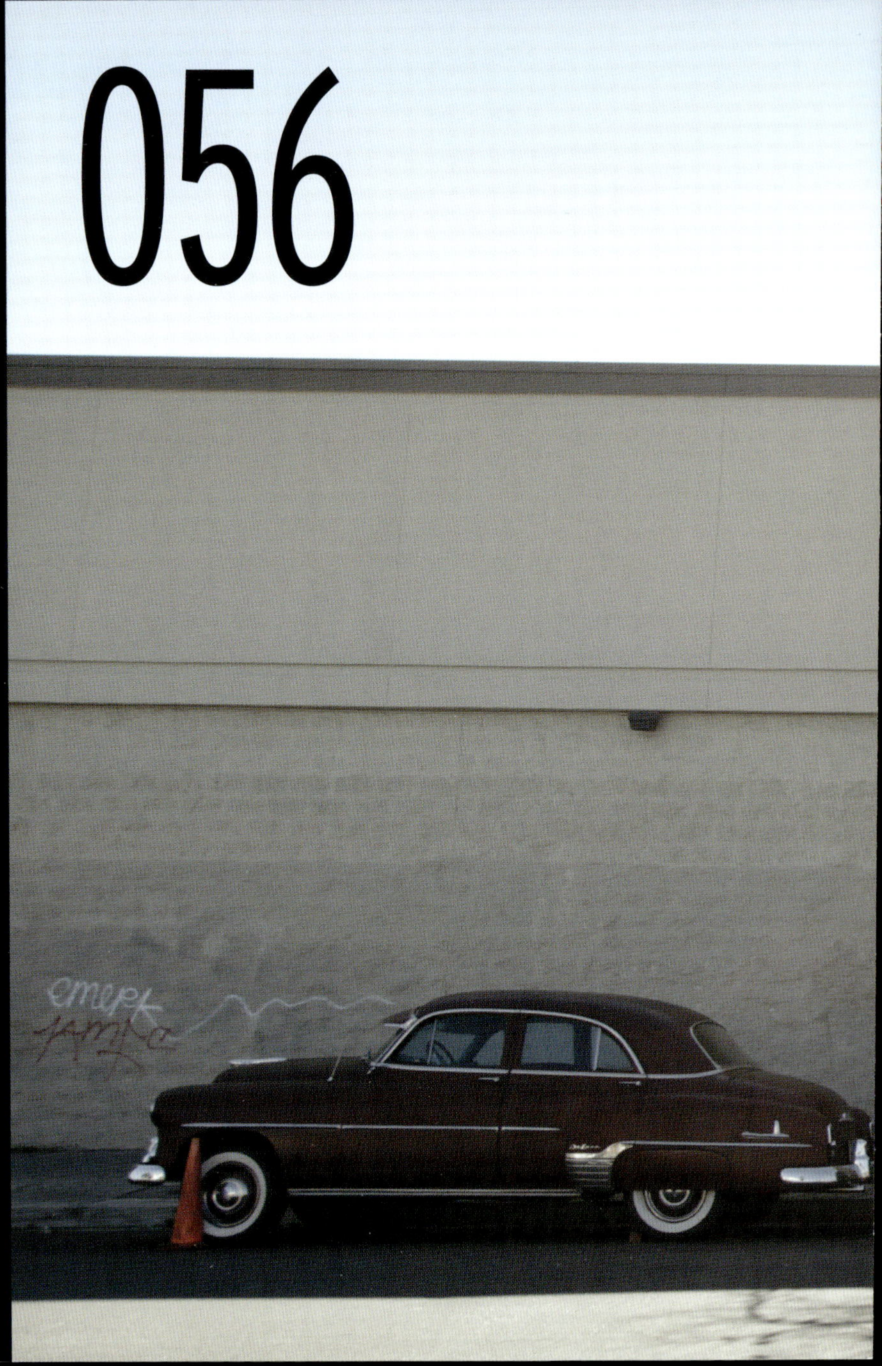

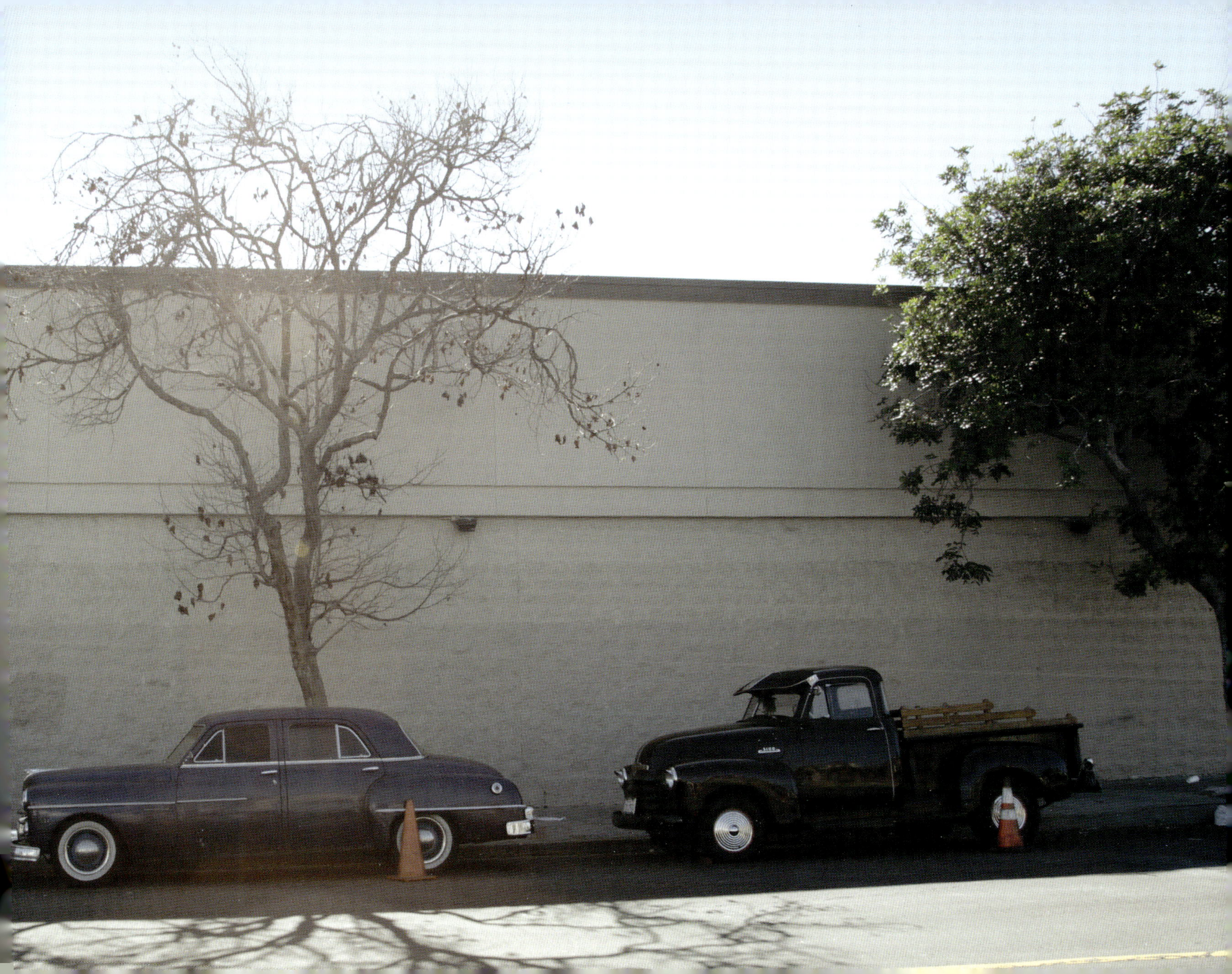

SILVER AND GREY. FAST. TECHNICAL. COOL. THE COLORS OF ROCKETS AND ICE CUBES.

SILBER UND GRAU. SCHNELL.

TECHNISCH. KÜHL.

DIE FARBEN VON RAKETEN UND EISWÜRFELN.

»High-speed drift on a prairie road. Hot tires sing like a string being bowed. Sudden town rears up, then explodes. Fragments resolve into white line code. Whirl on silver wheels.«
Bruce Cockburn

058

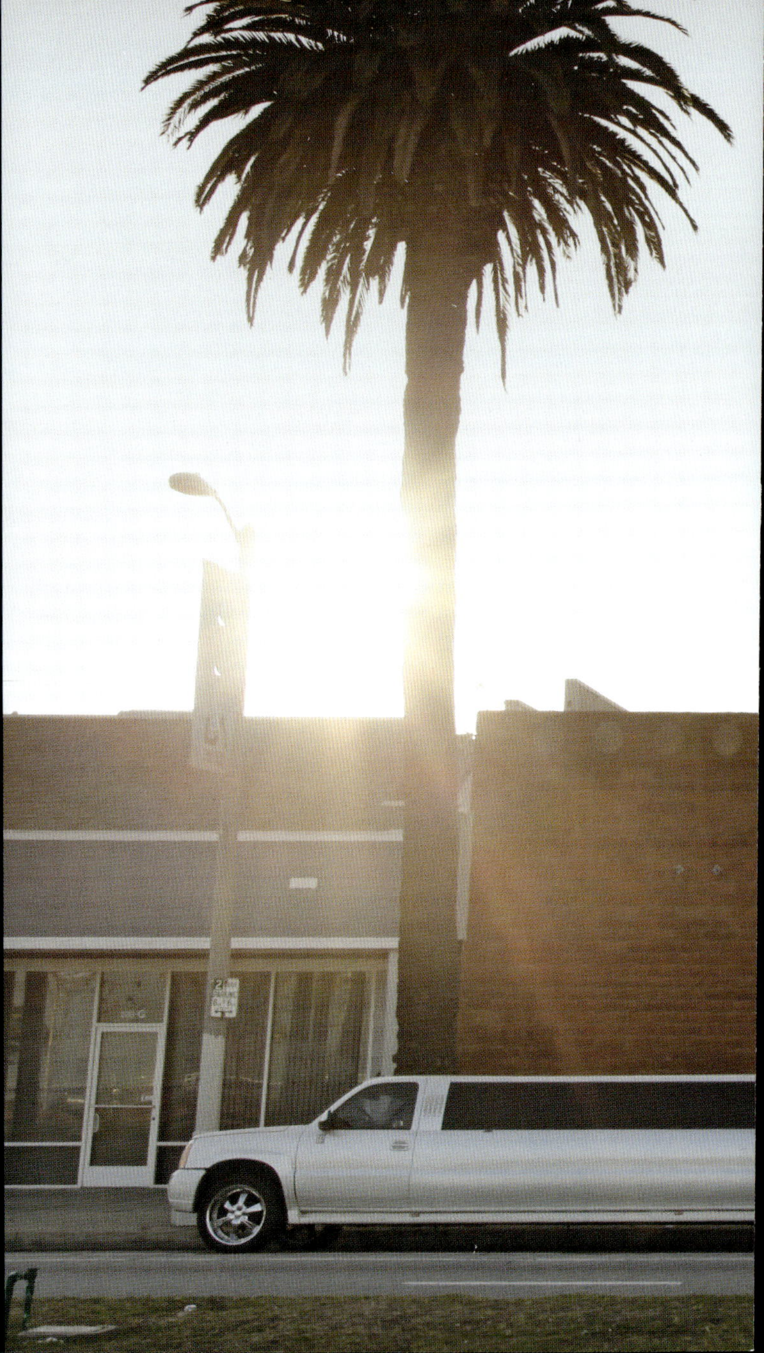

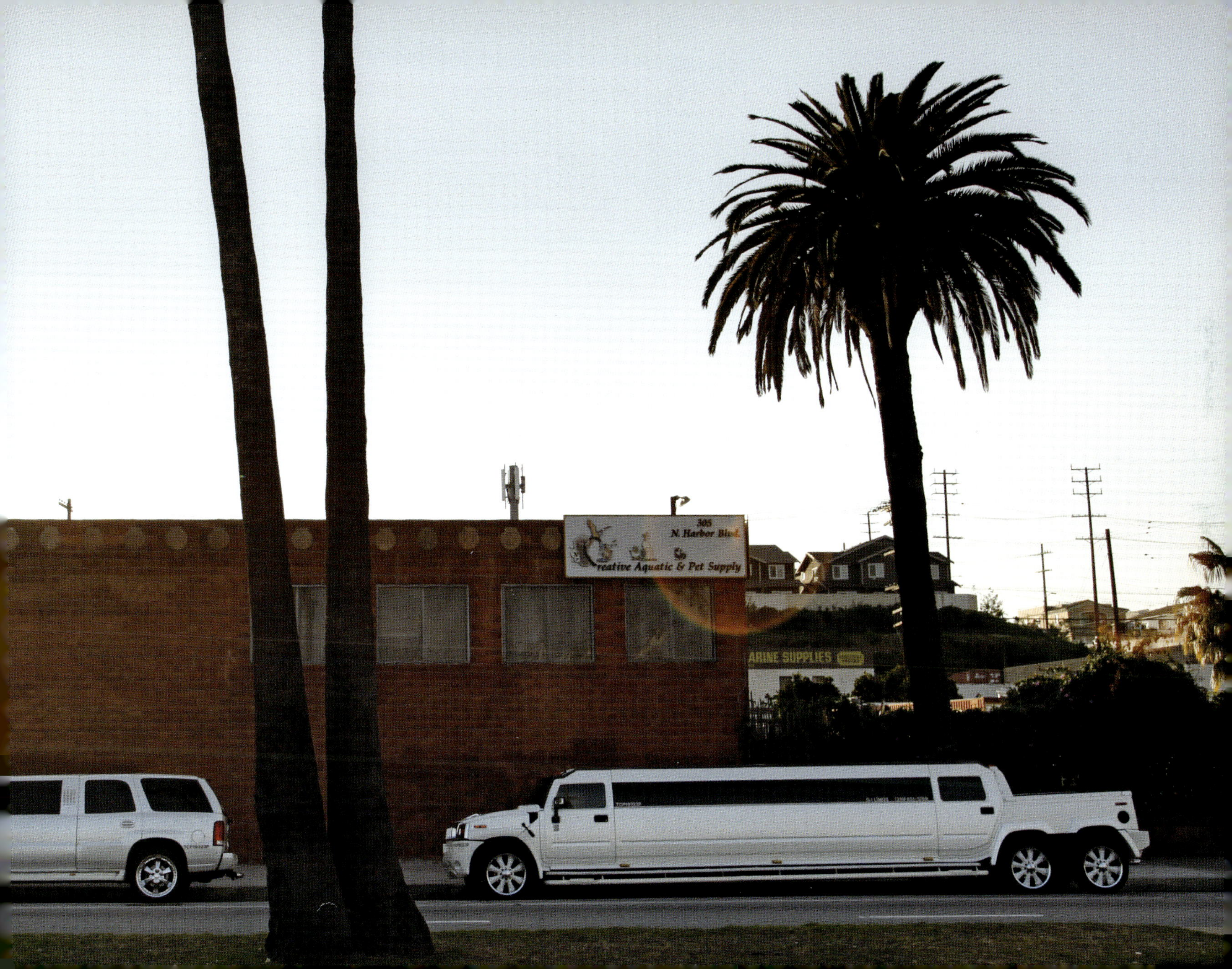
305
N. Harbor Blvd.
Creative Aquatic & Pet Supply
ARINE SUPPLIES

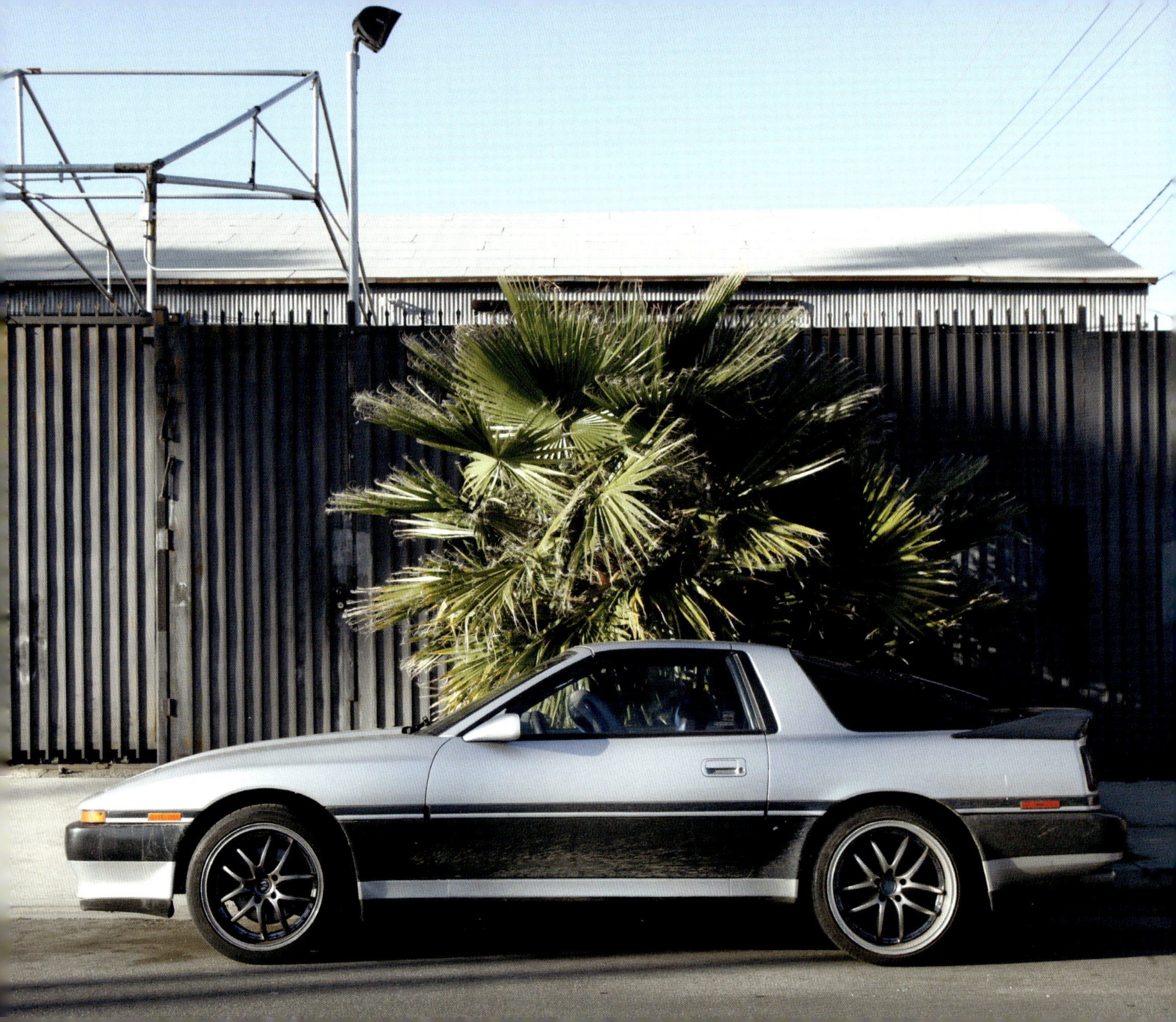

Kalifornische Blech-
architektur unterbro-
chen von Restgrün.
*Californian architecture
in sheet metal.*

Ben Hur 2.0: Streitwagen vor römischer Villa.
Ben Hur 2.0: Chariot in front of Roman villa.

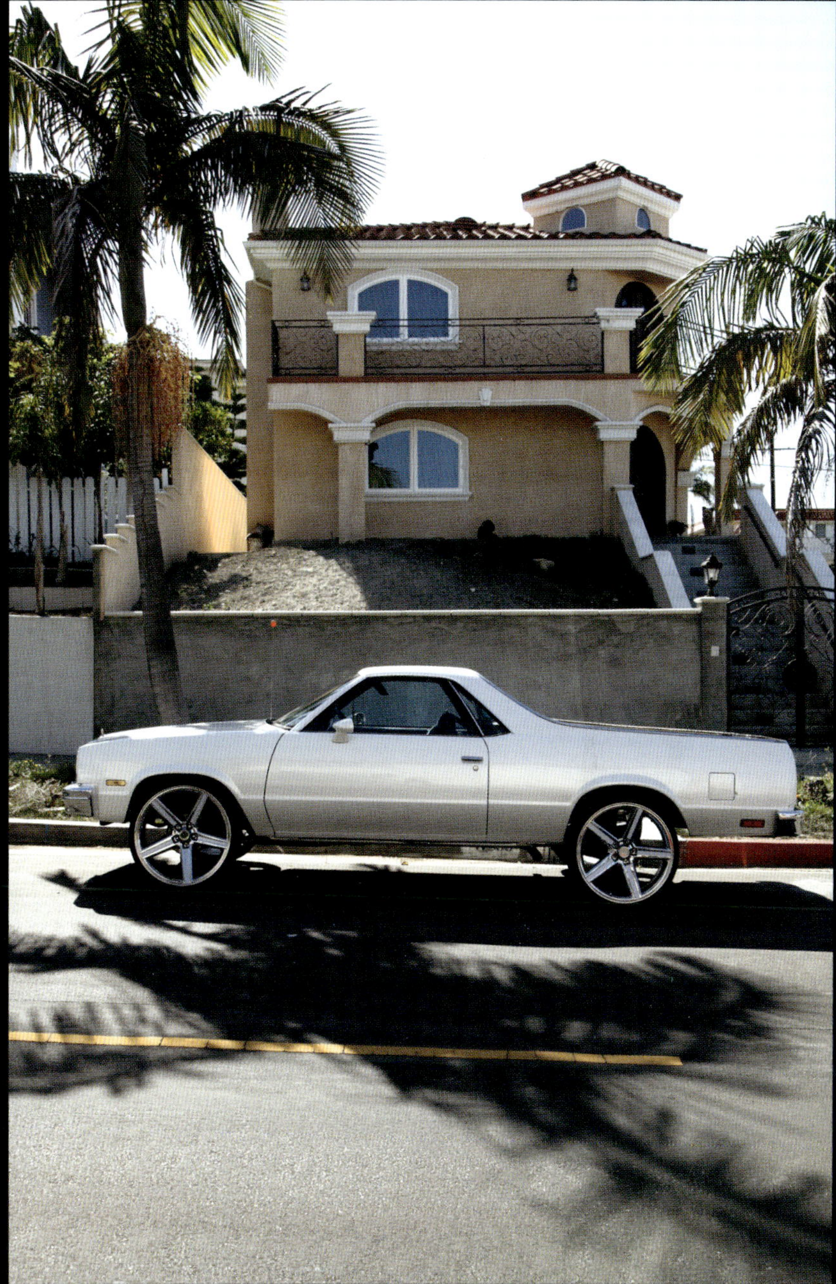

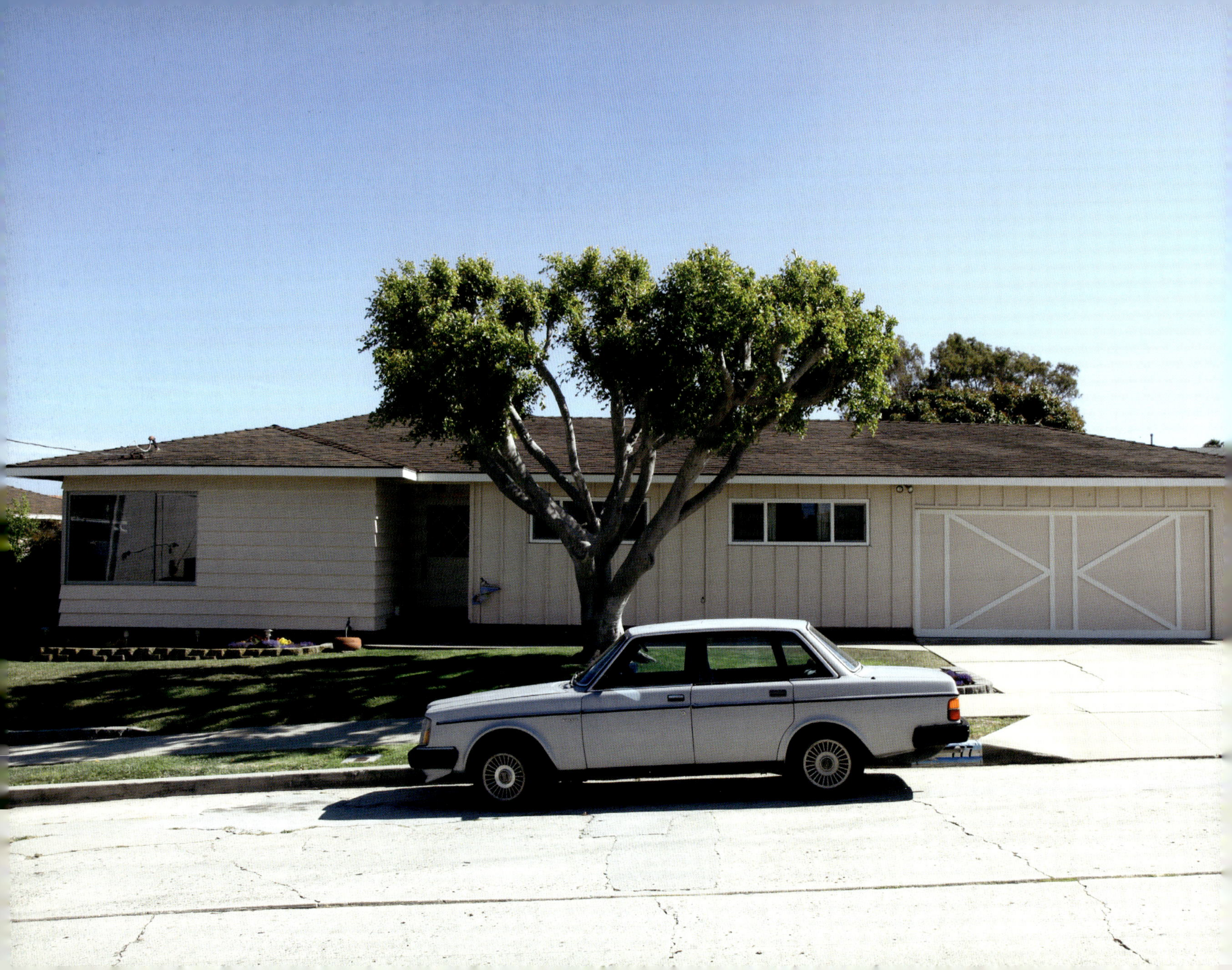

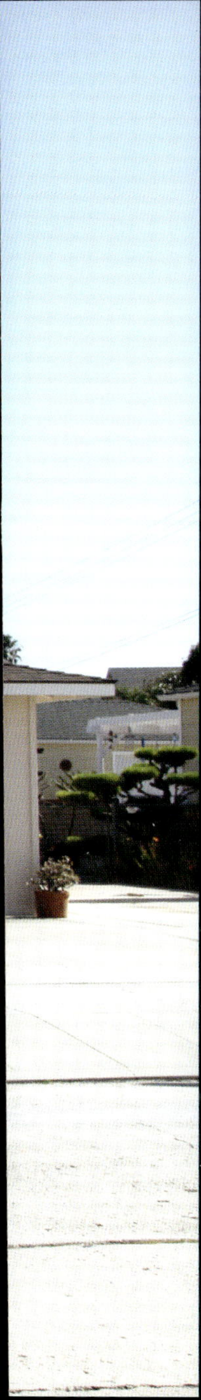

061

Volvo fahren ist Understatement. Ab einer gewissen Hausgröße darf man das.
Driving a Volvo is an understatement. This is allowed when your house is of a certain size

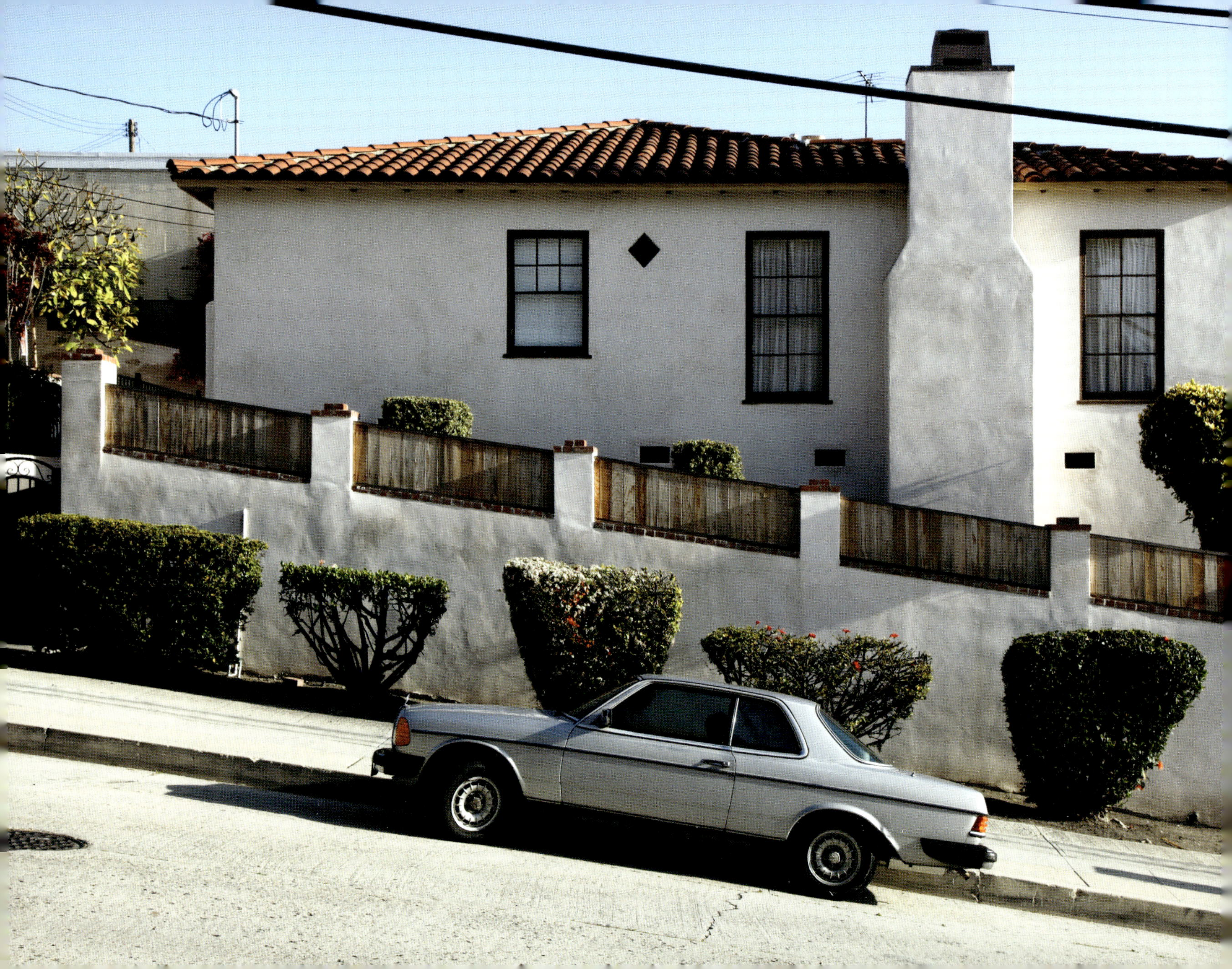

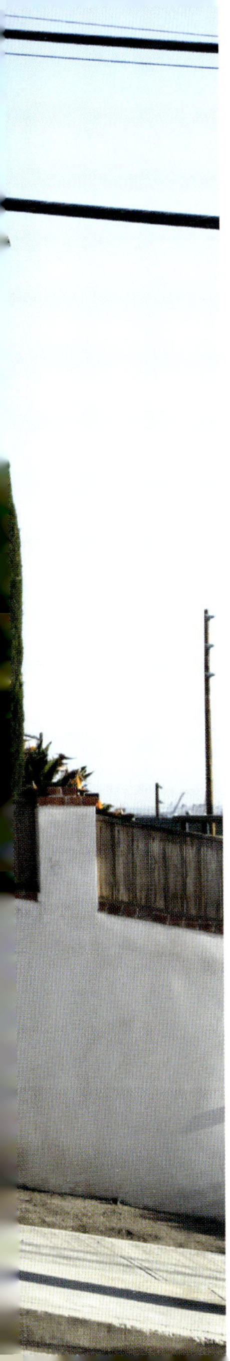

062

Das Mercedes Coupé wirkt vor diesem Haus wie ein geparktes Stilmöbel.
In front of this house, the Mercedes Coupé seems like parked period furniture.

063 064

Vorn parkt Mama, hinten Papa – oder umgekehrt?
Mom parks in front, Dad parks behind. Or is it the other way around?

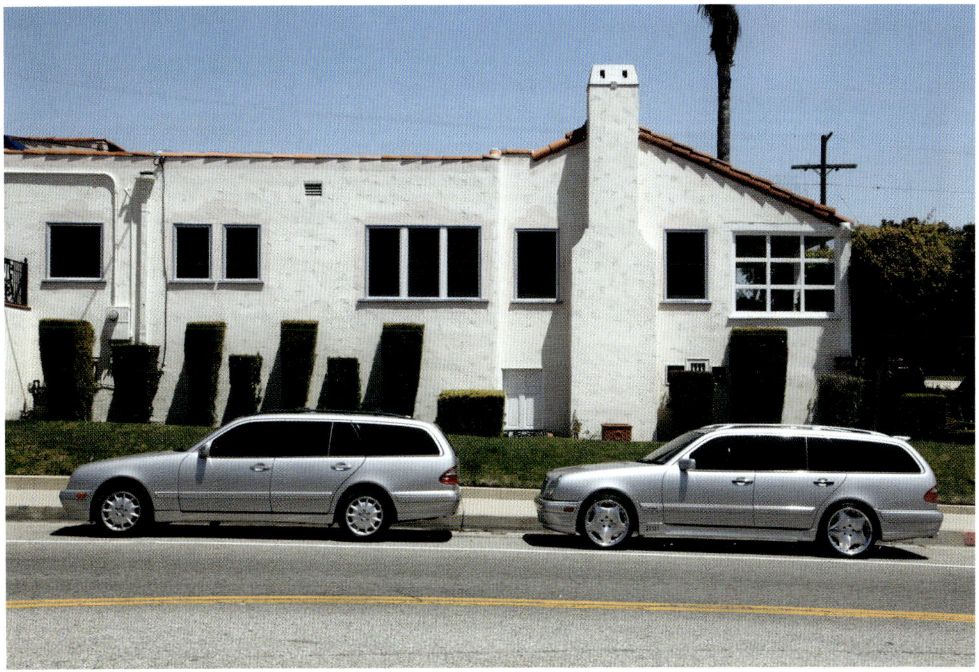

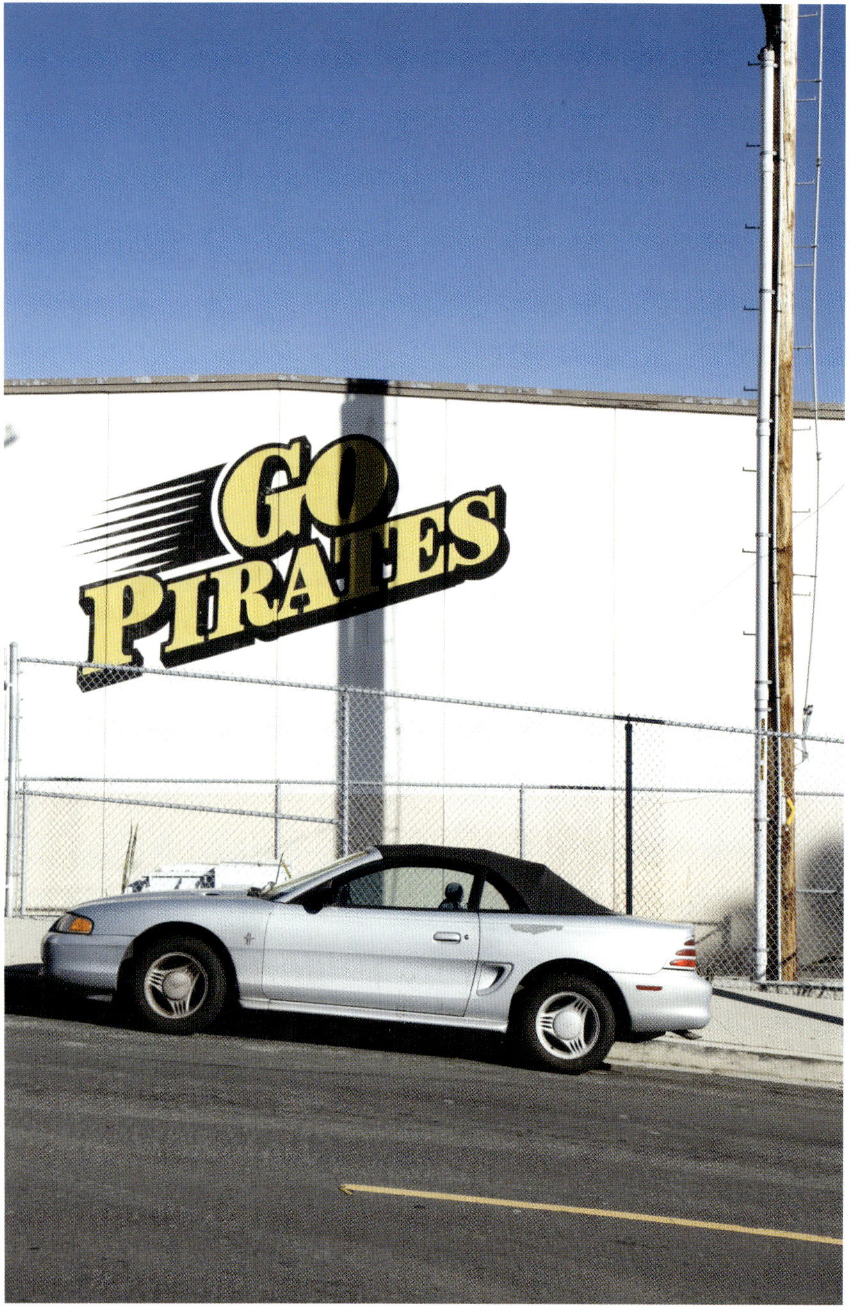

065

Der Sportwagen des Football Trainers. Go, Pirates, Go!
The football coach's sports car. Go, Pirates, go!

066

Mercedes »Strich Acht« sucht neues Zuhause.
Mercedes Slash Eight searching for a new home.

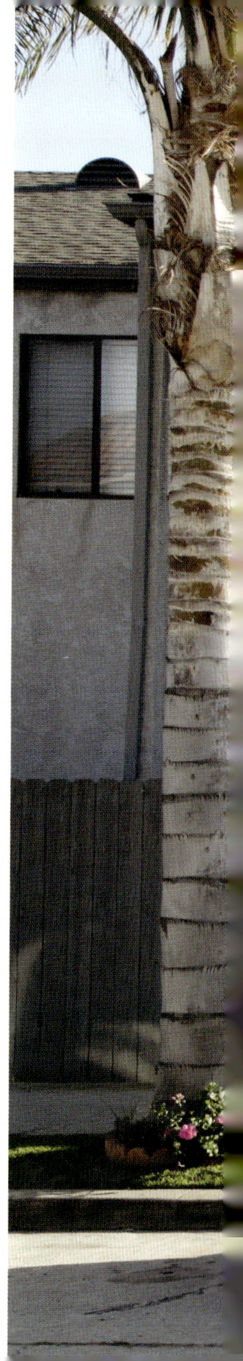

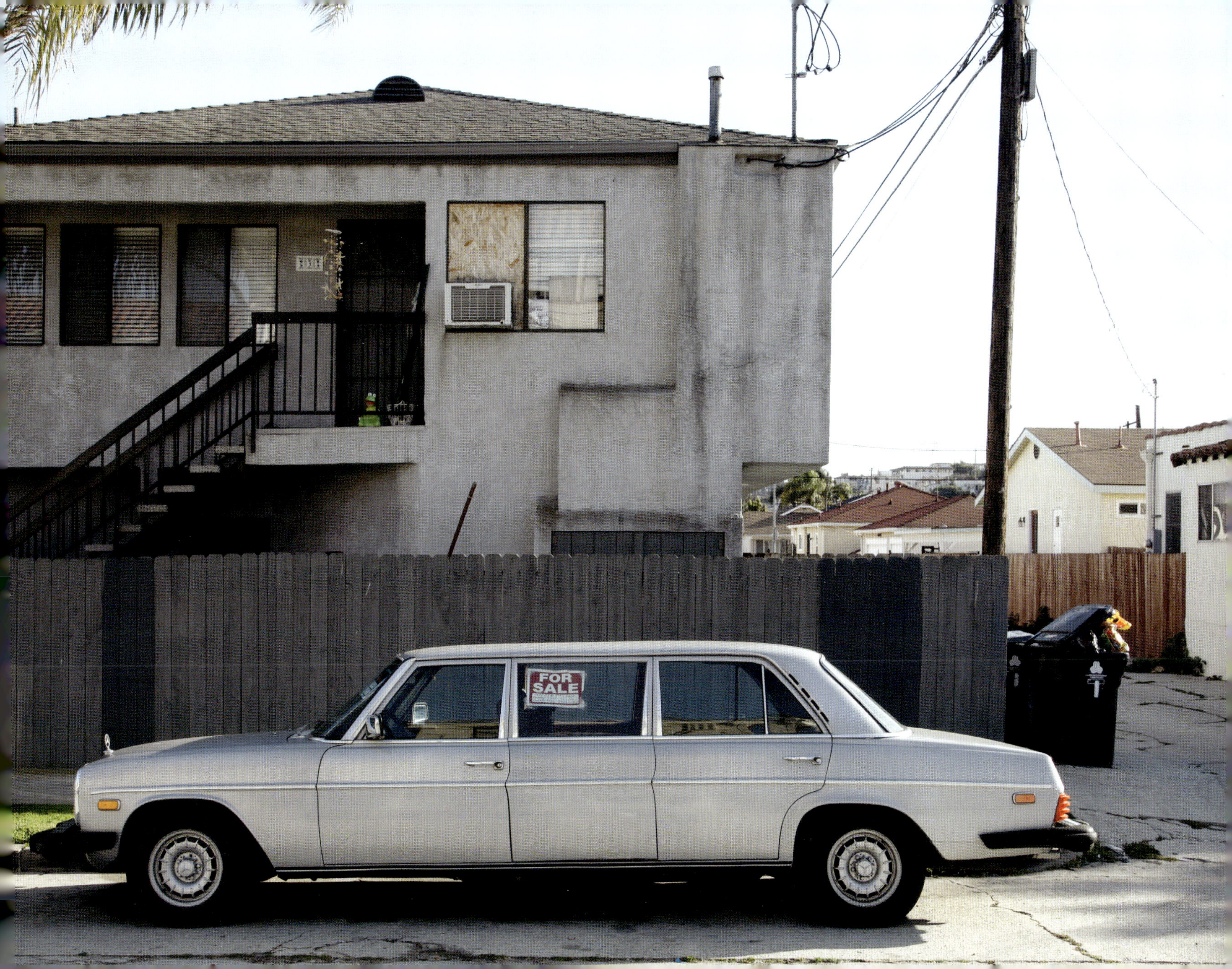
FOR
SALE

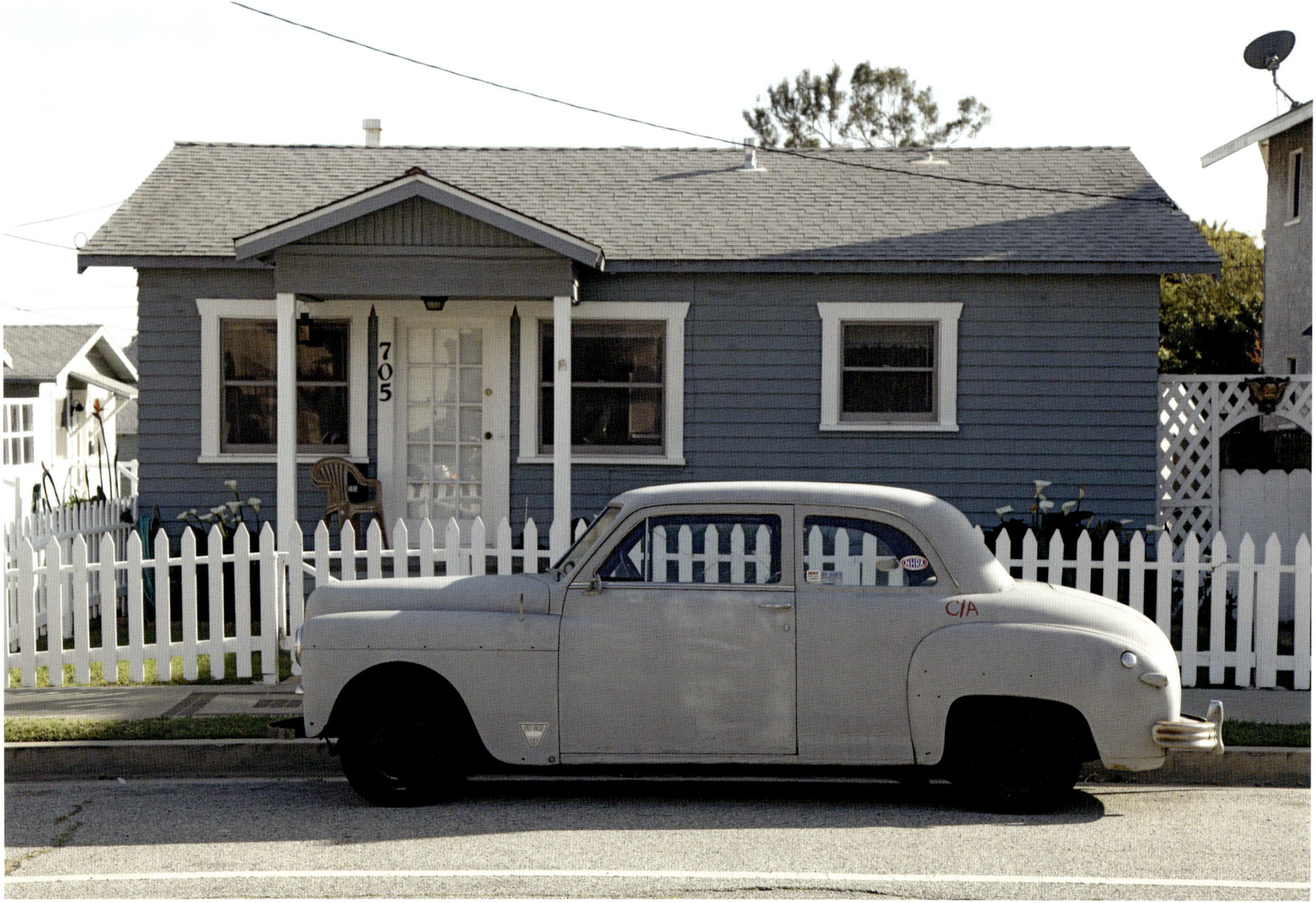

Dieses Bild zeigt den Willen zum Verzicht auf alles Überflüssige. *This photo demonstrates the will to do without all things unnecessary.*

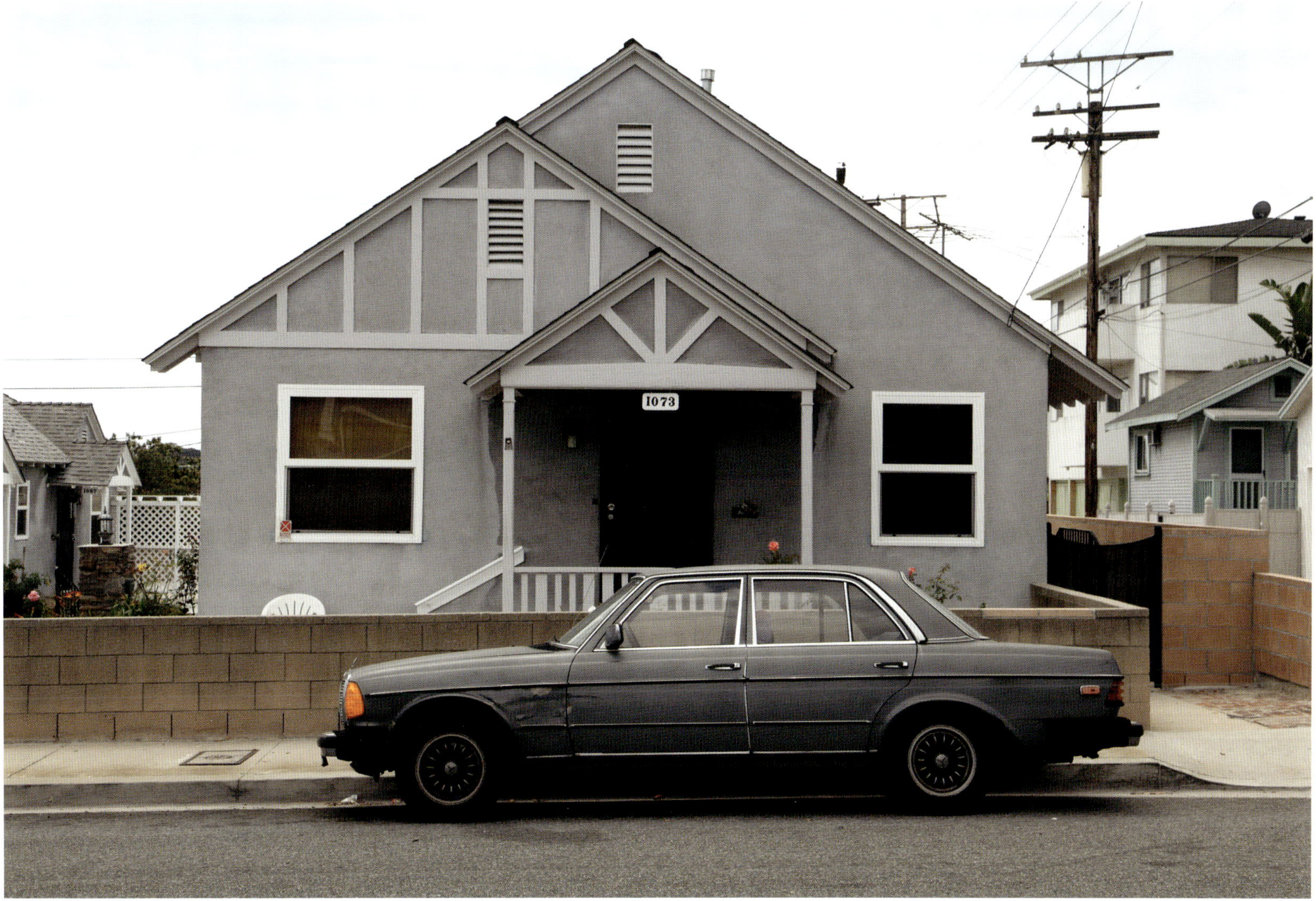

Hier lebt ein Liebhaber europäischer Altwagen. Aber wo ist der Saab (siehe 014)? *A lover of old European cars lives here. But where is the Saab (see 014) ?*

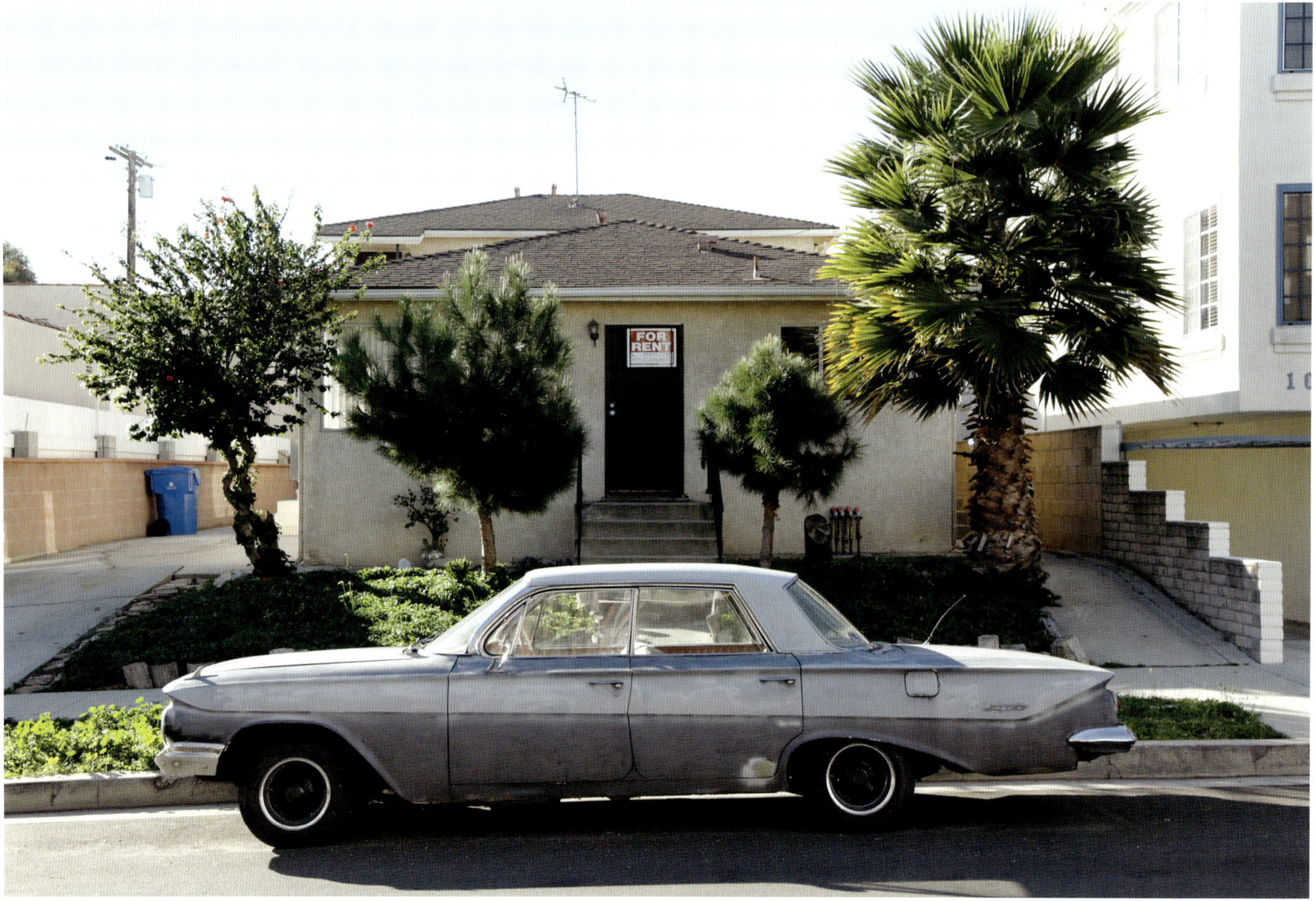

Typisch Amerika: dem Auto treu, dem Haus nicht. *Typically American: loyal to the car, but not to the house.*

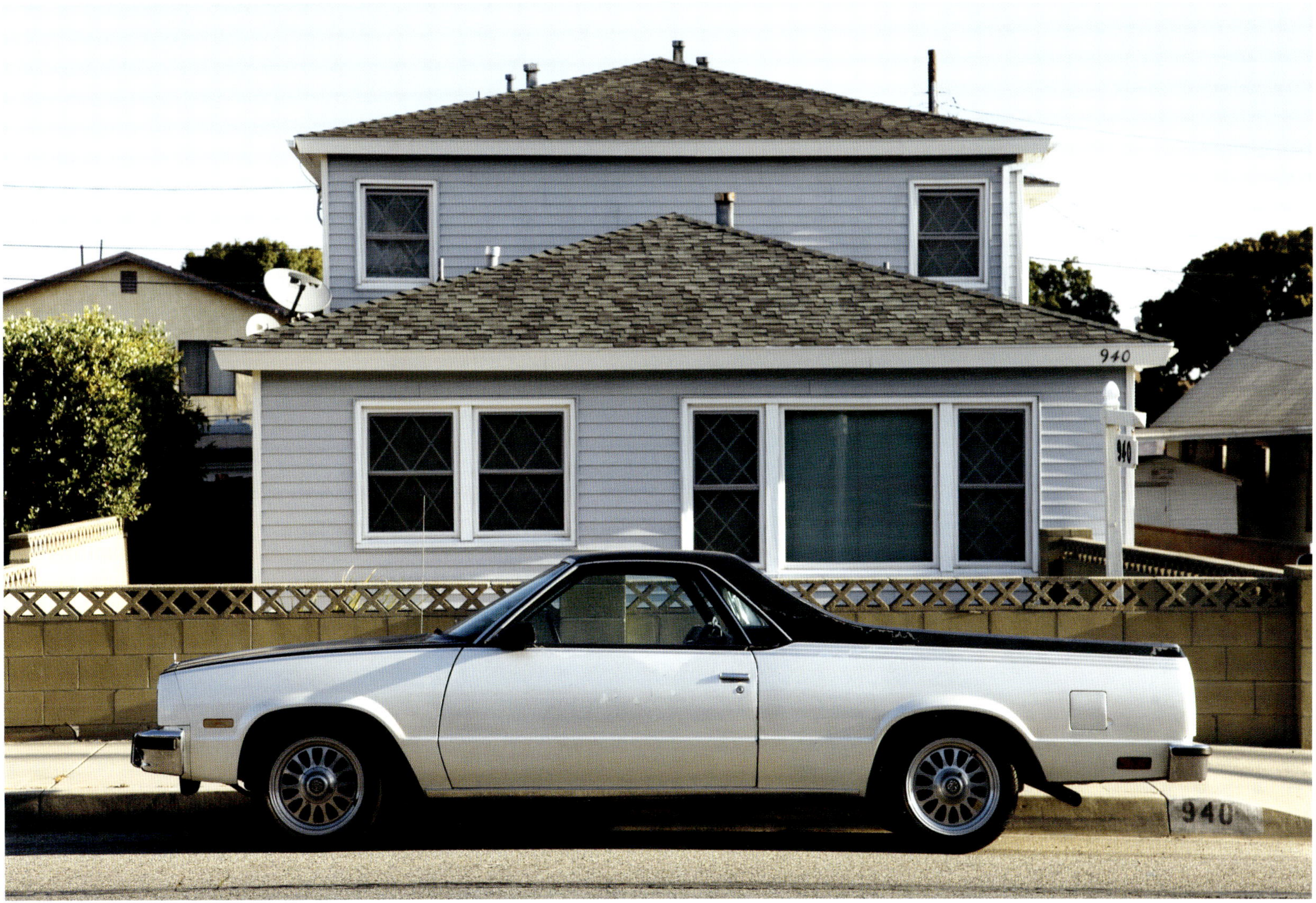

Man beachte die Symmetrie der drei Dächer. *Please note the three-roof symmetry.*

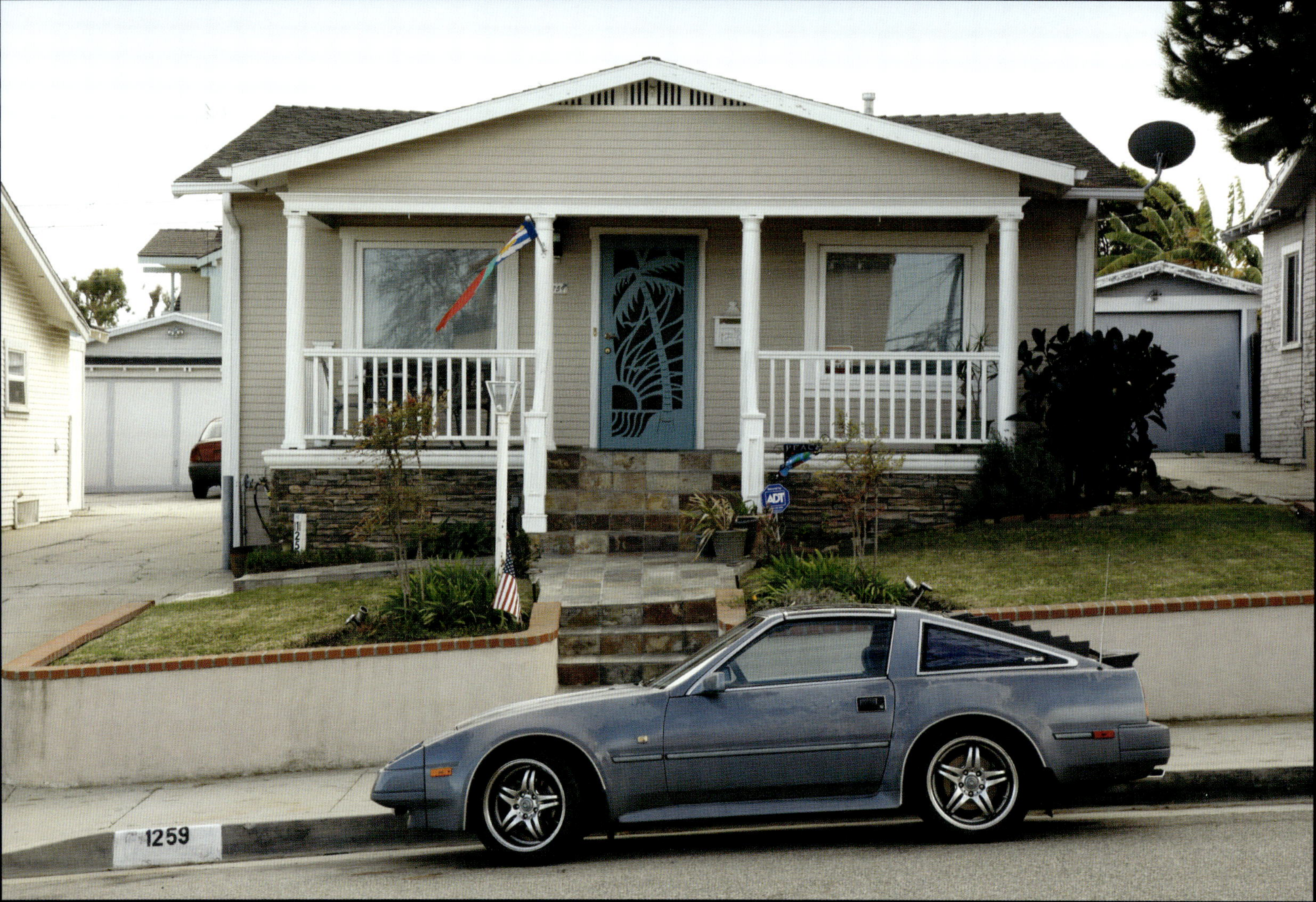

Amerikanischer Traum: Flaggen, Säulen, Palmen. *American Dream: flags, columns, palm trees.*

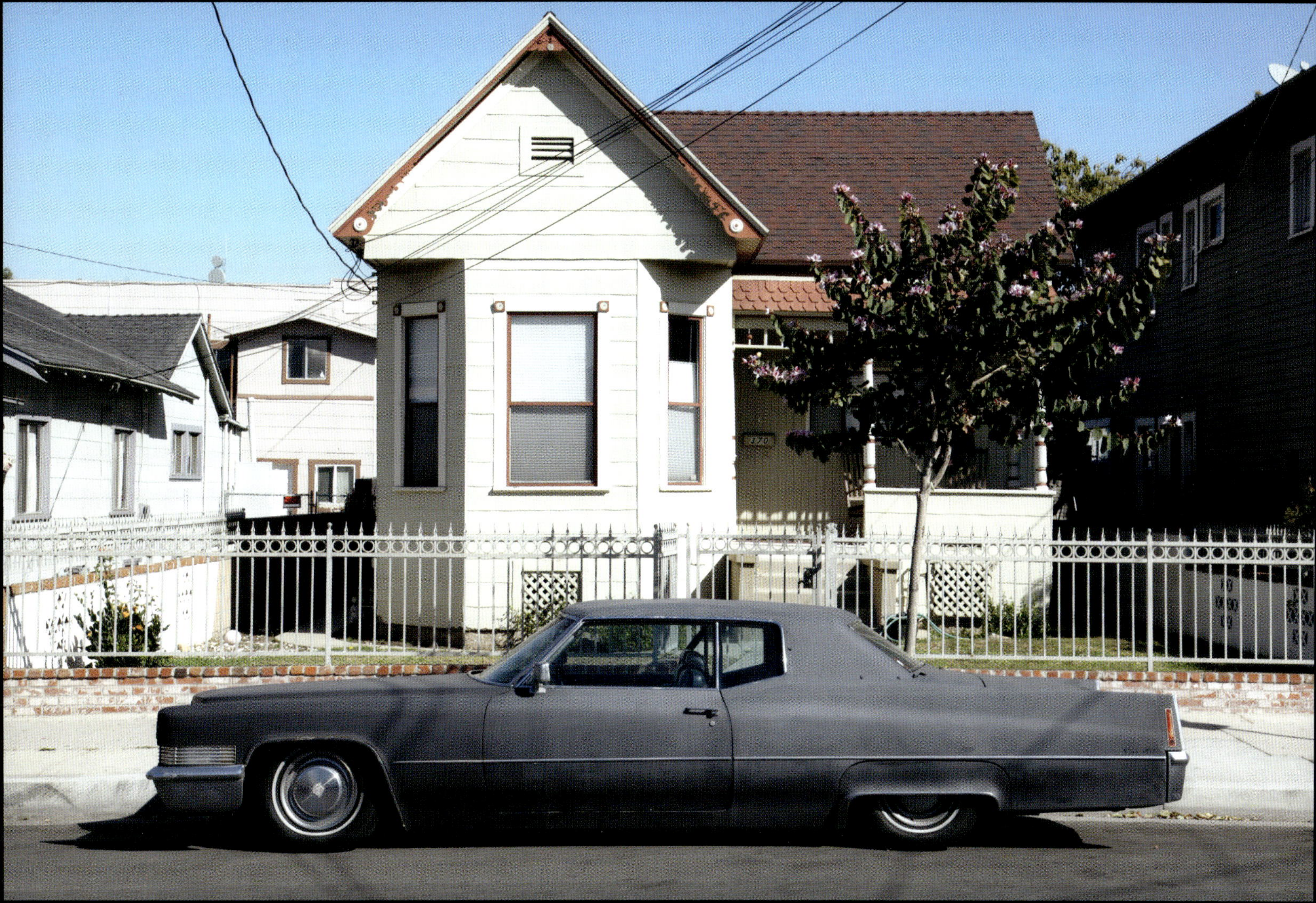

Schlafender Cadillac vor Spukschloss. *Sleeping Cadillac in front of haunted castle.*

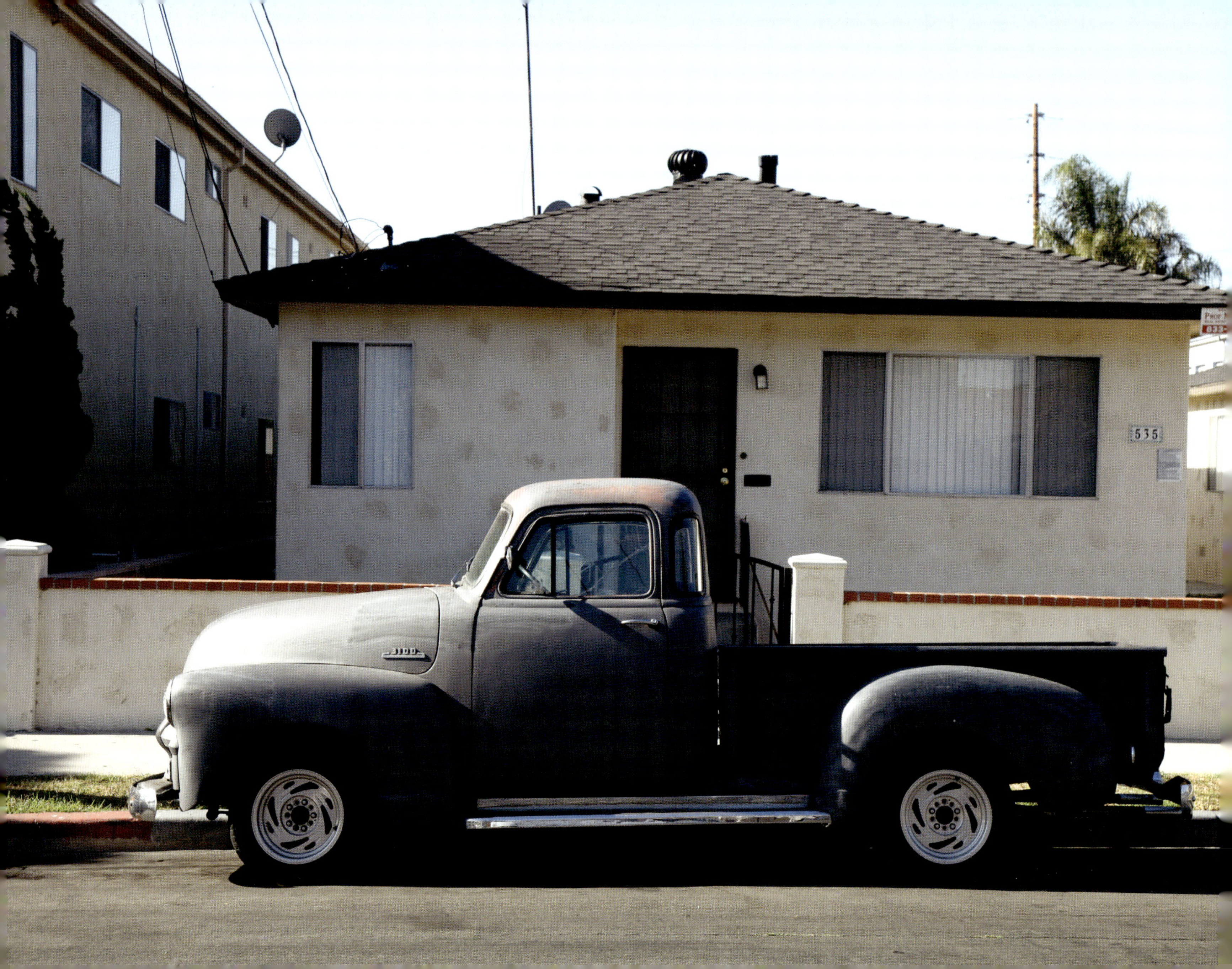
535
3100

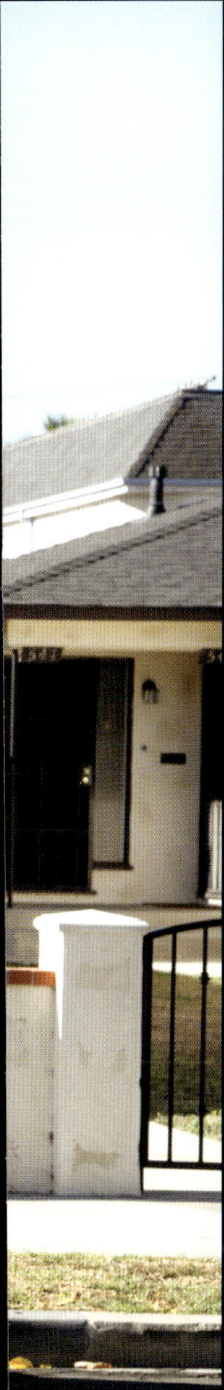

073

Ford F 100 Pickup in der Geschmacksrichtung »Ratte« vor Minimal-Architektur.
Ford F-100 in »rat« flavor in front of minimalist architecture.

074

Ein bisschen Rouge, ein bisschen Pink und ganz viel Ornamentik: Symphonie in der 25. Straße.
A bit of rouge, a bit of pink and lots of ornaments: symphony on 25th Street.

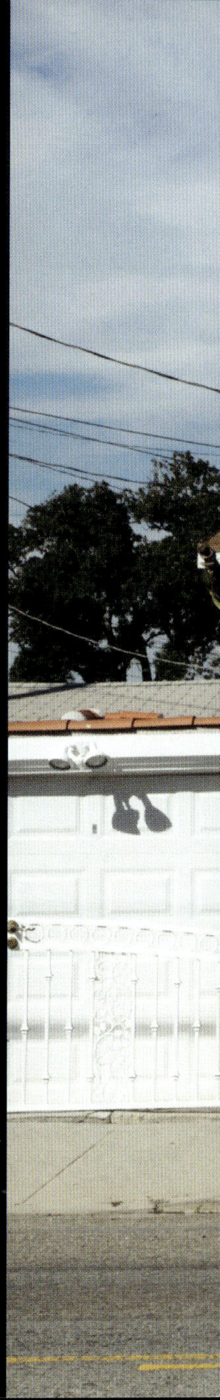

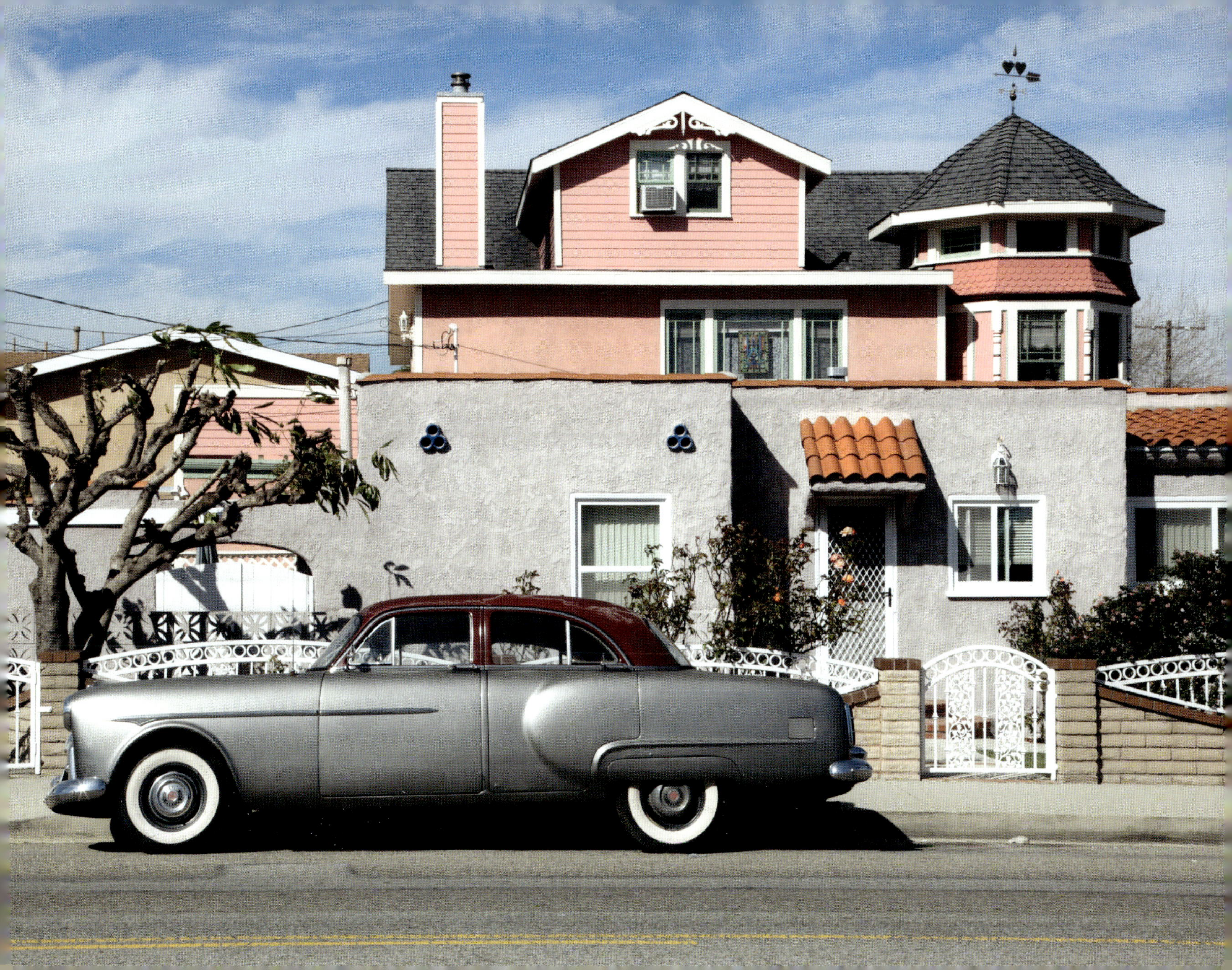

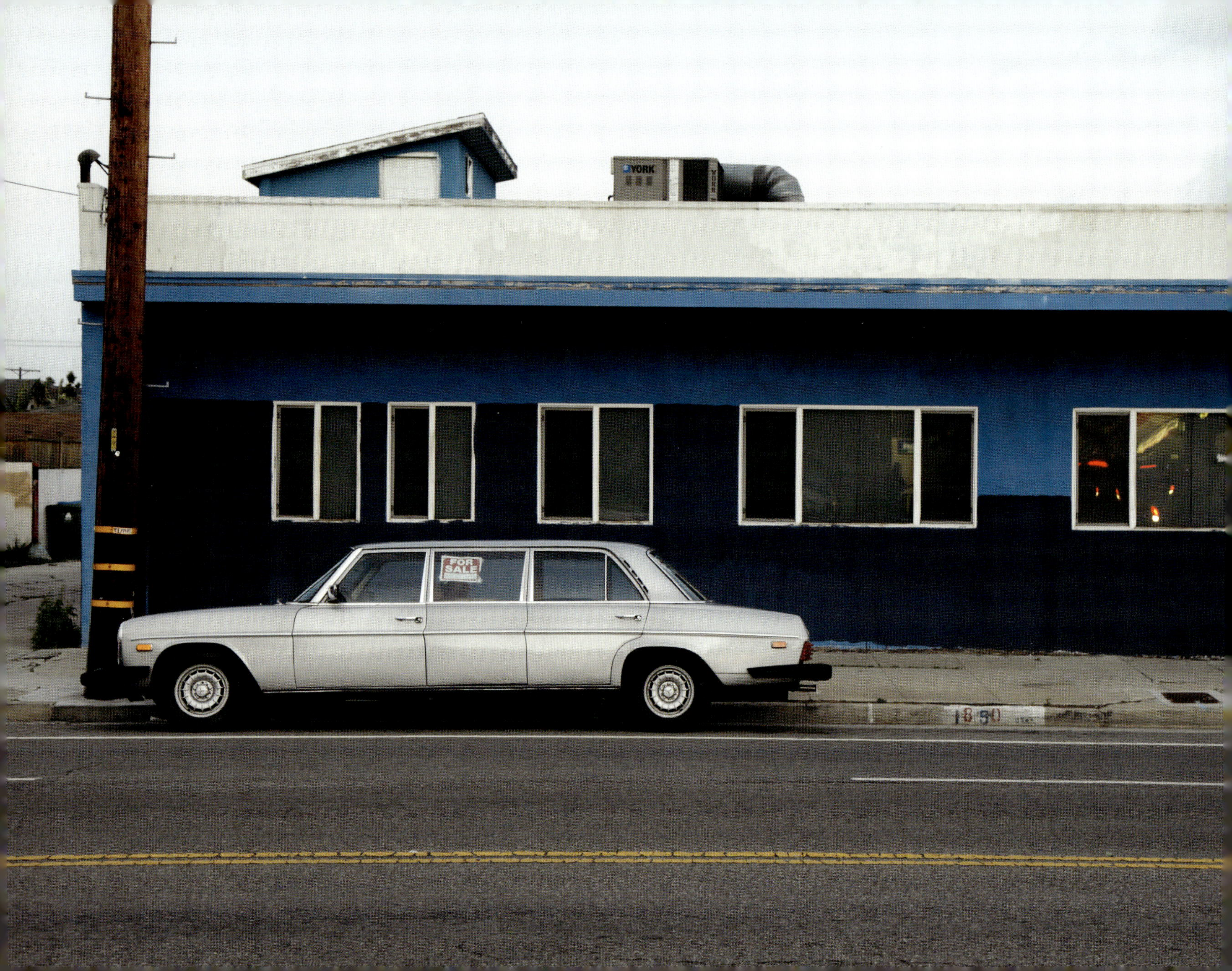
YORK
FOR
SALE

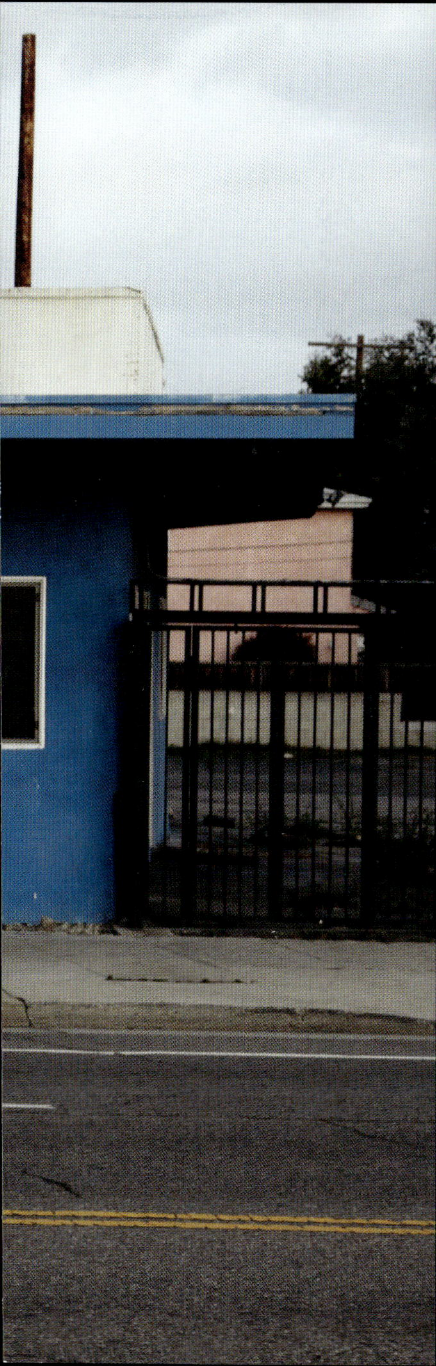

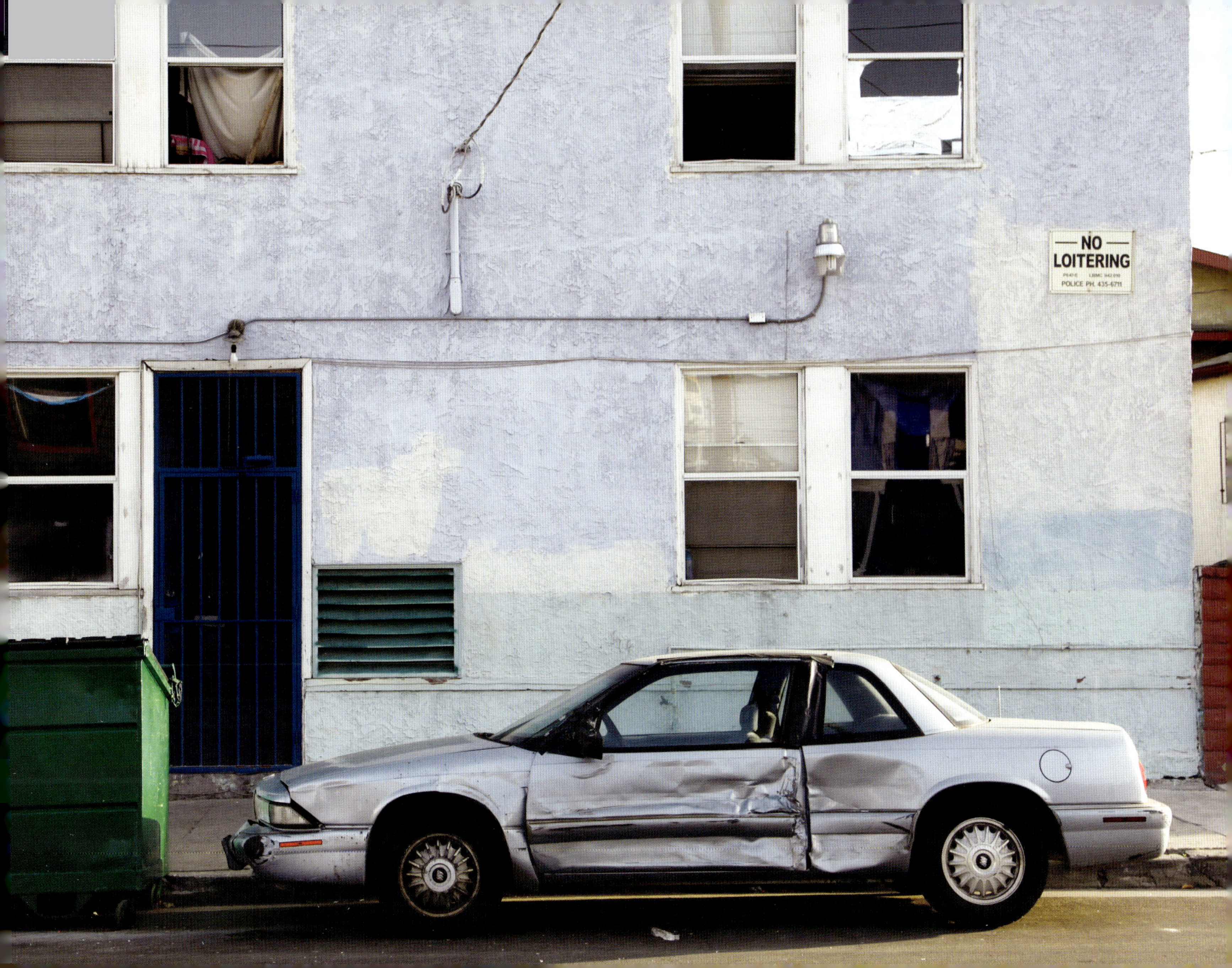
NO
LOITERING
POLICE PH. 435-6711

BLUE. BETWEEN SKY AND BLUE JEANS. THE COLOR OF BOUNDLESS DIMENSIONS IN THE LAND OF ENDLESS POSSIBILITIES.

BLAU. ZWISCHEN HIMMEL

UND BLUEJEANS.

DIE FARBE DER UNBEGRENZTEN DIMENSIONEN IM LAND DER UNBEGRENZTEN MÖGLICHKEITEN.

»Blue Hotel, on a lonely highway. Blue Hotel, life don’t work out my way. I wait alone each lonely night. Blue Hotel … Blue Hotel.«
Chris Isaak

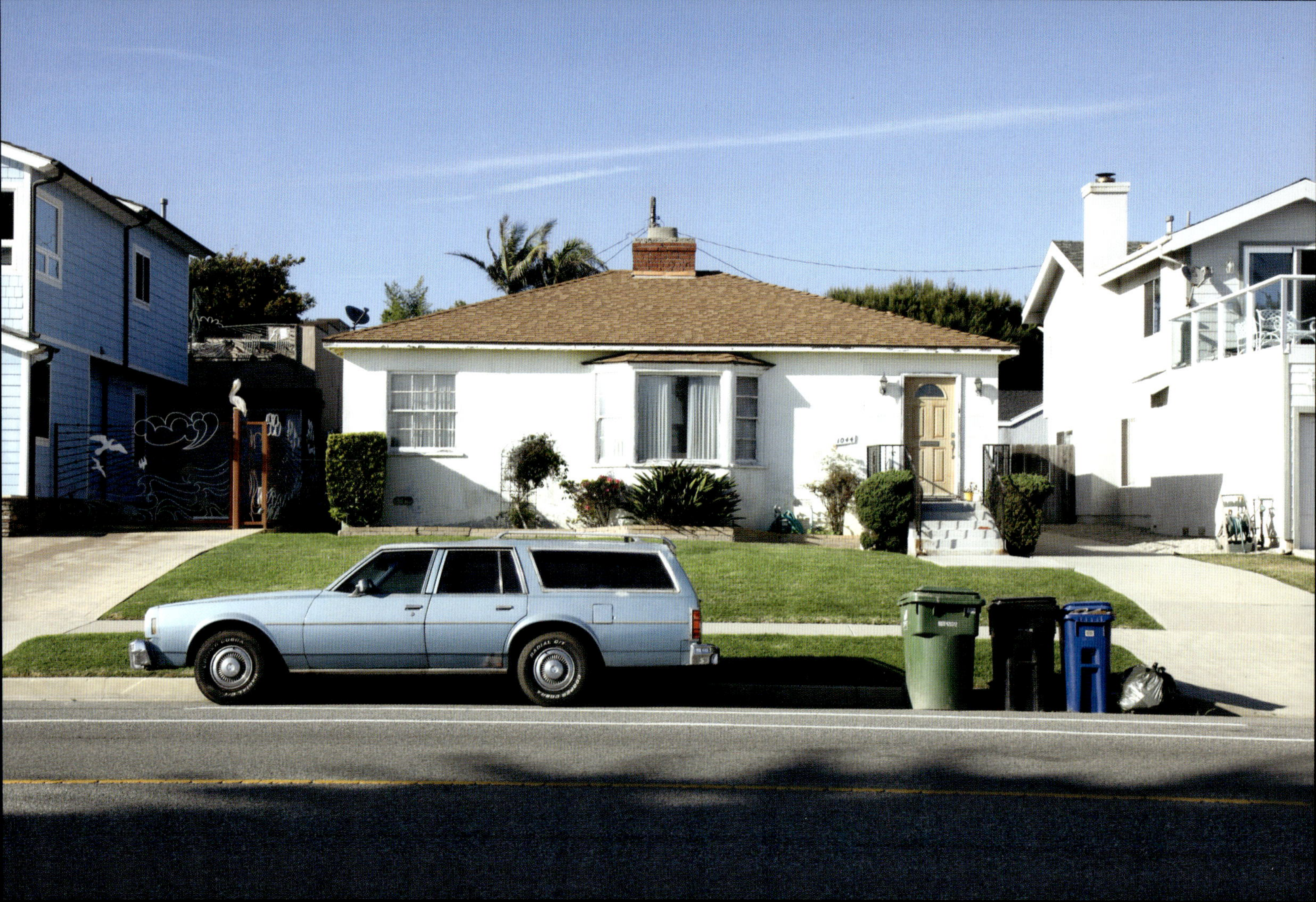

Chevy Caprice Kombi auf dem Paso del Mare. *Chevy Caprice station wagon on Paso del Mar.*

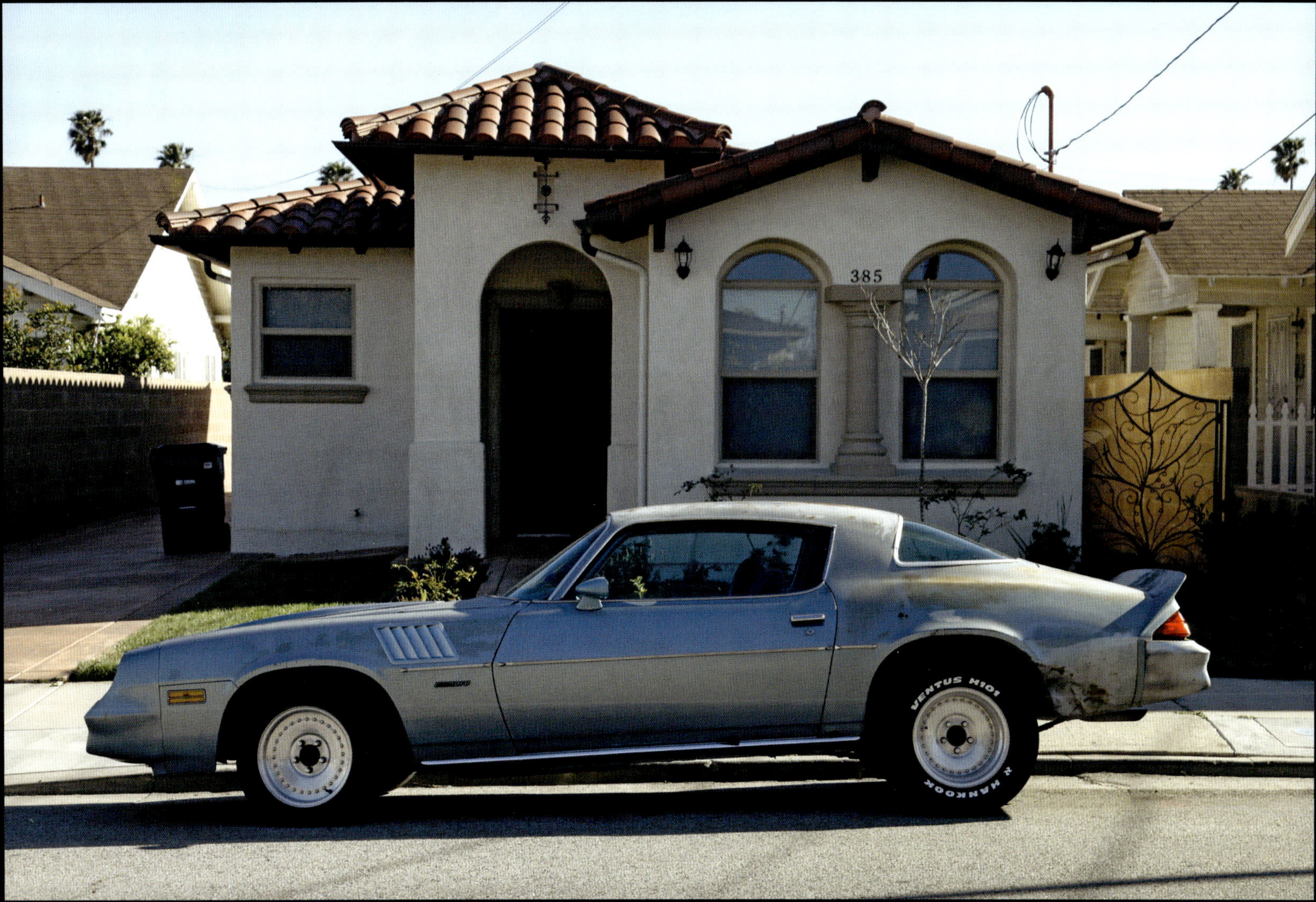

Pontiac Firebird in Lauerstellung. *Pontiac Firebird, lurking.*

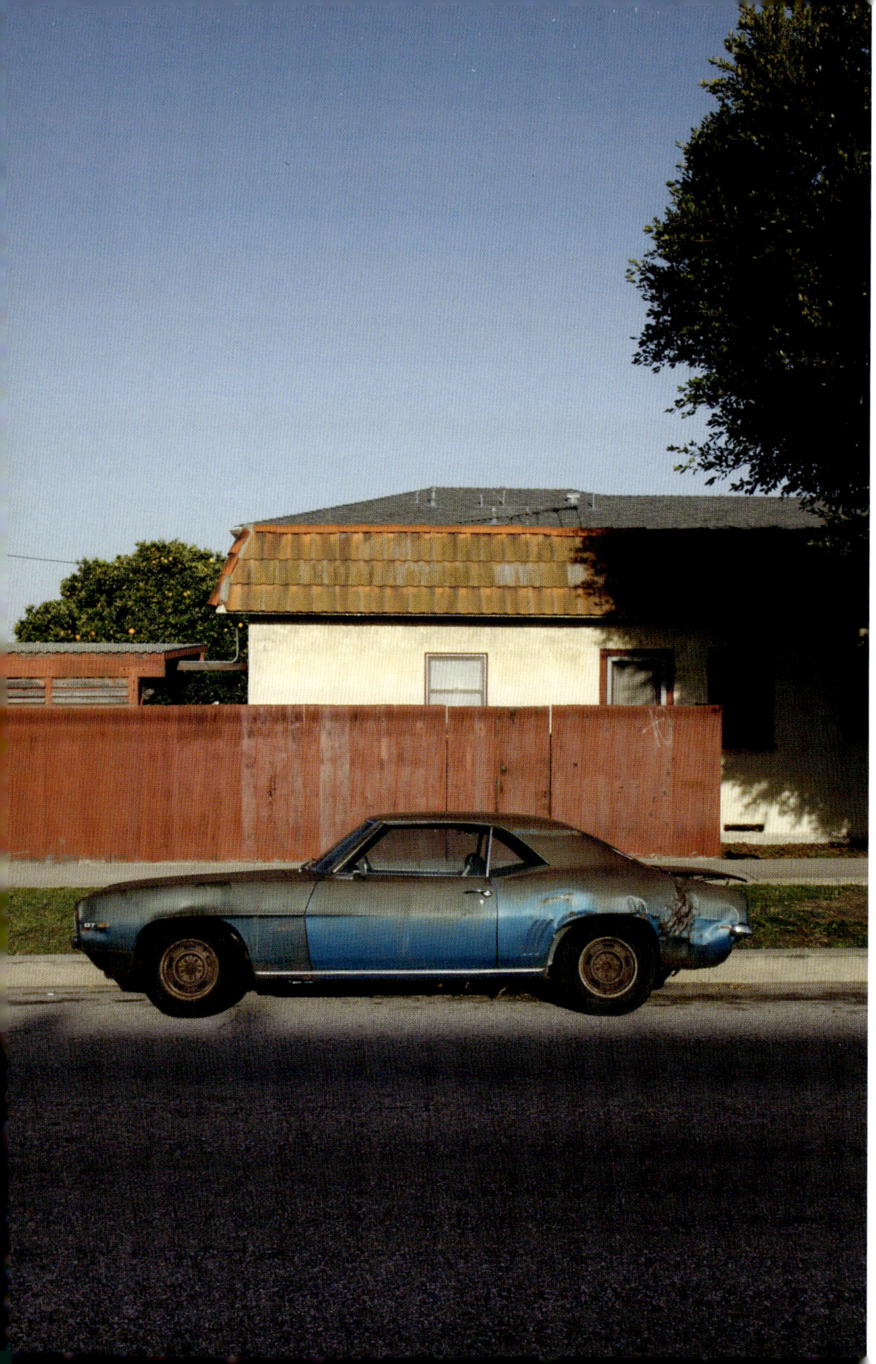

079

Wie ein streunender Hund: Camaro (siehe auch 031).
Like a stray dog: Camaro(see also 031).

080

Standfest: Schwedenstahl vor solider Mauer.
Steadfast: Swedish steel in front of solid wall.

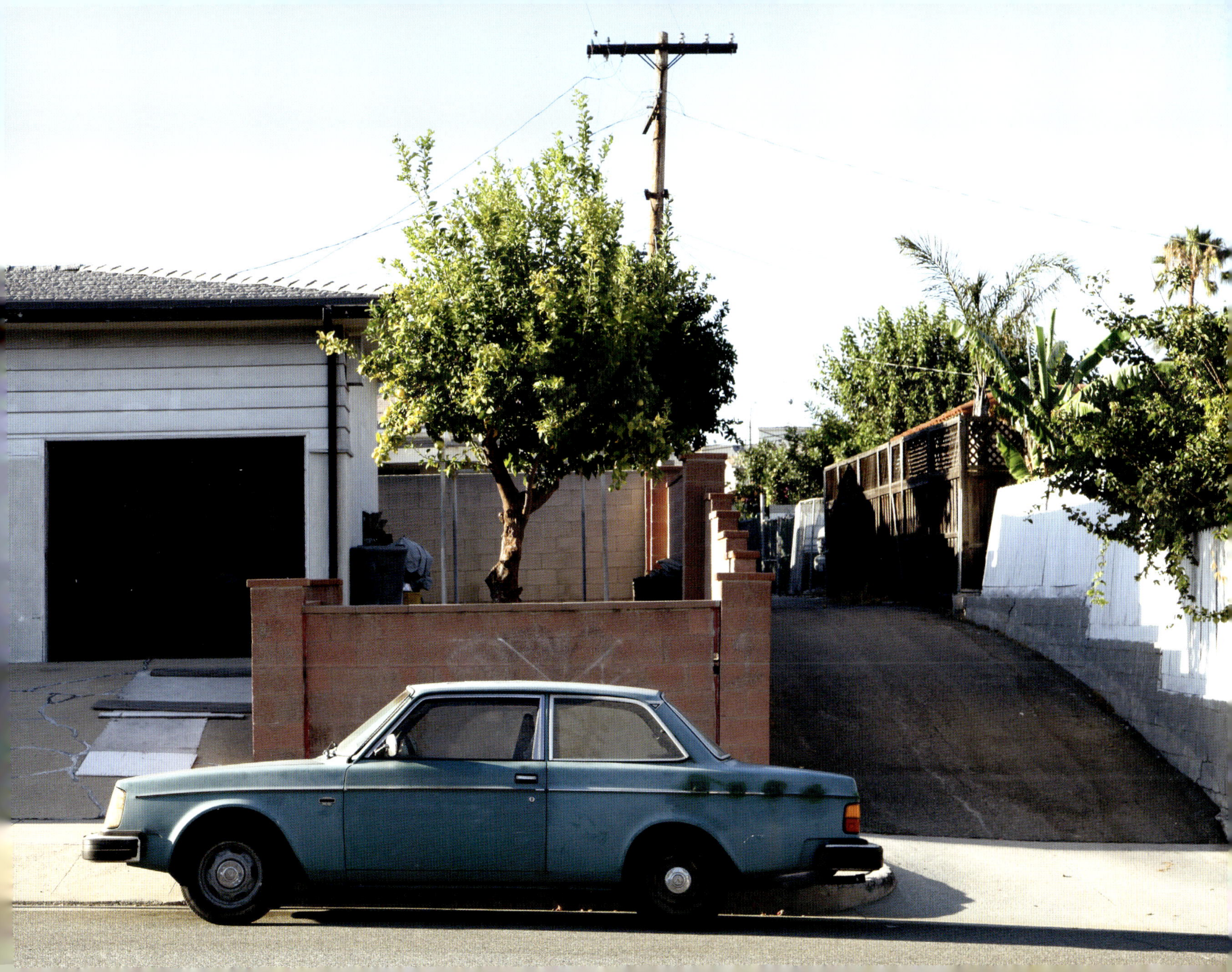

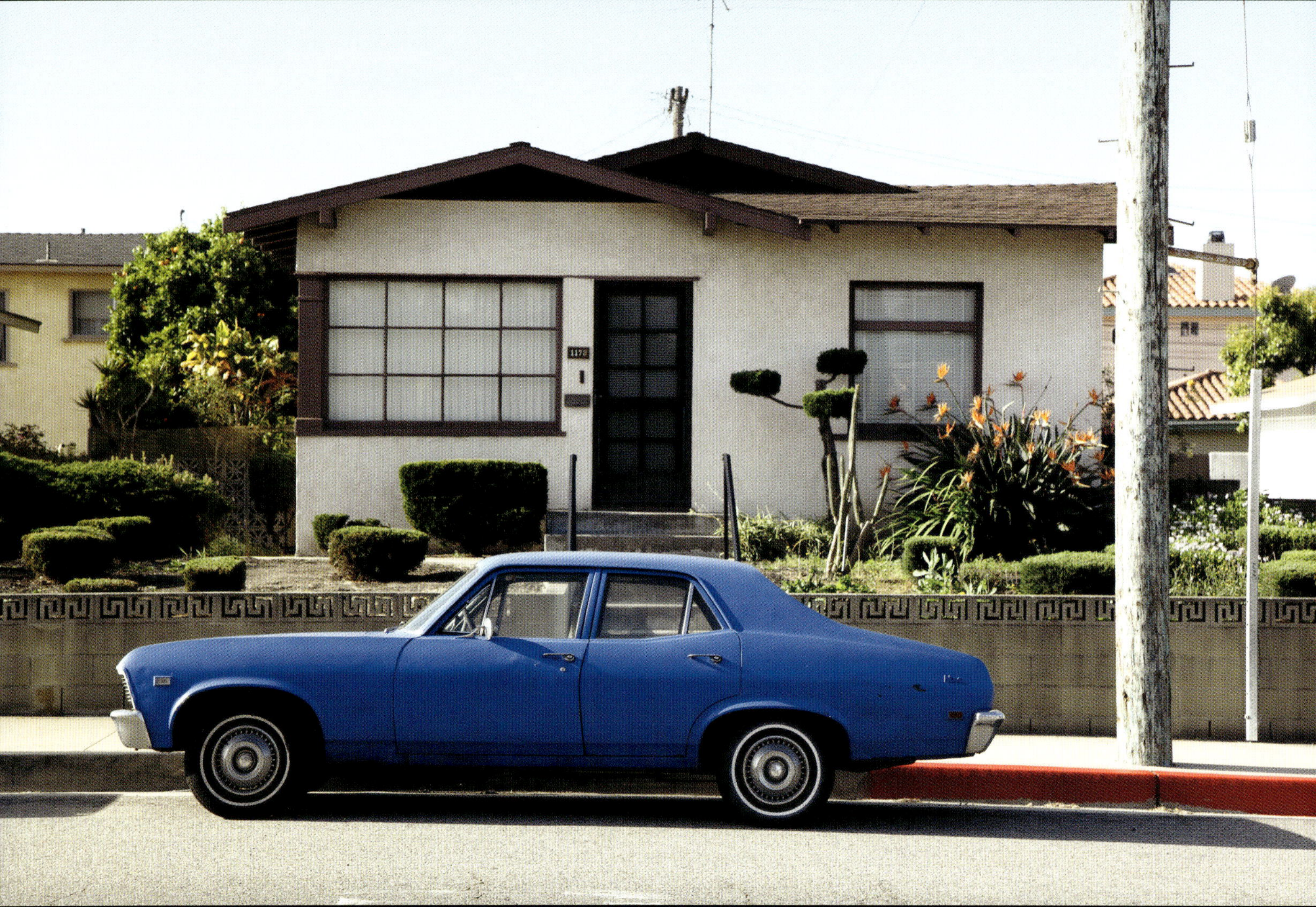

Blaue Limousine vor rotem Parkverbot. *Blue limousine and red »No Parking« zone.*

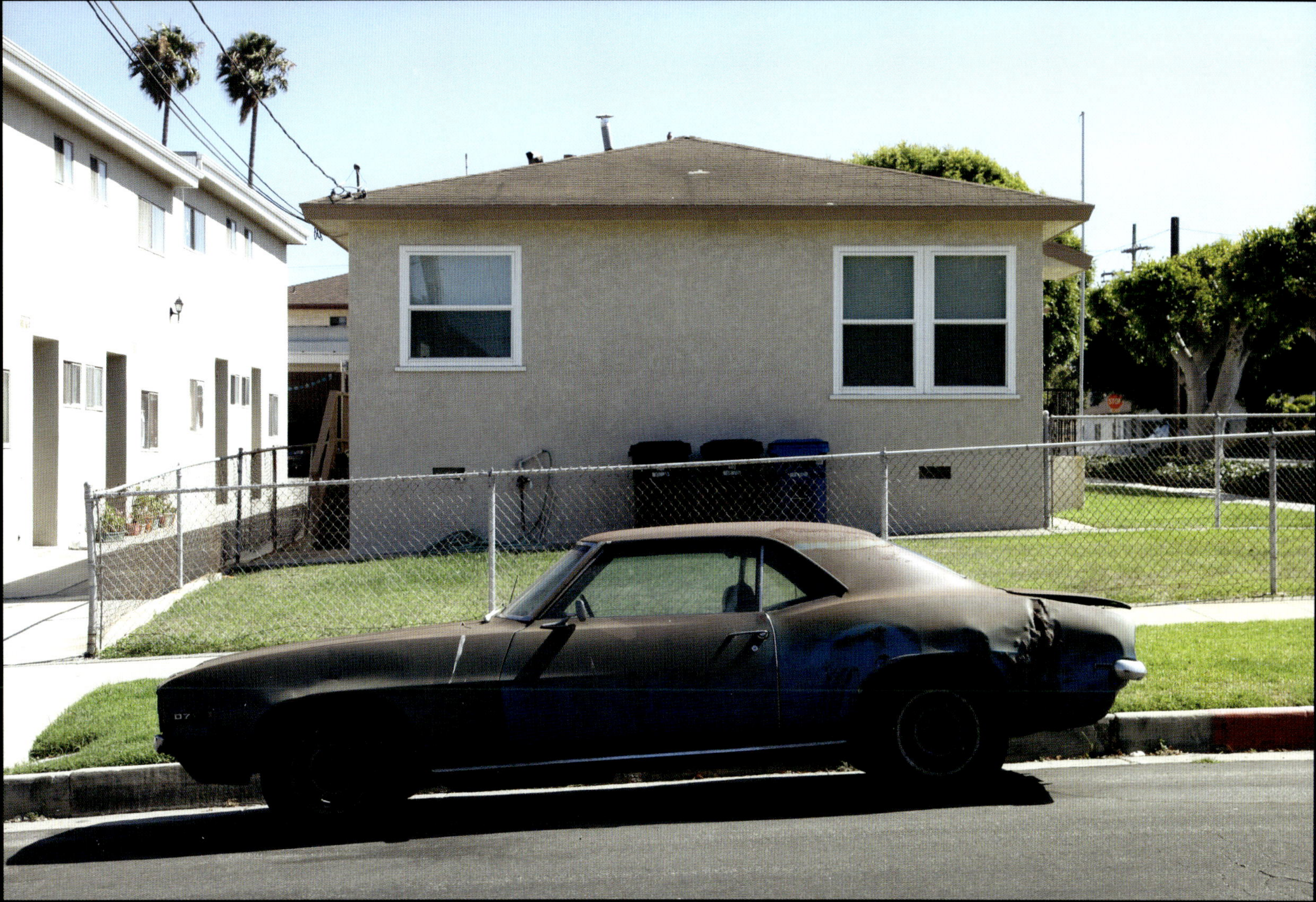

Wem gehört der bloß? Vagabundierender Camaro (siehe auch 031 und 079). *Who does this one belong to? A vagabond Camaro (see also 031 and 079).*

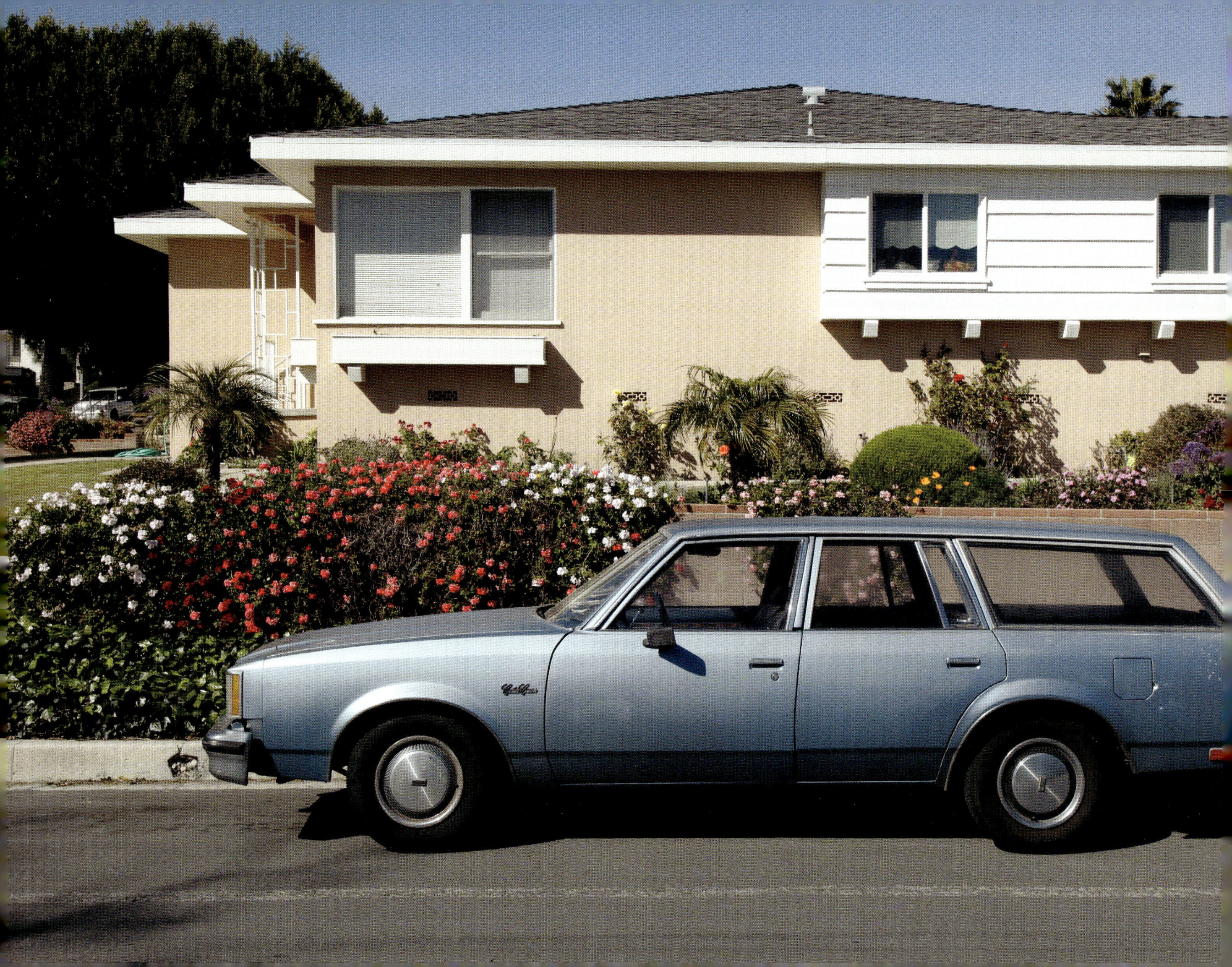

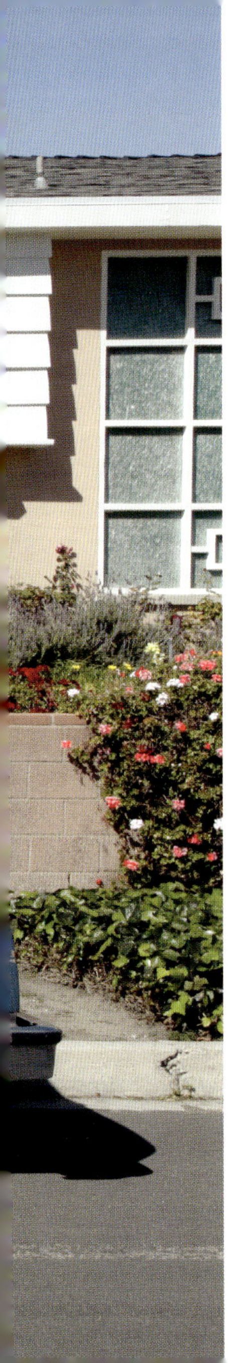

083

Das Auto des Gärtners?
Oldmobile Cutlass Kombi
vor Blumenmeer.
The gardener's car?
Oldsmobile Cutlass Station Wagon in front of a sea of flowers.

084

Autoähnliche Formation von Ersatzteilen vor Schattenspiel.
Auto-like formation of spare parts in front of a play of shadows.

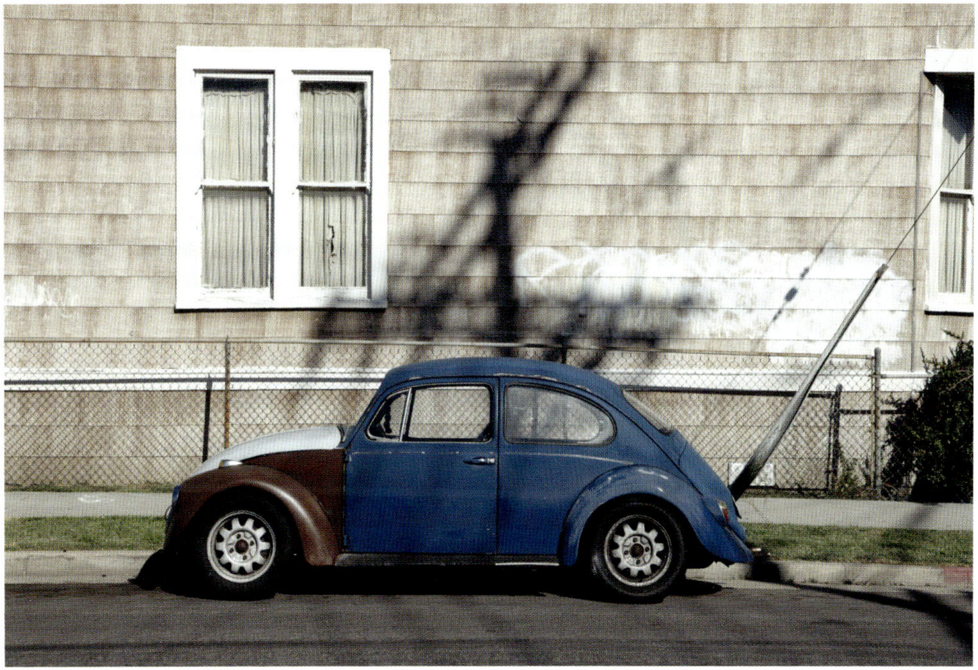

085

Der Übergang zwischen
Rost und Kunst ist fließend.
*The fluid transition from
rust to art.*

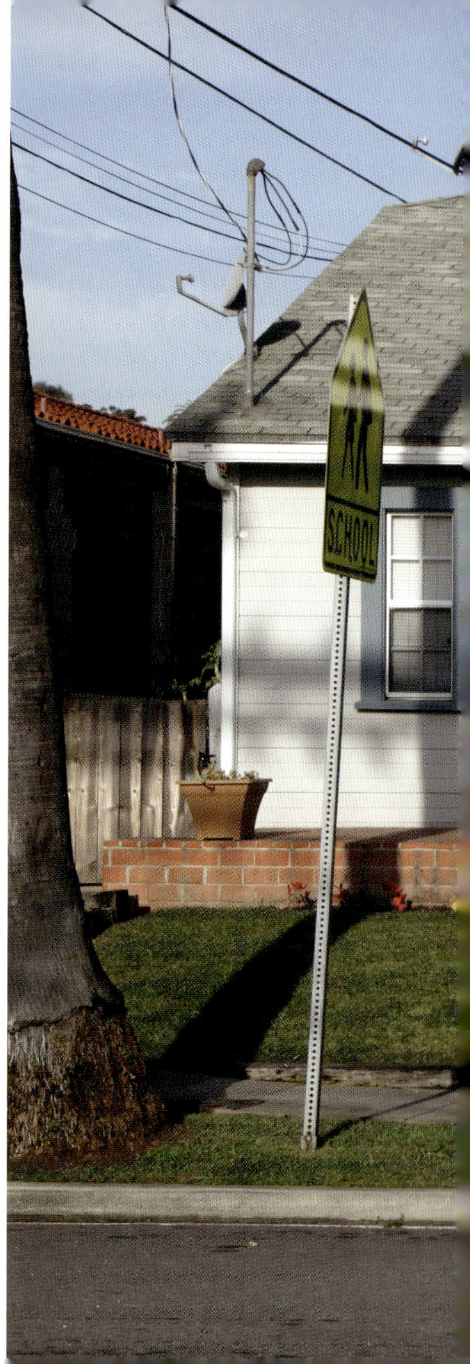

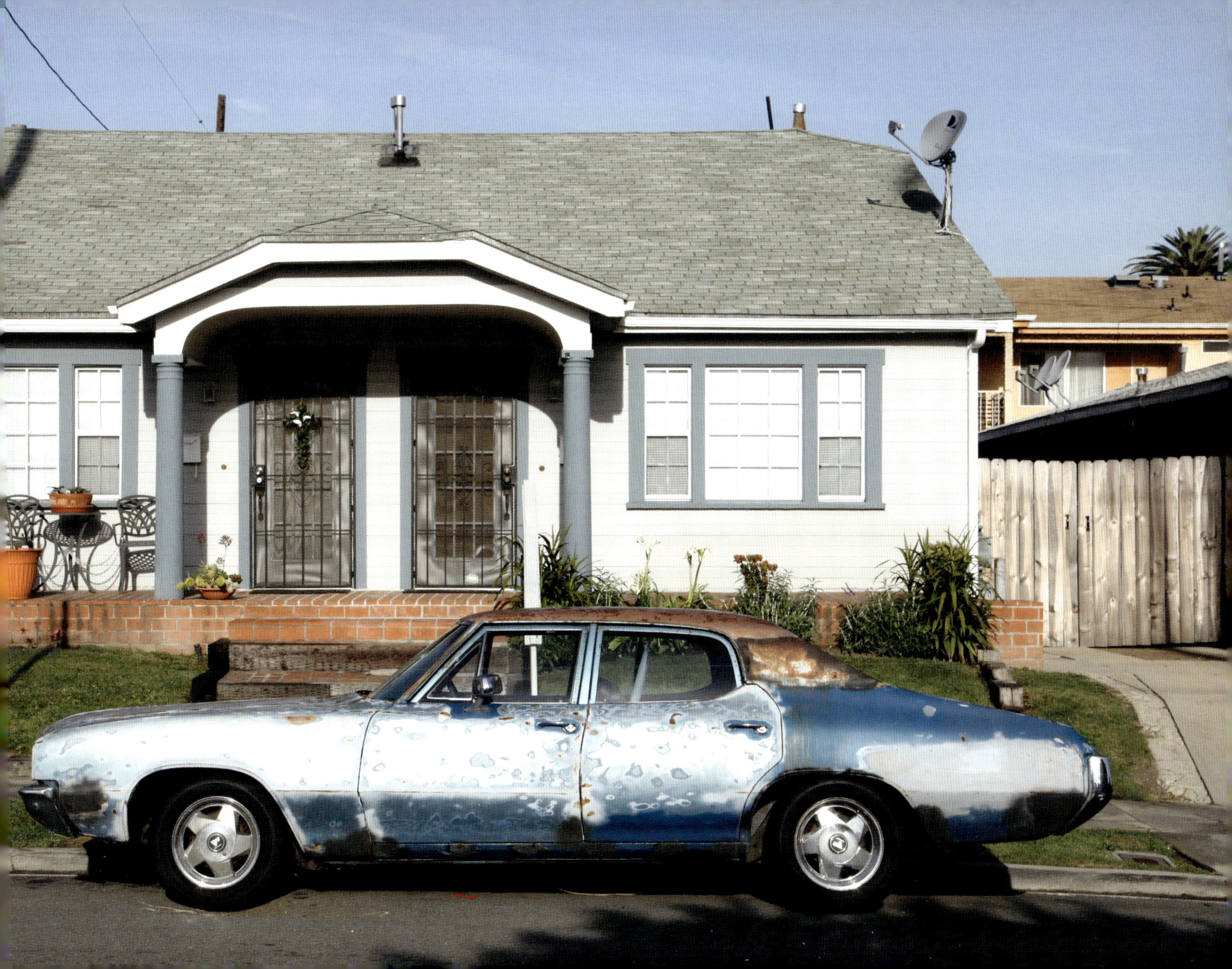

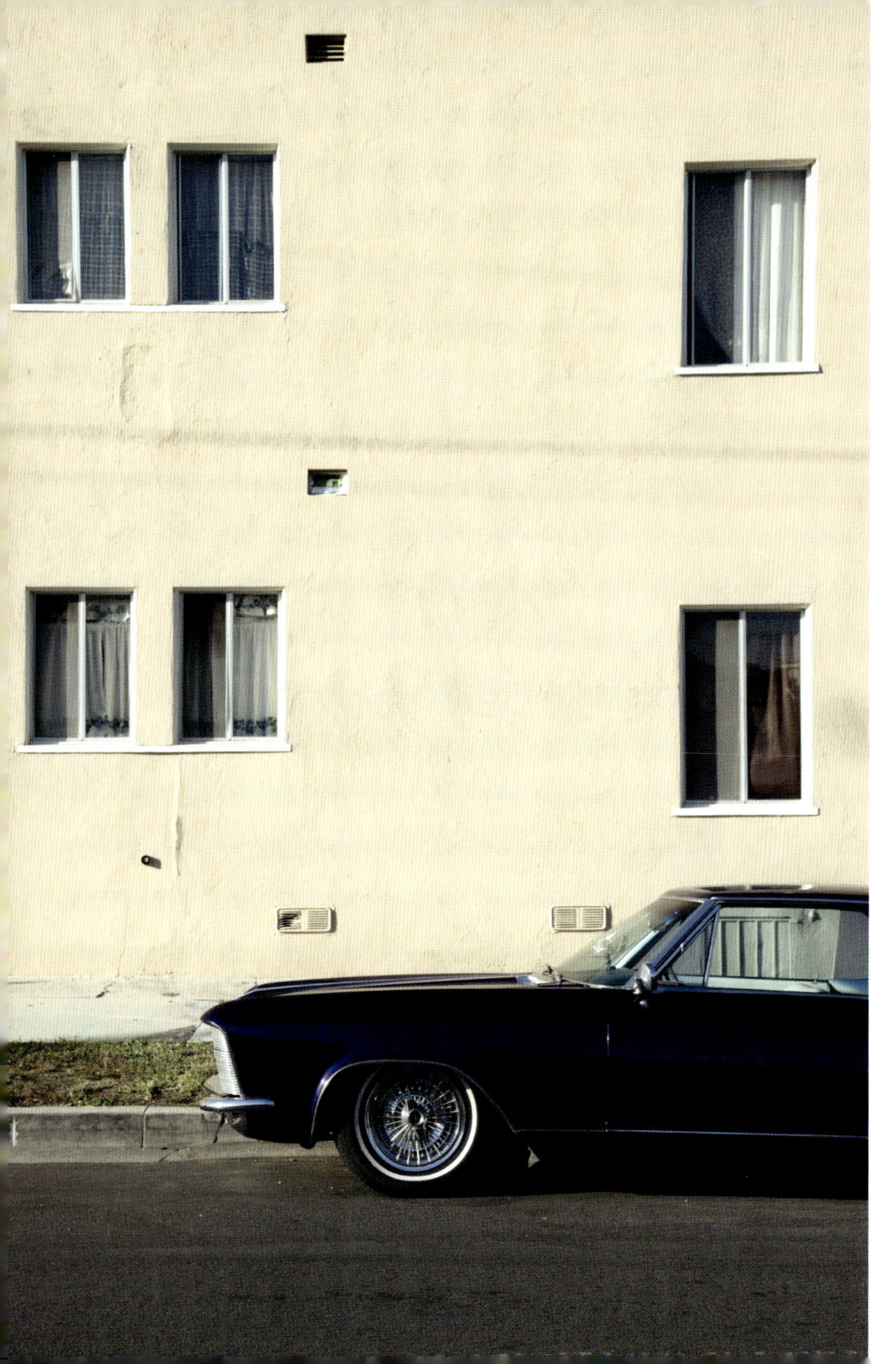

086

Lowrider in der kaliforni-
schen Abendsonne.
Lowrider in the California evening sun.

087

Zwei klassische amerika-
nische Holzbauten.
Two classic (American) wooden structures.

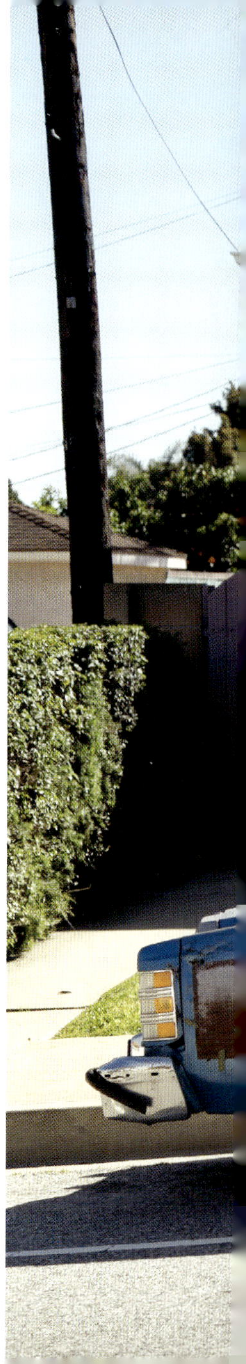

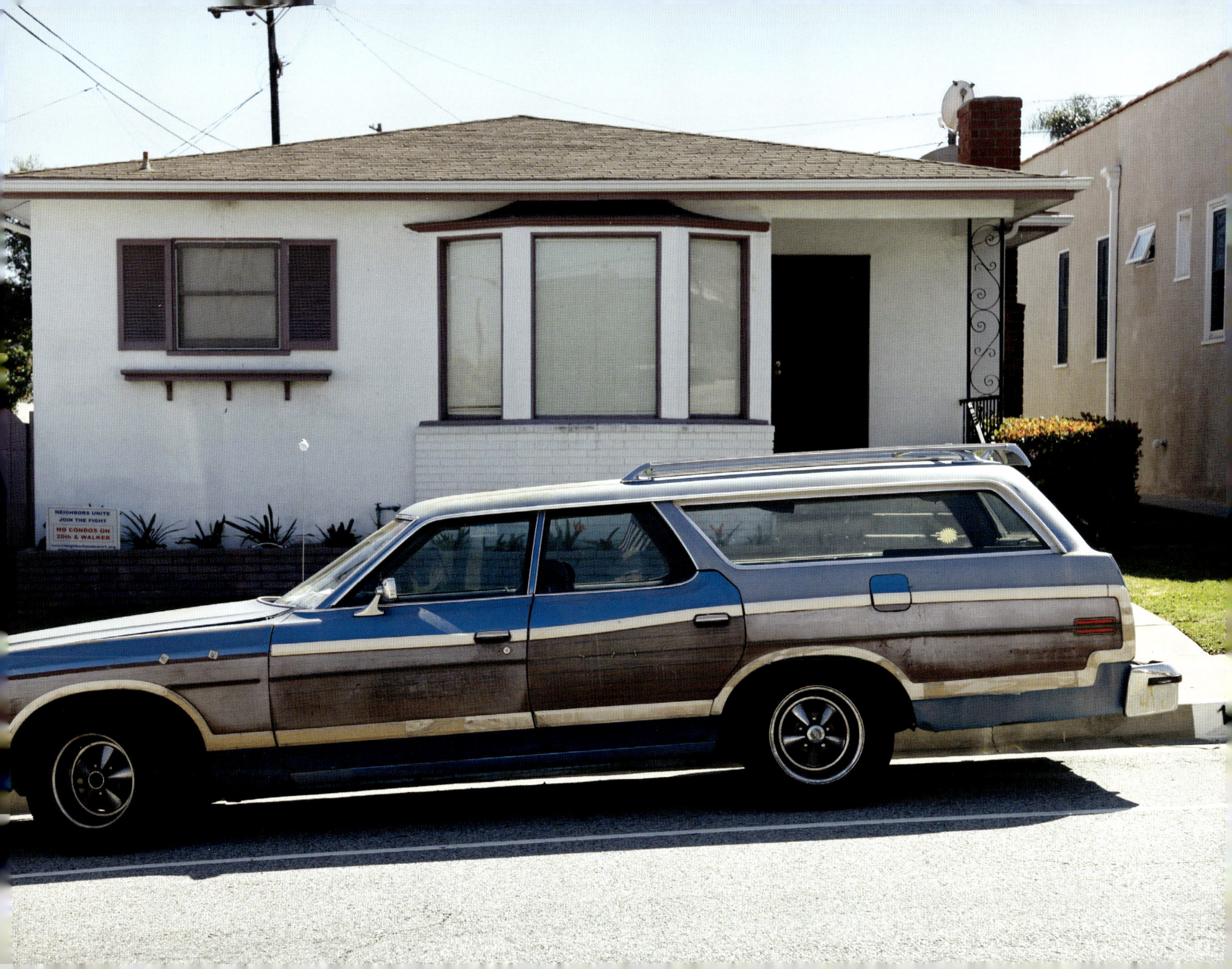
NEIGHBORS UNITE
JOIN THE FIGHT
NO CONDOS ON
20th & WALKER

GOLD. DAS TEURE REICHTUMS.

GOLD. MONEY. EXPENSIVE LUCK. THE COLOR OF WEALTH. ALSO THE COLOR OF IMITATION.

GLÜCK. DIE FARBE DES UND DER IMITATION.

»I wanna live, I wanna give. I've been a miner for a heart of gold. It's these expressions I never give, that keep me searching for a heart of gold. And I'm getting old. Keeps me searching for a heart of gold. And I'm getting old.«

Neil Young

088

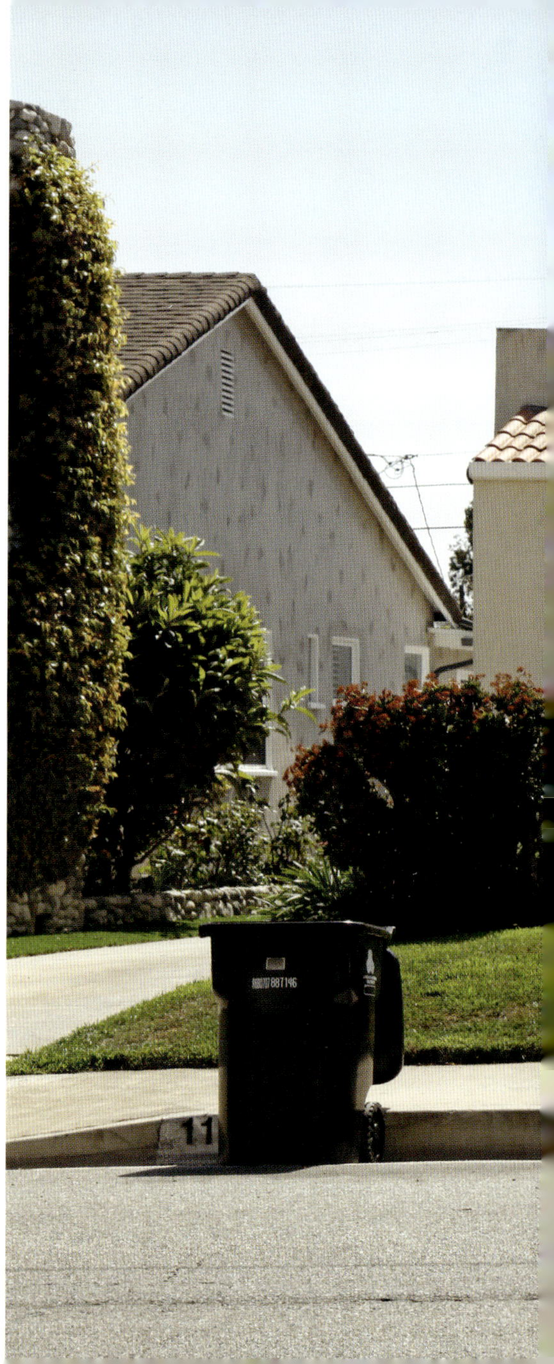

Volvo 240: automobiles Symbol für gehobenen Bildungsgrad.
Volvo 240: The automobile symbol for a higher level of education.

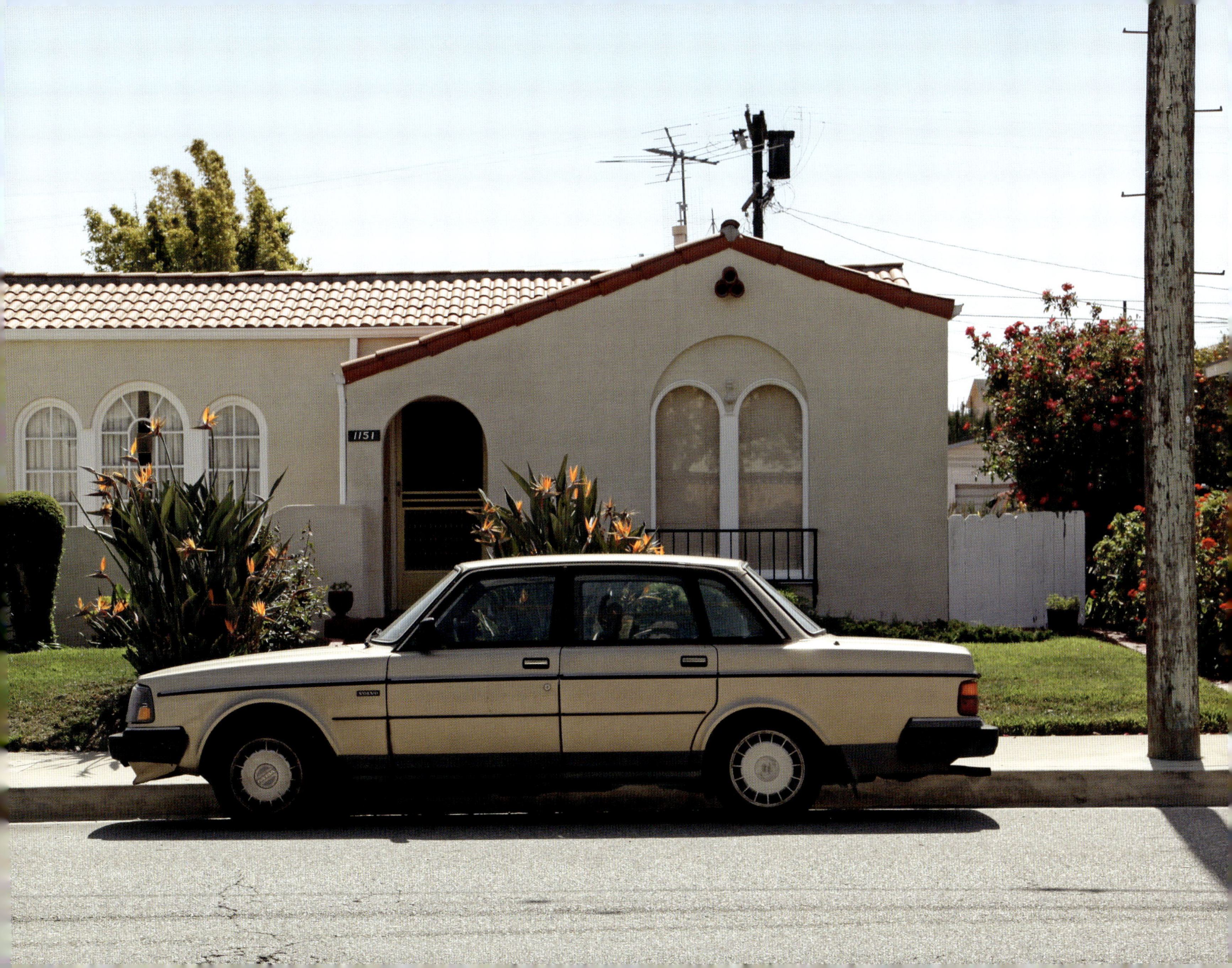
1151

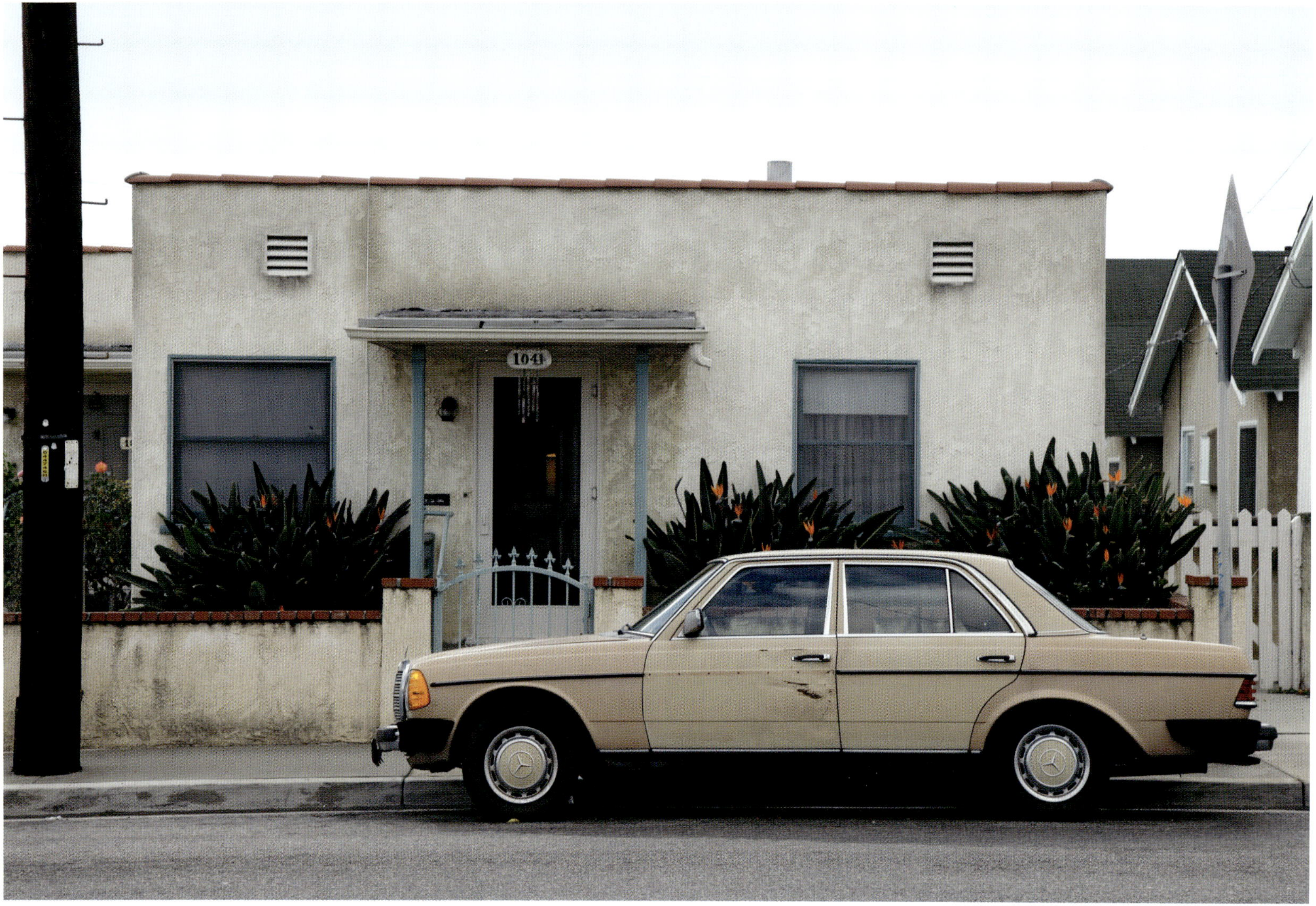

Mercedes 240 D-Bausatz vor Kakteenpracht. *Mercedes 240 D kit in front of cactus splendor.*

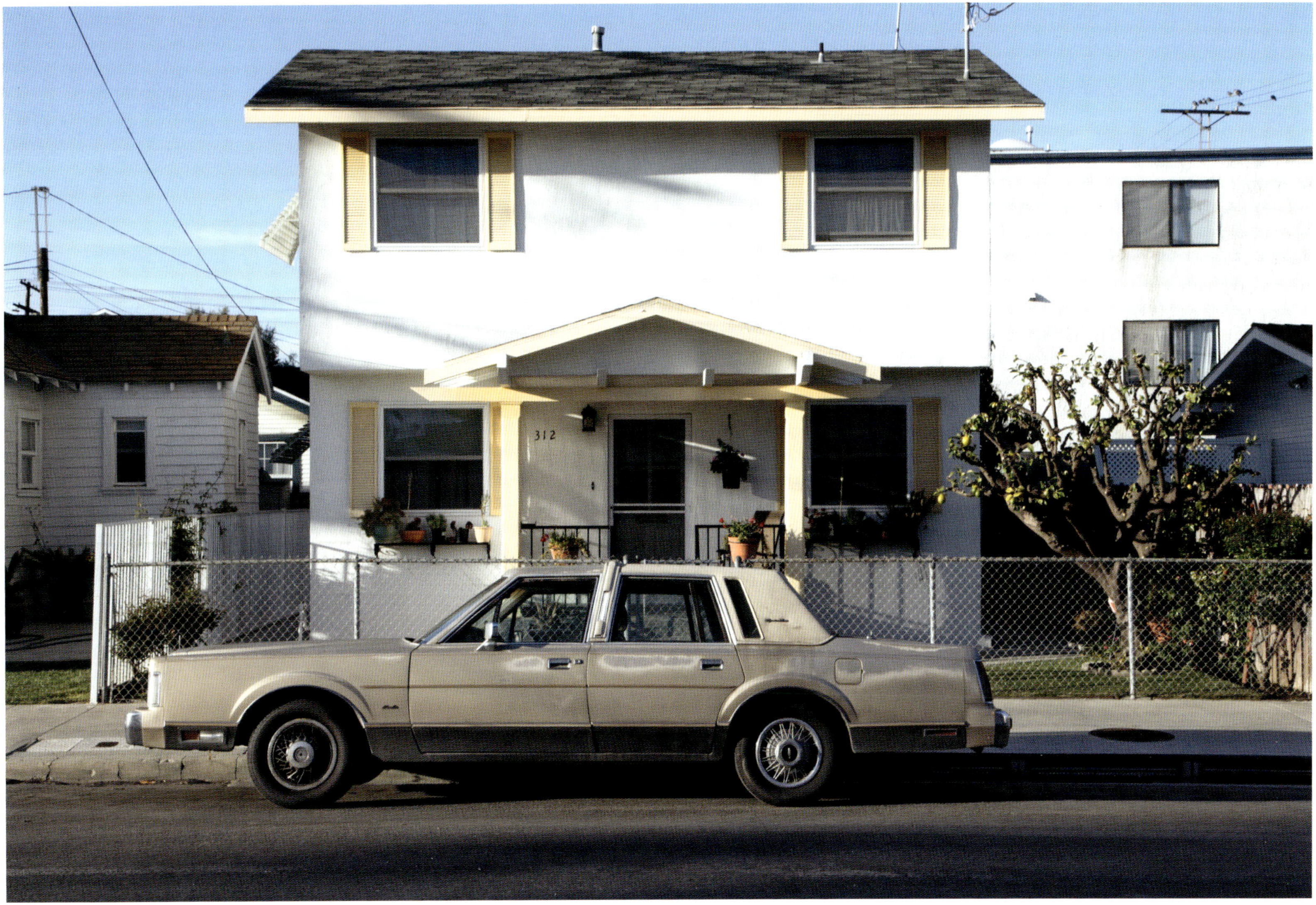

Mut zur geraden Linie: Lincoln Town Car vor Hausnummer 312. *Courage enough for straight lines: Lincoln Town Car at No. 312.*

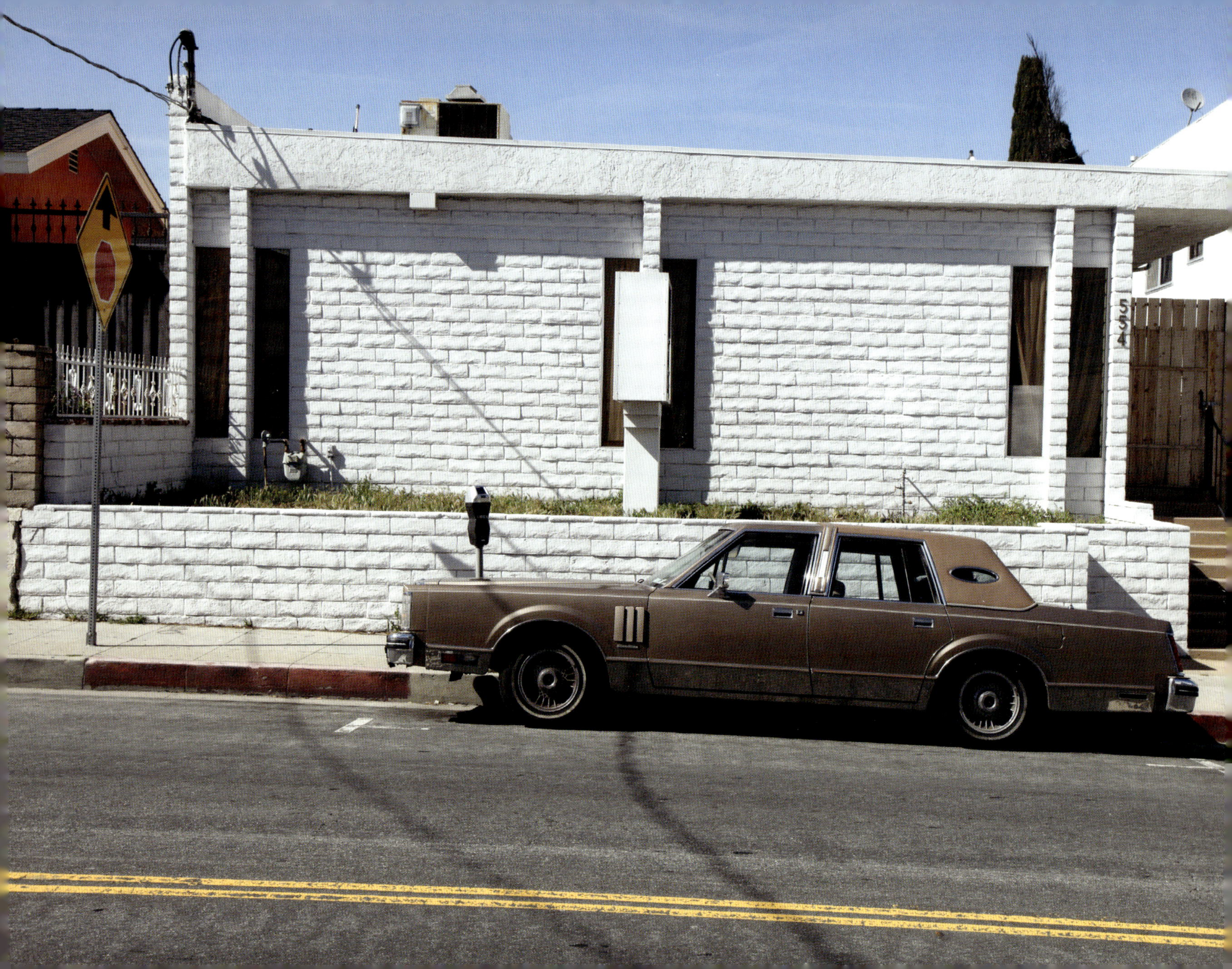
534

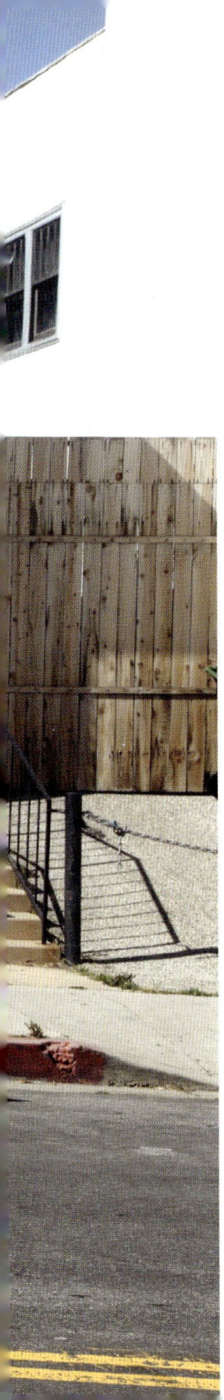

091

Lincoln Town Car mit Opern-
fenster vor Bauhaus-Replika.
*Lincoln Town Car with opera win-
dows in front of Bauhaus replica.*

092

Klare Grundstücksgrenzen mit voller Raumausnutzung.
Clear property lines and maximum utilization of space.

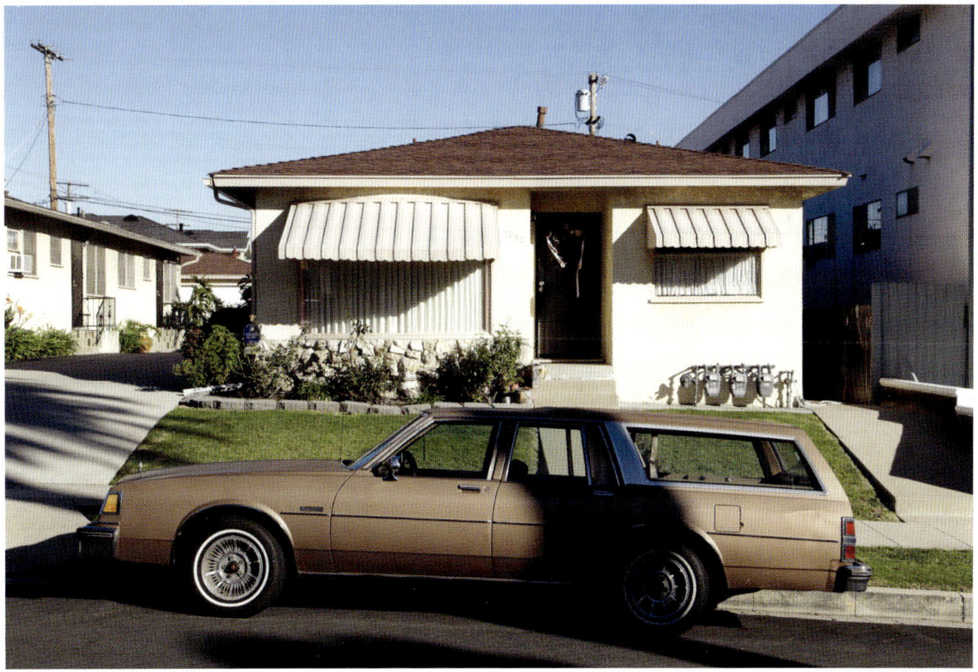

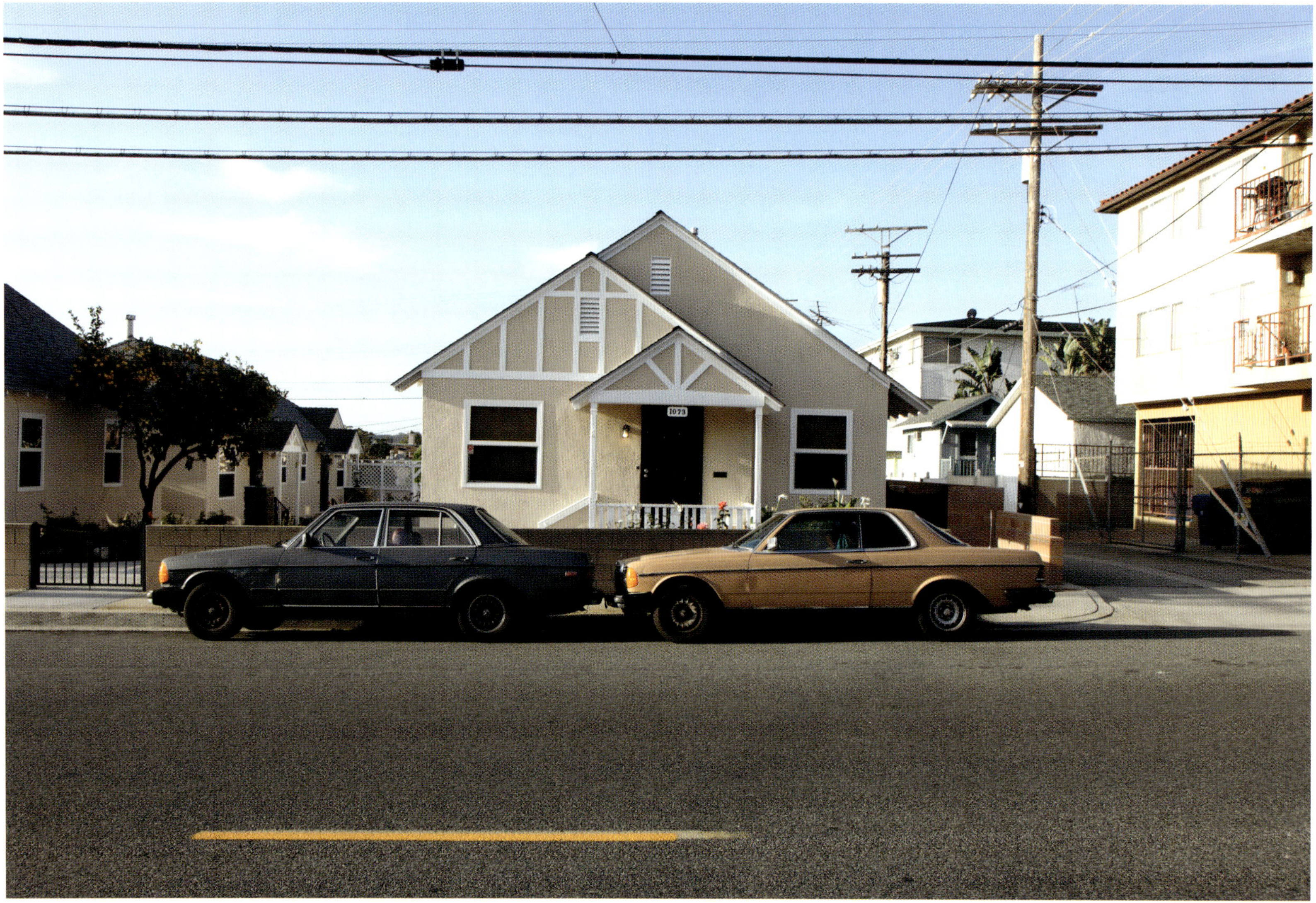

Rendezvous an der Bordsteinkante: Zwei Mercedes haben sich gefunden. *Rendezvous on the curb: the meeting of two Mercedes.*

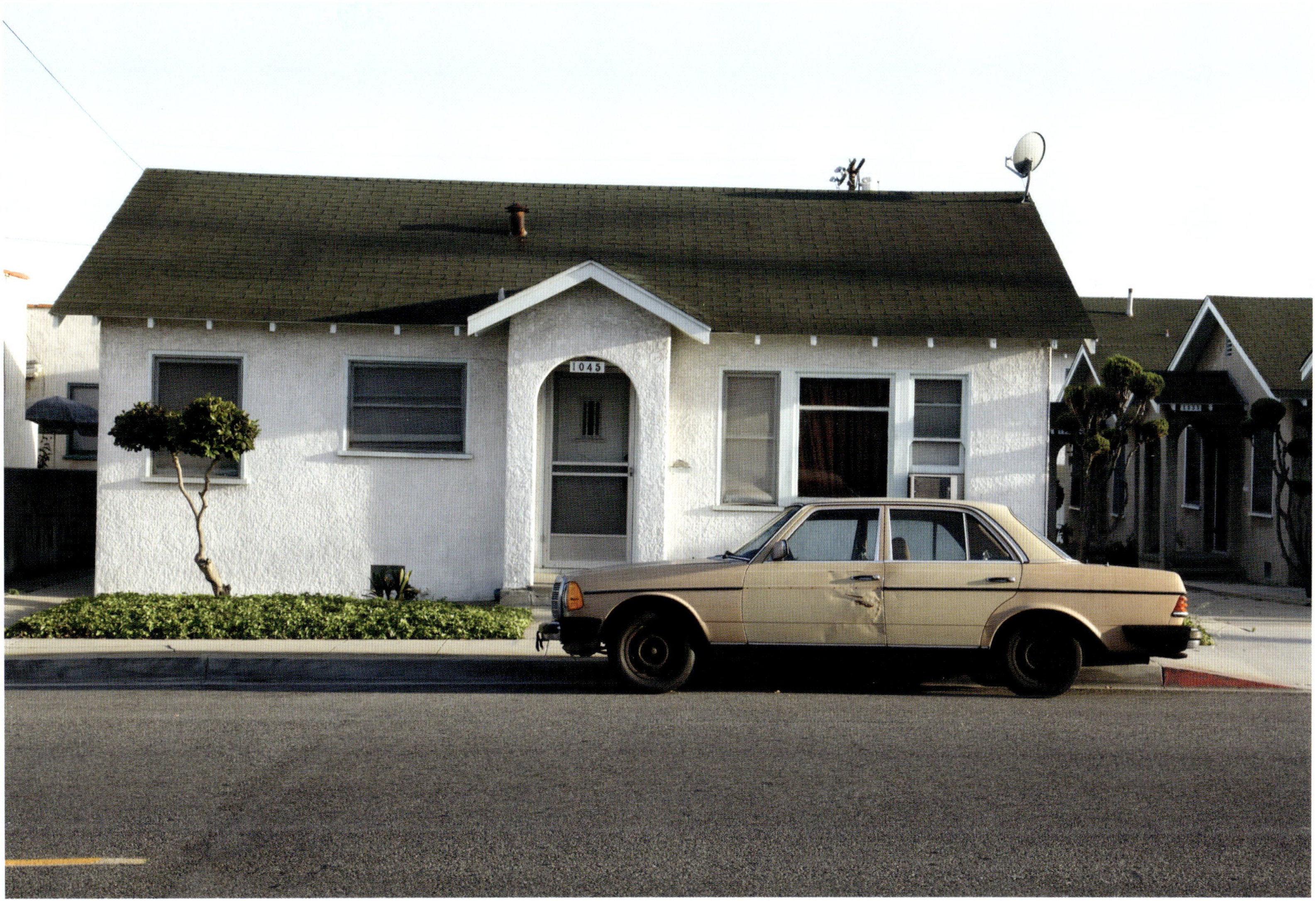

Dieser sucht noch einen Partner. *This one is still searching for a partner.*

GRÜN. ZWISCHEN

GREEN. BETWEEN HOPE AND POISON. THE COLOR THAT DEFIES CONCRETE.

HOFFNUNG UND GIFT.

DIE FARBE, DIE DEM BETON TROTZT.

»Just a little bit of green. Oh, clouds my eyes to what I've seen. Just a little bit of green. When I see you with someone new. And knowing that there's nothing I can do.«
Elvis Presley

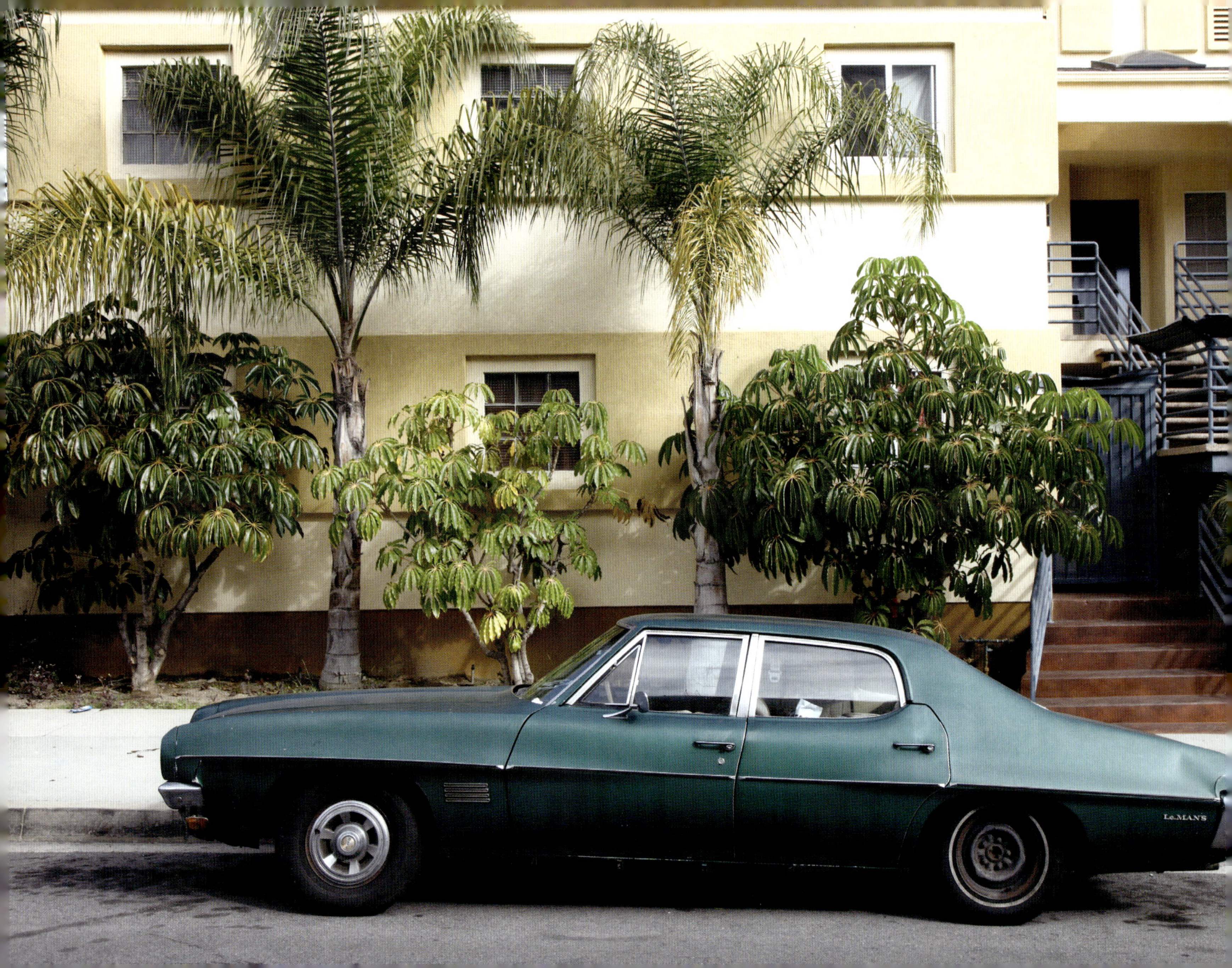
Le MANS

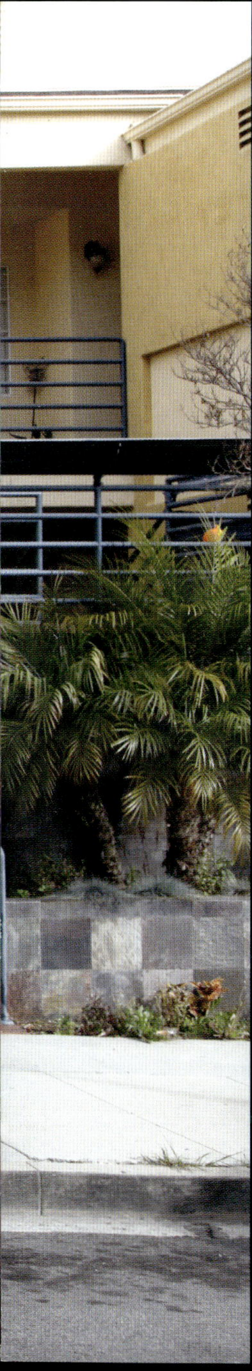

096

Gut getarnter Pontiac im Urwald von San Pedro. *Well-camouflaged Pontiac in the jungles of San Pedro.*

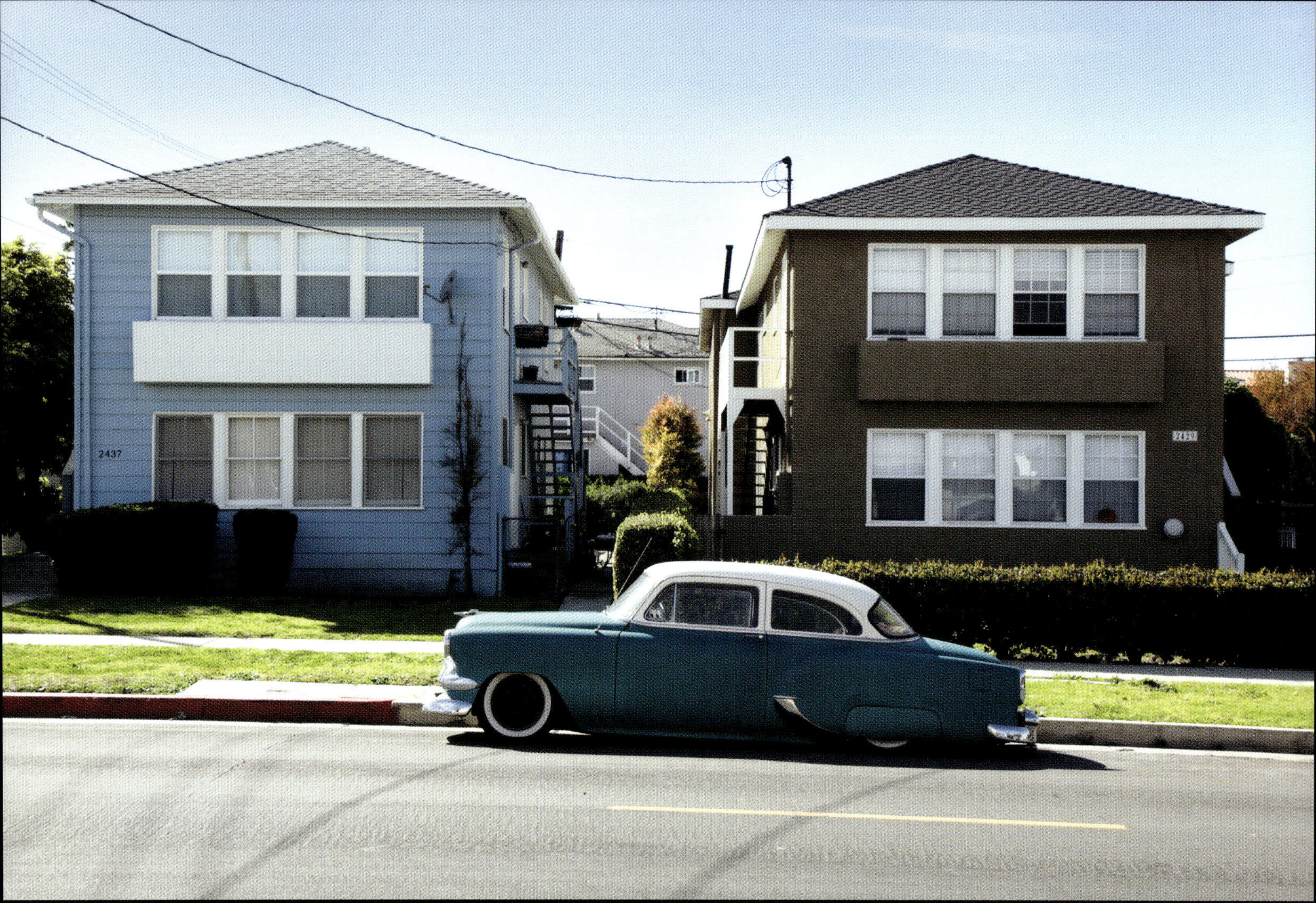

Symmetrisches Häuserduo mit Pastellfarben und mittigem Lowrider. *Symmetrical duo in pastel colors and centered lowrider.*

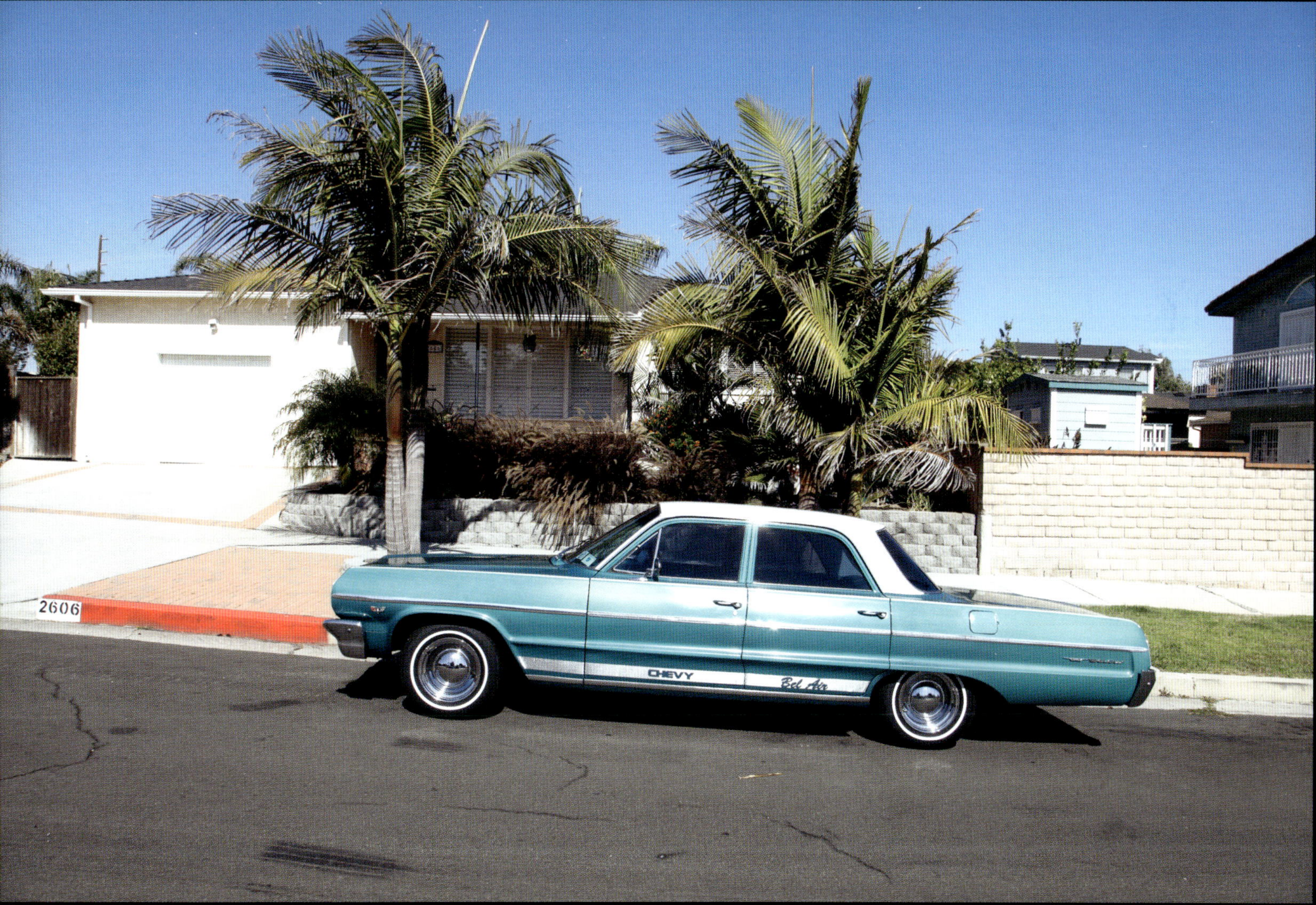

Nomen est omen: Chevrolet Bel Air in Höhenlage abgestellt. *Nomen est omen: Chevrolet Bel Air parked in the hills.*

099

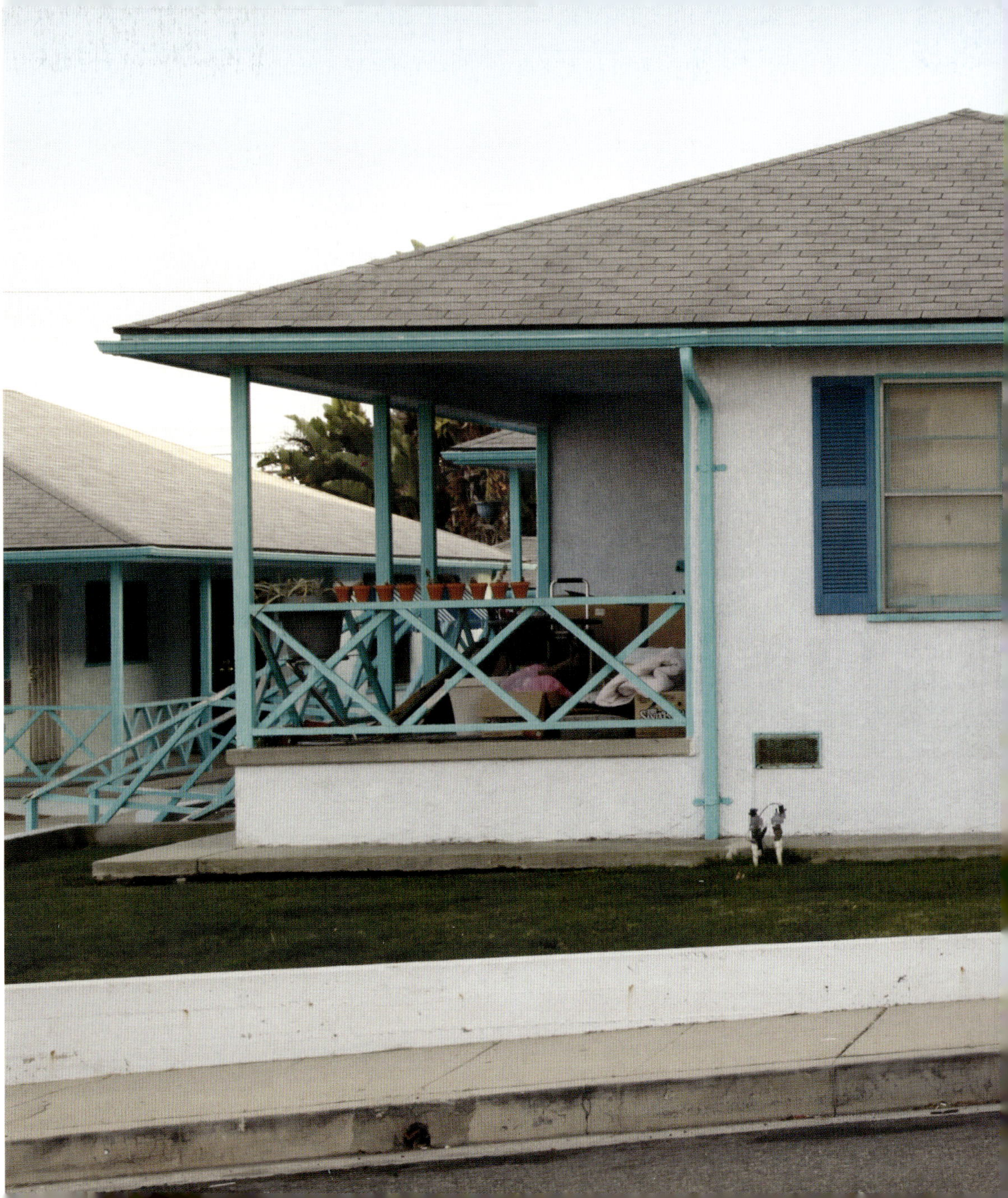

Giftgrüner Strandläufer vor Bungalow mit Wohnterrasse.
Toxic-green sandpiper in front of bungalow with terrace.

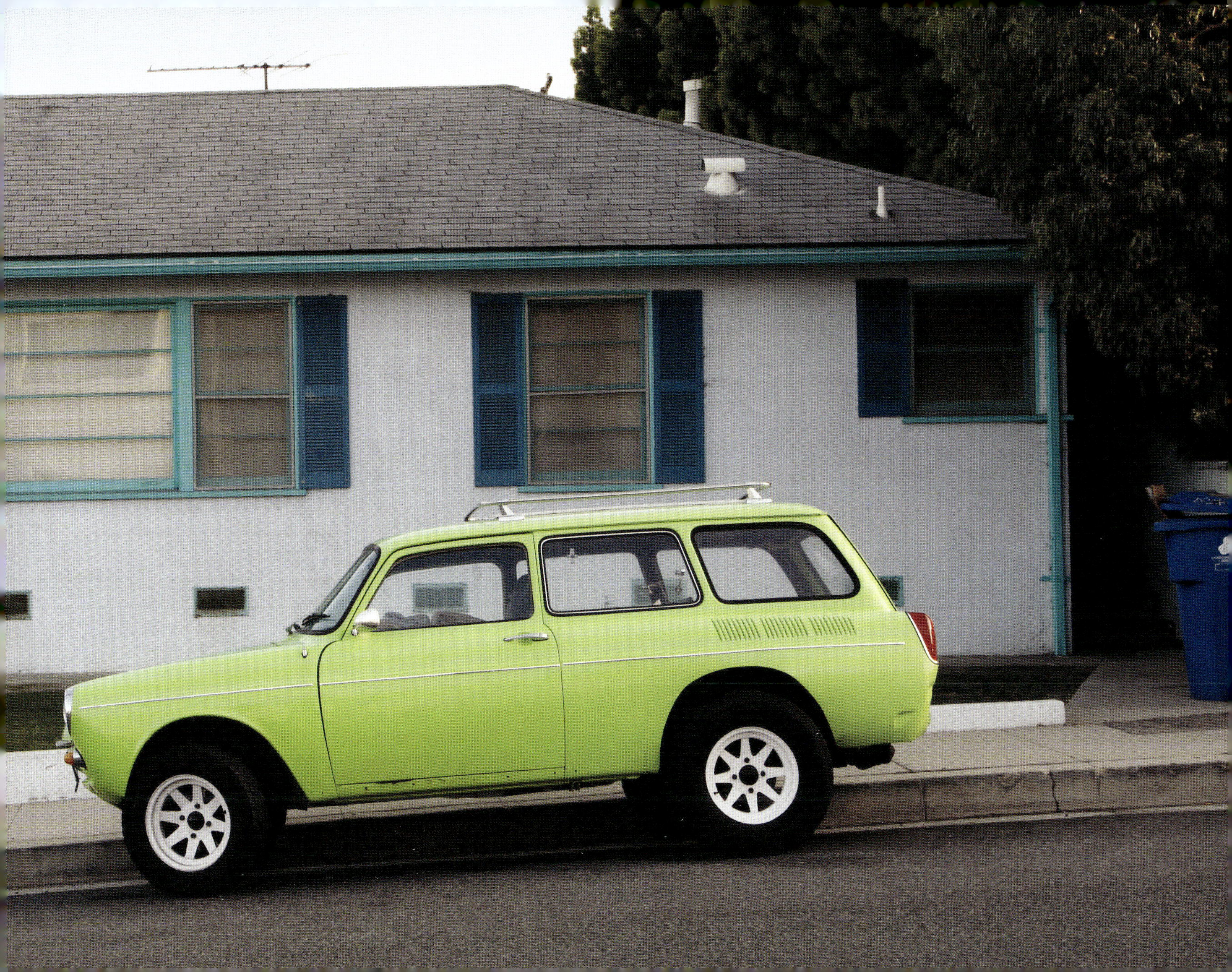

Bibliografische Information der Deutschen Nationalbibliothek
Die Deutsche Nationalbibliothek verzeichnet diese Publikation in der Deutschen Nationalbibliografie; detaillierte bibliografische Daten sind im Internet über http://dnb.d-nb.de abrufbar.

1. Auflage
ISBN 978-3-7688-3597-8

Text und Fotos: Tim Maxeiner
Lektorat: Alexander Failing, Nicole Hille-Priebe
Gestaltung: Jörg Weusthoff, Weusthoff Noël, Hamburg
Reproduktionen: Lithotronic, Berchtesgaden
Druck und Bucheinband: Westermann-Druck, Zwickau
Printed in Germany 2013

Delius Klasing Verlag, Siekerwall 21, D - 33602 Bielefeld
Tel.: 0521/559-0, Fax: 0521/559-115
E-Mail: info@delius-klasing.de
www.delius-klasing.de

A METAPHOR FOR THE AMERICAN LIFESTYLE

EINE METAPHER FÜR DEN AMERIKANISCHEN LEBENSSTIL

Haus, Auto und Benutzer bilden eine Verbindung auf Zeit. Auch die Immobilien gehen von Hand zu Hand. Ewig ist nur die Parkplatzsuche. *House, car and user form a bond for a limited time. Even real estate properties are passed from one owner to the next. The search for a parking space, however, never ends.*

»Eldorado fins, whitewalls and skirts. Rides just like a little bit of heaven here on earth. Well buddy when I die, throw my body in the back and drive me to the junkyard in my Cadillac.«
Bruce Springsteen

001 002 003 004 005 006 007 008 009

019 020 021 022 023 024 025 026 027

037 038 039 040 041 042 043 044 045

055 056 057 058 059 060 061 062 063

073 074 075 076 077 078 079 080 081

091 092 093 094 095 096 097 098 099

010	011	012	013	014	015	016	017	018
028	029	030	031	032	033	034	035	036
046	047	048	049	050	051	052	053	054
064	065	066	067	068	069	070	071	072
082	083	084	085	086	087	088	089	090